英汉双语对照

作家篇

百位名人
校园原声演讲集锦

王瑞泽 周文博 编译

北京航空航天大学出版社
BEIHANG UNIVERSITY PRESS

U0604853

图书在版编目（CIP）数据

百位名人校园原声演讲集锦．作家篇：英汉对照 /
王瑞泽，周文博编译．-- 北京：北京航空航天大学出版
社，2015.10

ISBN 978-7-5124-1891-2

Ⅰ.①百…　Ⅱ.①王…　②周…　Ⅲ.①英语 - 汉语 -
对照读物　②演讲 - 汇编 - 世界　Ⅳ.① H319.4：I

中国版本图书馆 CIP 数据核字（2015）第 234020 号

版权所有，侵权必究。

百位名人校园原声演讲集锦——作家篇

王瑞泽　周文博　编译
责任编辑　秦莹　周美佳
*
北京航空航天大学出版社出版发行
北京市海淀区学院路 37 号（邮编 100191）　http://www.buaapress.com.cn
发行部电话：（010）82317024　传真：（010）82328026
读者信箱：bhpress@263.net　邮购电话：（010）82316936
中国铁道出版社印刷厂印装　各地书店经销
*
开本：710×960　1/16　印张：13.5　字数：308 千字
2015 年 10 月第 1 版　2015 年 10 月第 1 次印刷
ISBN 978-7-5124-1891-2　定价：25.80 元

若本书有倒页、脱页、缺页等印装质量问题，请与本社发行部联系调换。

联系电话：（010）82317024

译者序

伟大的演讲产生伟大的力量，它能够让人觉醒催人奋进，它能够震撼人们的灵魂，它能够粉碎人世间的丑恶，它能够激扬人世间的美善，它能够改变人们的精神风貌，它甚至能够改变历史的进程。马丁·路德·金的《我有一个梦想》让横行了美国 200 年之久的种族隔离制度土崩瓦解，约翰·肯尼迪的《想想你能为国家做什么》激励一代代美国人前赴后继勇赴国难，巴拉克·奥巴马的《无畏的希望》把一个默默无闻的政治家变成了世界舞台上的超级政治明星……

伟大的演讲不但会对政治家产生不可估量的影响，同样会也对我们这些普通百姓产生巨大的激励作用。2008 年 11 月 3 日晚上夜深人静的时候，我照常打开了美国广播公司新闻网站，一个历史性画面映入了我的眼帘——奥巴马在发表胜选演讲！透过互联网，我注视着万里之外的奥巴马的眼神，聆听着他的声音，我忽然忘记了自己身在太平洋此岸的中国大陆，仿佛已经置身于太平洋彼岸的演讲现场，奥巴马的声音如同神奇的手指撩拨着我的心弦。他的演讲在万众欢呼声中结束了，但是我的心情却久久不能平静，我突发奇想，为什么不把他的精彩演讲汇集成册，让爱好英语爱好演讲的国人也和我一样聆听名人演讲感受蓬勃力量呢？于是便有了 2009 年英语读物销售冠军的《奥巴马演说集》，于是便有了 2010 年广受读者喜爱的《我有一个梦想》，于是便有了后来一系列的英语演讲书，于是便有了今天摆在读者面前的这套丛书。

本套丛书共有 6 册，精选了英语世界里的 108 篇精彩校园演讲，按照分类分为影视明星篇、作家篇、企业家篇、政治家篇、教育家篇和媒体达人篇。读者朋友在这 108 篇演讲中必定找到最开心的演讲、最励志的演讲、最具正能量的演讲、最有意思的演讲、最具智慧的演讲、最具启发性的演讲。

影视明星篇的演讲者包括 18 位明星，他们是：金·凯瑞（Jim Carrey）、查理·戴（Charlie Day）、敏迪·卡灵（Mindy Kaling）、艾德·赫尔姆斯（Ed Helms）、朱莉·安德鲁斯（Julie Andrews）、简·林奇（Jane Lynch）、罗伯特·德尼罗（Robert De Niro）、丹泽尔·华盛顿（Denzel Washington）、斯蒂芬·科尔伯特（Stephen Tyrone Colbert）、乌比·戈德堡（Whoopi Goldberg）、梅丽尔·斯特瑞普（Meryl Streep）、丽莎·库卓（Lisa Kudrow）、艾伦·狄珍妮（Ellen DeGeneres）、阿诺德·施瓦辛格（Arnold Schwarzenegger）、多莉·帕顿（Dolly Parton）、比尔·考斯比（bill cosby）、威尔·法瑞尔（Will Ferrell）和博诺（Bono）。

作家篇的演讲者包括 18 位著名作家，他们是：戴维·雷姆尼克（David Remnick）、阿图·葛文德（Atul Gawande）、乔斯·韦登（Joss Whedon）、比尔·麦克基本（Bill McKibben）、狄巴克·乔布拉（Deepak Chopra）、乔治·桑德斯（George Saunders）、乔纳森·福阿（Jonathan Foer）、尼

尔·盖曼（Neil Gaiman）、迈克尔·刘易斯（Michael Lewis）、阿伦·索尔金（Aaron Sorkin）、托马斯·弗里德曼（Thomas L. Friedman）、阿里安娜·赫芬顿（Ariana Huffington）、艾丽·维塞尔（Elie Wiesel）、约翰·格里沙姆（John Grisham）、苏·蒙克·基德（Sue Monk Kidd）、路易丝·俄德里克（Louise Erdrich）、戴维·福斯特·华莱士（David Foster Wallace）和安娜·昆德兰（Anna Quindlen）。

企业家篇的演讲者包括18位著名企业家，他们是：杜邦CEO爱伦·库尔曼（Ellen Kullman）、汤丽柏琦品牌创始人汤丽·柏琦（Tory Burch）、通用汽车CEO玛丽·博拉（Mary Barra）、Youtube公司CEO苏珊·沃西基（Susan Wojcicki）、AOL创始人史蒂夫·凯斯（Steve Case）、纽交所CEO邓肯·尼德奥尔（Duncan L. Niederauer）、推特CEO迪克·科斯特洛（Dick Costolo）、特斯拉CEO埃隆·马斯克（Elon Musk）、耐克基金会主席兼CEO玛丽亚·艾特尔（Maria Eitel）、LinkedIn联合创始人雷德·霍夫曼（Reid Hoffman）、微软公司前CEO史蒂夫·鲍尔默（Steve Ballmer）、亚马逊CEO杰夫·贝佐斯（Jeff Bezos）、苹果公司CEO提姆·库克（Tim Cook）、谷歌CEO拉里·佩奇（Larry Page）、雅虎原CEO杨致远（Jerry Yang）、家得宝公司创始人伯尼·马库斯（Bernie Marcus）、风投资本家约翰·多尔（John Doerr）和惠普前CEO卡莉·菲奥莉娜（Carly Fiorina）。

政治家篇的演讲者包括17位著名政治家，他们是：美国前总统乔治·沃克·布什（George Walker Bush）、美国总统巴拉克·奥巴马（Barack Obama）、美国外交部长约翰·克里（John Kerry）、美联储主席珍妮特·耶伦（Janet Yellen）、美国前总统比尔·克林顿（Bill Clinton）、美国参议员科里·布克（Cory Booker）、纽约市前市长迈克尔·布隆伯格（Michael Bloomberg）、诺贝尔和平奖得主昂山素季（Aung San Suu Kyi）、美国前外交部长科林·鲍威尔（Colin Powell）、利比亚总统瑟利夫夫人（Ellen Johnson-Sirleaf）、美联储前主席本·伯南克（Ben Bernanke）、美国副总统乔·拜登（Joe Biden）、美国前外交部长希拉里·克林顿（Hillary Clinton）、美国最高法院首位女大法官桑德拉·奥康纳（Sandra Day O'Connor）、美国最高法院大法官安东尼·肯尼迪（Anthony Kennedy）、美国前外交部长马德琳·奥尔布赖特（Madeleine Albright）和美国前外交部长康多莉莎·赖斯（Condoleezza Rice）。

教育家篇包括18位大学校长、教授以及教育工作者，他们是：美国教育部长阿恩·邓肯（Arne Duncan）、普林斯顿大学教授乔伊斯·欧茨（Joyce Oates）、斯坦福大学校长约翰·亨尼斯（John Hennessy）、耶鲁大学校长彼得·沙洛维（Peter Salovey）、哈佛大学经济学教授格利高里·曼昆（N. Gregory Mankiw）、普林斯顿大学经济学教授本·伯南克（Ben Bernanke）、匹兹堡大学传播学教授约翰·施利姆（John Schlimm）、政治学教授梅丽莎·哈里斯·佩里（Melissa Harris-Perry）、普林斯顿大学校长雪莉·蒂尔曼（Shirley Tilghman）、哈佛大学生物学教授E.O.威尔逊博士（E.O. Wilson）、弗吉尼亚大学校长泰瑞莎·沙利文（Teresa Sullivan）、斯坦福大学物理学教授朱棣文（Steven Chu）、宾夕法尼亚大学校长艾米·古德曼（Amy Gutmann）、哥伦比亚大学经济学教授杰弗里·萨克斯（Jeffrey Sachs）、美国前教育部长玛格丽特·斯佩林斯（Margaret

Spellings）、经济学教授穆罕默德·尤努斯（Muhammad Yunus）、卡内基梅隆大学计算机教授兰迪·鲍许（Randy Pausch）和布朗大学前校长瓦谭·格里格瑞恩（Vartan Gregorian）。

媒体达人篇包括18位电视节目主持人、报刊编辑、新媒体创始人、专栏作家，他们是：《纽约时报》前总主编吉尔·爱博松（Jill Abramson）、CBS新闻主播鲍勃·西弗（Bob Schieffer）、《华盛顿邮报》执行主编马丁·巴隆（Martin Baron）、《华盛顿周报》执行编辑格温·艾费尔（Gwen Ifill）、《纽约时报》专栏作家大卫·布鲁克斯（David Brooks）、《纽约时报》专栏作家尼格拉斯·克里斯托弗（Nicholas Kristof）、CBS主播夏琳·阿尔方西（Sharyn Alfonsi）、《赫芬顿邮报》合伙人阿里安娜·赫芬顿（Ariana Huffington）、CNN主播坎蒂·克劳利（Candy Crowley）、资深体育节目解说里兰德·柯尔索（Leland Corso）、CNN主播索莱达·奥布莱恩（Soledad O'Brien）、脱口秀节目主持人奥普拉·温佛瑞（Oprah Winfrey）、脱口秀节目主持人柯南·奥布莱恩（Conan O'Brien）、CBS新闻主播凯蒂·库里克（Katie Couric）、NBC主播布莱恩·威廉姆斯（Brian Williams）、体育节目资深解说迪克·恩伯格（Dick Enberg）、资深政治评论员詹姆斯·卡维尔（James Carville）和NBC主播汤姆·布罗考（Tom Brokaw）。

本套丛书有三大特点：一、注释详细。本套丛书除了包括英文文本外，我们还提供了参考译文，重要的是我们对难词和常用短语予以了详细注释，我们对和西方文化有关的圣经故事、历史事件和历史名人进行了详细注解。我们相信多达3000余条的注释一定会让你多掌握一些英语单词和英语习语，一定会让你多了解一些西方文化，充实自己的精神世界；二、奉送全部演讲的原声音频。正因为有原声音频，我们才能体会演讲者的激情和力量；三、本套丛书的大部分演讲都是第一次被译成中文，第一次与广大国内读者见面，例如好莱坞明星金·凯瑞的演讲、特斯拉CEO埃隆·马斯克、经济学家格利高里·曼昆的演讲等。

108位名人就像《水浒传》里的108将一样，个个有自己精彩的故事，个个有自己精彩的人生，个个有自己精彩的至理名言。您还等什么？打开本套丛书，跟随着名人的演讲去探索他们非凡的人生和思想吧。

王瑞泽　2015年9月3日写于中国大阅兵之际

目 录

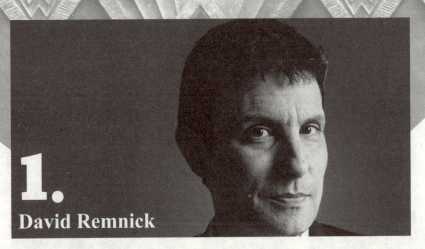

1.
David Remnick

戴维·雷姆尼克
在雪城大学的演讲（2014年）

扫一扫

 人物档案

　　戴维·雷姆尼克（David Remnick，1958年10月29日—），美国著名作家，曾担任《华盛顿邮报》记者达10年之久，期间4年常驻莫斯科。1992年，他加盟《纽约客》杂志。1998年以来，一直担任该刊主编。他之前出版的关于拳王穆罕默德·阿里的传记著作《世界之王》，1998年被《时代》杂志评选为非虚构类图书第一名。1994年，他撰写的《列宁墓：苏联最后的日子》获得普利策奖。

 场景介绍

　　雪城大学（Syracuse University），也称为锡拉丘兹大学，成立于1870年，位于美国纽约州雪城，是一家私立研究型大学。最早可以追溯到由卫理公会于1832年成立的神学院。1920年，雪城大学宣布自己为无宗派学校，但仍保持着与美国卫理公会的联系。雪城大学在1966年加入美国大学联盟。雪城大学是一所多样化的高等教育学府，致力于一流的师资力量和学术水平，吸引及支持充满进取心的学生前来求学，并努力实现本地、全美及国际范围的沟通和交流。

As of Today You Are Inescapably Citizens of the World
从今天开始你们不可避免地成为了世界公民

经典原文
Original Text

1　Good morning and happy Mother's Day! Let's hear it for the mothers.

2　I'd like to begin with an announcement: To the Chancellor, to the trustees, to the faculty, to the parents and grandparents who are smiling so hard their faces are starting to ache. To the siblings texting descriptions of their mad impatience up in the **bleachers**①, to all of you my announcement is this: I hereby declare the Class of 2014 to be, without question, the greatest graduating class in the history of Syracuse University.

3　The most intelligent. The most accomplished. And certainly, the best looking. (Yes, I thought you would agree.) By the way, I think you graduates are **off the hook**② for Mother's Day. The vision of you in a cap and gown, trust me, beats a nice 'Best mom ever' mug any old day. The mothers agree.

中文译文
Suggested Translation

1　大家早上好，母亲节快乐！让我们听听献给母亲们的祝福声。

2　我想首先声明一下：校长、各位理事、各位老师、脸上笑得都开始发疼的学生家长们、在看台上等得不耐烦开始疯狂发送短信的学生的兄弟姐妹们，我对你们所有人声明：我特此宣布，2014届毕业班毫无疑问是雪城大学历史最好的毕业班。

3　你们是最聪明的。你们是最有成就的。当然，你们也是最好看的。（是的，我想你们会同意我的这个说法。）顺便说一下，我想你们不用为了母亲节而苦恼了。请相信我，你们戴着学位帽、身穿学位袍的样子胜过以往任何母亲节送给妈妈的精致杯子，尽管杯子上面印有"最佳妈

---

① bleacher ['blɪtʃəz] *n.* 漂白剂；漂白业者；露天看台
② off the hook 摆脱困境；电话没挂好；连续不断；很棒，很酷

4   At least for one day your parents feel, and I've felt it, an immeasurable sense of relief.

5   First of all, they know where you are. And second, no kidding, their hearts are absolutely overflowing with joy.

6   So good, I've now officially fulfilled the most important initial requirement of a proper commencement speech, pandering shamelessly to the graduating class and to motherhood and mothers everywhere. I hope you appreciate it because this is a pretty scary gig.

7   This place is known as the loud house. I have no idea why. And it's been the scene of many Orange triumphs.

8   As most of you know, Syracuse has been the scene of two of the most celebrated speeches delivered anywhere in recent years, speeches by two gifted writers, **Aaron Sorkin**③ and **George Saunders**④. Not only were Aaron and George particularly eloquent, they're also Syracuse people.

9   Family. Which leads to the absolutely sensible question: What in God's name is this outsider doing here?

妈"的字样。母亲们会同意我的这个观点。

4   至少有这么一天，你们的父母觉得如释重负，我已经感受到了。

5   首先，他们知道你们在哪里。第二，不开玩笑，他们的心里绝对满怀欣喜。

6   太好了，我现在已经正式满足了一个恰当的毕业典礼演讲的最重要的初步要求，即厚着脸皮迎合毕业班的学生们以及无处不在的母亲们。我希望你们喜欢我的演讲，因为这是一场非常可怕的现场演出。

7   这个地方被称为喧哗之屋。我不知道为什么会起这样一个名字。这里是多次见证雪城大学橘子人队取得胜利的地方。

8   正如你们大多数人都知道的那样，近年来最著名的毕业典礼演讲中，有两个就发生在雪城大学，是由两位有才华横溢的作家发表的演讲，他们是阿伦·索尔金和乔治·桑德斯。阿伦和乔治不仅发表了极有说服力的演讲，关键是他们也是雪城大学的人。

9   他们和你们是一家人。那么一个绝对合情合理的问题来了：我这个局外人到底来这里干什么？

③ Aaron Sorkin 阿伦·索尔金，美国作家，详见本书他的演讲
④ George Saunders 乔治·桑德斯，美国作家，详见本书他的演讲

10   I can't know for sure, but I doubt it's because as the editor of *The New Yorker* I'm the world's foremost judge of talking dog cartoons. By the way, I am.

11   And I'm pretty certain that I'm the only person alive whose job in large measure is based on an ability to distinguish a funny talking **spaniel**⑤ from a really boring talking spaniel.

12   There are jobs and there are jobs. But I think it's something else.

13   I think part of the reason I'm here has something to do with the family for whom I work. The Syracuse family that runs *The New Yorker* and much else. The Newhouse family. Even on winter days with your eyes tearing from the cold, you must have noticed the buildings on campus, the Newhouse School of Public Communications, **cue**⑥ the cheering of the communications school. The Newhouse family is a press family that is press shy. But let me thank them just this once publicly not only for the gifts they've provided to your great institution, but for the gift of absolute editorial freedom that they have provided to my colleagues and to me.

14   Now, the remaining obligation of a Commencement address is to have, well, something to say. And this is what I would say three decades after I threw

10   我真的不知道是什么原因，但我怀疑这是因为作为《纽约客》的编辑，我是世界上最重要的对有会说话的狗狗的卡通进行鉴赏的人。顺便说一下，我就是。

11   我敢肯定，在活着的人中，我是唯一一个在很大程度上靠分辨一个会说话的西班牙猎犬是有趣还是很无聊为工作的人。

12   有工作方面的原因。但我认为这有别的原因。

13   我认为我来这里的部分原因和我为之工作的那个家族有关。一个运营着《纽约客》以及还有很多其它杂志和报纸的锡拉丘兹市家族，它就是纽豪斯家族。即使在冬天里你冻得眼睛直流泪，你一定也会注意到校园里那些属于纽豪斯公共传播学院的建筑物，让我们听听来自纽豪斯公共传播学院毕业生们的欢呼声。纽豪斯家族是一个羞于面对媒体的媒体家族。但请让我仅借这个场合公开向他们表示一次感谢，不仅因为他们为你们这所伟大的院校捐赠了这么多礼物，还因为他们给予我的同事和我如此大的编辑自由。

14   一个毕业典礼演讲者的其余义务就是要说点什么东西。下面的话，就是在我将自己那顶绝

---

⑤ spaniel ['spænjəl] *n.* 西班牙猎犬；恭顺的人
⑥ cue [kju] *vt.* 给……暗示

my own absolutely ridiculous graduation hat up into the air. And by the way, there's some great ones out there.

15 I have every hope for all of you as individuals. I hope for your good health. I hope that you are blessed with family and friends to love. I hope you're able to care for your parents, and for your children. I hope you find a way to make a living that thrills and nourishes you. I hope, in other words, that your lives are happy and deep and interesting and loving lives.

16 But I also hope you know as of today you are inescapably citizens of the world.

17 Last year at convocation George Saunders spoke of the virtue of kindness. And he spoke of kindness for the most part as a private virtue, a texture of human interaction, a way of being, really between and among friends, family, colleagues, and even strangers. And he was absolutely right. To be kind-to be the opposite of heedless or cruel-is a simple sounding but wholly essential, virtue.

18 But all of us are also members of a community, many kinds of communities that stretch from the local to the global. And this demands of you many things. Being a member of a community demands that you pay taxes, obey the law, maybe join a school board, volunteer to help the poor and disabled. But the one demand of living in a community and in the world that I want to talk about today is the demand placed

对可笑的毕业帽抛向空中的 30 年后，我想要说的话。顺便说一下，我的话里还真有一些重要的东西。

15 我对你们每一个人都满怀希望。我希望你们身体健康。我希望你们沐浴在家人和朋友的爱中。我希望你们能照顾你们的父母和你们的孩子。我希望你们找到谋生的方式并以此振奋和激励自己。换句话说，我希望你们的生活是快乐的、深刻的、有趣的并充满爱意的。

16 但我也希望你们知道，从今天开始，你们不可避免地成为了世界公民。

17 在去年的毕业典礼大会上，乔治·桑德斯谈到了善良的美德。他说，善良在很大程度上是一种私德，是人类交流的构成部分，是一种存在方式，真正存在于朋友之间，家人之间，同事之间，甚至是陌生人之间。他说的完全正确。对人善良——即对人漠视或残忍的反面——是一个说起来简单却必不可少的美德。

18 但我们每个人也都是某一个社会的成员，从地方到全球我们有很多社会。这就要求你做很多事情。作为一个社会成员，你必须纳税，遵守法律，或许还要加入一个学校董事会，自愿帮助穷人和残疾人。但要在社会和世界上生活，就要求你要有远见，

on you for vision.

19　It's traditional on graduation day for your elders to admit, as if it were ever a secret to you, that we, the old and the soon-to-be-so have screwed up the world on a colossal scale. We then go on to say we're very sorry but now we're going fishing and now we're depending on you to fix everything. **Have a ball**⑦!

20　In fact, that's a **dodge**⑧, a dumb show of civilizational false modesty. In so many ways modern life is immensely better than ever before. Over time, we human beasts or at least the large and lucky percentage of us, have emerged from the state of nature that was in the words of **Thomas Hobbs**⑨, "solitary or nasty, brutish, and short." And through the development of law and political organizations, science and culture, our lives are less solitary, less poor, less nasty, brutish, and short. Not for a second do I want to suggest that life is better for everyone. We have not eliminated cruelty, stupidity, poverty, or violence. Oppression reigns from Damscus to Pyongyang, to even Moscow, but the movement forward, while full of **detours**⑩ and disasters, the stuff we call history, is unmistakable.

这也是我今天要谈论的话题。

19　毕业典礼这一天的一个惯例就是，你们的长辈承认，老一辈们和即将老去的人把这个世界搞得乱七八糟，好愿你们以前不知道似的。接下来我们就要说声我们很抱歉，但是我们现在要去钓鱼了，而我们相信你们能修正这一切。我们狂欢去了！

20　事实上，这是一种托词，是一出用文明的方式假意谦虚的哑剧。在很多方面，现代人的生活比以前是好多了。随着时间的推移，我们这些野蛮人，或者至少说我们中很大一部分幸运儿，从托马斯·霍布斯口中"孤独或肮脏、野蛮、贫困"的自然状态中挣脱出来。而通过法律和政治组织以及科学和文化的发展，我们的生活变得不那么孤独、不那么贫穷、不那么肮脏、不那么野蛮、也不那么粗暴。我毫不犹豫地想说，我们每个人的生活都变得更好了。尽管我们未能彻底消除残忍、愚蠢、贫困或暴力。从大马士革到平壤甚至再到莫斯科，压迫统治依然存在，但时代

⑦ have a ball　狂欢；玩得开心

⑧ dodge [dɑdʒ] *n.* 躲闪；托词

⑨ Thomas Hobbs 托马斯·霍布斯（1588—1679），英国政治家、哲学家。他在著作《维利坦》中试图要建立一个属于自由人的自然秩序，其实质是理性的人们资源交出个人的自然权利而自发形成的自然秩序

⑩ detour ['dɪtʊr] *n.* 绕道；便道

21   Think of it, the percentage of the world's population destined to live in a state of absolute poverty has in just the past 50 years dropped by half. The percentage of the world that lives in some form of relative political liberty has vastly expanded, from Eastern Europe, to Latin America. And although a modern media guarantees we are at least dimly aware of bloody conflict from Ukraine to the Central African Republic, the scale of the world's conflicts according to scholars like Stephen Pinker, is, overall, markedly less than any time in human history.

22   And we are healthier. My colleague at *The New Yorker* **Atul Gawande**[11] has written about a typical medical operation in the 19th century performed by a surgeon named Liston. Because there was no effective **anesthesia**[12] at the time, Liston had to work at fantastic speed. But while trying to amputate a patient's leg, he also managed to amputate the fingers of his assistant. Whoops. Both the patient and the assistant died of subsequent infections. The sight of all this medical **mayhem**[13] was so disgusting that a spectator in the **operating theater**[14] died of shock. Thereby as Gawande writes, this was a surgical procedure with a 300% mortality rate. A big **body count**[15]. And not at all unusual for the times.

21   想想看，注定要生活在绝对贫困状态里的世界人口比例在过去的 50 年里下降了一半。从东欧到拉丁美洲，生活在某种形式的相对政治自由状态里的世界人口比例已大大增加。尽管现代传媒保证我们至少能了解到从乌克兰到中非共和国的流血冲突，但据史蒂芬·平克等学者的分析，现在世界冲突的规模总的来说明显低于人类历史上的任何时期。

22   我们也更加健康了。我在《纽约客》的同事阿图·葛文德写了一个发生在十九世纪的典型医疗手术事件，手术是由一位名叫利斯顿的外科医生实施。由于当时没有有效的麻醉药，利斯顿不得不以极快的速度进行手术。但当他试图截掉病人的一条腿时，他还成功地锯掉了他助手的手指。哎呀乖乖。病人和助理都死于了继发性感染。这种医疗重大事故的景象是如此让人感到恶心，以至于在手术室里的一位旁观者也死于了休克。因此，正如葛文德所写，这是一个死亡率高

在向前发展，尽管其间充满曲折和灾难，但我们称之为历史的东西是不会错的。

---

⑪ Atul Gawande 阿图·葛文德，美国作家，详见本书他的演讲部分

⑫ anesthesia [ˌænəsˈθɪʒə] *n.* 麻醉；麻木（等于 anaesthesia）

⑬ mayhem [ˈmeɪhem] *n.* 故意的伤害罪；重伤罪；蓄意的破坏

⑭ operating theater 手术室

⑮ body count 死亡人数统计

23 So we've gotten better at these things. So much of what used to kill us is now a matter of an antibiotic or a pill. Operations on the heart, the brain can often be performed without blood at all.

24 As Gawande writes, we are now in an era in which a teenage boy can undergo **aorta**[16] surgery on a Thursday and be well enough to **sprain**[17] his ankle playing sports the following Saturday. The technological refinement of our abilities to care for the human body has been **nothing short of**[18] miraculous. **At the height of**[19] the Roman Empire, life expectancy was about as old as you are now, 22. By 1900, no so long ago, global life expectancy was 32. Now it's close to 70 and in the United States we live into our 80s and some of you, God help you, will **limp**[20] past 100.

25 As for technological advance, I hardly need to tell you: The capacity to communicate efficiently and instantly, to compute, to navigate, to take 5,000 graduation pictures as you will today, to record a

达 300% 的外科手术。一个庞大的死亡人数统计数字在那个时代不足为奇。

23 所以我们在这些事情上变得更好了。有太多过去可以致我们以死地的东西现在只需要一粒抗生素或药丸就可解决。对心脏和大脑实施手术往往可以在根本见不到一滴血的情况下进行。

24 如葛文德写到的，我们现在处于这样一个时代：一个十几岁的小男孩可以在星期四接受主动脉手术，而在接下来的星期六就恢复得好到足以在运动时扭伤膝盖。我们照顾人体的能力在技术上得到了奇迹般的提升。在罗马帝国鼎盛时期，人们的平均寿命和你们现在的年龄差不多，22 岁。到了距离现在并不久远的 1900 年，全球的平均寿命是 32 岁。现在全球平均寿命接近 70 岁，而美国人的平均寿命高达 80 多岁，而你们中的一些人，托上帝的福，将会活过 100 岁。

25 至于科技方面的进步，我甚至无需告诉你们：人类能即时有效地交流，计算，导航，像你们今天这样为 5000 名毕业生拍

⑯ aorta [eɪˈɔːtə] *n*. [解剖] 主动脉
⑰ sprain [spreɪn] *vt.* 扭伤
⑱ nothing short of 简直就是；无异于……；简直不比……差
⑲ at the height of 在……顶点；在……的顶峰或鼎盛时期
⑳ limp [lɪmp] *vi.* 跛行，一拐一拐地走；缓慢费力地前进

voice, to read the news in any language and then share it, to access the literary and musical wealth of all of human history, to do all of these things is as simple as reaching into your pocket.

26　You have a remote control for your life waiting for you.

27　We have also, locally and globally made advances in the quality and range of human empathy. Take the life of the great Lou Reed, who studied here at Syracuse. He was not some distant historical figure, he and his band The Velvet underground were pivotal figures in rock'n roll in the New York art scene, and he died just last October. And yet when he was a teenager in the late'50s, his parents tried to, quote, solve, unquote, his bisexuality by submitting him to electric shock therapy. Try to imagine that. Many years later he said about the treatment they put **electrodes**[21] on your head and the effect is that you lose your memory and become a vegetable. You can't read a book because you get to page 17 and you have to start right back on Page 1 again.

28　It was around the same time that American magazines advertised a hideous burning cream that could lighten the skin so that African Americans could somehow pass more easily into white racist

照，录音，用任何语言阅读新闻然后与人分享，探访人类历史上所有的文学和音乐财富——人们做所有这些事情都简单得如同探囊取物。

26　你们未来生活的遥控器撑握在你们手中。

27　在人类同理心的品性和范围方面，我们在本地区和全球范围内都取得了进展。以摇滚巨星卢·里德的一生为例，他就在雪城大学搞研究。他并非是年代久远的历史人物，他和他的地下乐队"地下丝绒乐队"在纽约摇滚乐坛举足轻重，他在去年十月刚刚去世。然而，在 20 世纪 50 年代末当他还是一个十几岁的少年的时候，他的父母试图通过电击疗法来（引用原话）"解决"（结束引用）他的双性恋问题。大家试着想象一下当时的情形。许多年以后，他说起了那段治疗过程：他们把治疗电极缠在你头上，其效果就是让你失去记忆，让你变成植物人。你不要这样读书，你已经翻到第 17 页了，你需要回过头来从第 1 页开始看。

28　差不多就在同一时期，美国杂志为一支可恶的烧伤膏做广告，它说该药膏能够漂白皮肤，以便让非裔美国人可以更容易地

㉑ electrode [ɪˈlektrəʊd] *n.* [电] 电极；电焊条

society. Now we live in a world where the gains of the Civil Rights Movement of the'50s and'60s and the women's movement of the'70s at least seem to be well established. And we're deep into a liberation movement of the 21st century, the LGBT movement. Marriage freedom, unthinkable so recently, opposed by absolutely everyone but a small number, is now, I'm happy to say, a national inevitability. In 50 years, in other words, we have gone from putting electrodes on the head of a teenager to, quote, cure his homosexual feelings, to a growing national consensus that celebrates the marriages, the equality, and the humanity of gay men and lesbians. **Hallelujah**[22].

29 And yet, if the world is on such upward trajectories, aren't you just free to pursue your own private lives and tend your private gardens? Needless to say, my **triumphalist**[23] description of global advance is full of holes and gigantic, horrifying exceptions. If you think racism in America is disappeared, you know nothing of **Trayvon Martin**[24]. If you think racism in America is disappeared, you haven't tried to drive or **hail a cab**[25] while black

融入白人种族主义者的社会。现在我们生活在一个由 20 世纪 50 年代和 60 年代的美国民权运动以及 70 年代的妇女运动所种下的树似乎开始开花结果的时代。我们正在深入开展 21 世纪的解放运动，即同性恋权利运动。就在不久前，婚姻自由还是不可想象的，它遭到了绝大多数人的反对，只得到了极少数人的拥护；但是现在，我很高兴地说，婚姻自由成了国人的必然选择。换句话说，50 年来，我们已经从通过把电极缠在一个少年头上来"治愈"他的同性恋倾向，走到了越来越多的国人对男同性恋和女同性恋的婚姻、平等和人性应予以庆祝达成共识这一步。哈利路亚，赞美上帝。

29 然而，如果世界在如此向上的轨道上前进的话，是不是说你就可以自由自在地过自己的私人生活、照料自己的私人花园了呢？不用说，我对全球进步过于乐观的描述充满了漏洞以及大量可怕的例外。如果你认为种族主义在美国已经消失了，你就是对特雷沃恩·马丁一事一无所知。

---

[22] hallelujah [ˌhælɪˈluːjə] *int.* 哈利路亚，赞美你上帝
[23] triumphalist [traɪˈʌmfəlɪst] *adj.* 为向败者夸耀而大肆庆祝的
[24] Trayvon Martin 美国黑人青年，2012 年 2 月 16 岁的他被白人保安射杀，这件事引发了美国各地大规模的游行示威
[25] hail a cab 叫出租车

or brown. If you think sexism is dead in America, you haven't taken note of the unbearable maleness of corporate boardrooms in New York or Silicon Valley. If you think sexism in America is dead, you haven't noticed that women are still paid markedly less than men for comparable work. If you think homophobia is dead, you are not watching the last round of Republican primary debates when a gay combat soldier in Afghanistan asked the candidates about his rights in the military and members of the crowd booed him and the candidates, cowards one and all, failed to stand up for him.

30   But all of that is self evident. I said I wanted to speak of the demands on you of vision. What I mean is that the rate and the way the world advances is dependent on us and now most definitely as of this day on you. Nothing is inevitable. If this day means anything, it means that you are now in the **contingent**[26] of the responsible. You must be kind, yes, but you must also look beyond your own house. We're depending on you for your efforts and your vision. We are depending on your eye and your imagination to identify what wrongs exist and persist, and on your hands, your backs, your efforts to right them.

如果你认为种族主义在美国已经消失了，那你就是没有以一个有色人种的身份试过驾车或叫出租车。如果你认为性别歧视在美国已经完蛋了，你就是还没有注意到在纽约或硅谷的公司董事会里几乎清一色地全是男性的情况简直让人无法忍受。如果你认为性别歧视在美国已经消失了，那你就是没注意到做同等的工作女性得到的报酬仍然远比男性的少。如果你认为同性恋恐惧症在美国已经死了，那你就是没有看到最后一轮的共和党初选辩论中，当一名在阿富汗服役的同性恋士兵问候选人他在军队有何权利时，人群中对他发出的嘘声，而候选人个个都是懦夫，竟然没有一个人站出来声援他。

30   但所有的这一切都是不言而喻的。我说过我想谈谈对你们在远见方面的要求。我的意思是，世界前进的步伐和方式取决于我们，而于今日，无疑更多地是依赖你们。没有什么是必然的。如果说这一天意味着什么，那就意味着你们现在加入了负责者的队伍。你必须心地善良，是的，但你也必须看到自己房子以外的天空。我们依赖于用你们的努力和远见。我们依赖于用你们的视野和想象力去辨别什么样的

㉖ contingent [kən'tɪndʒənt] *n.* 分遣队；偶然事件；分得部分；代表团

31　All of us have **20/20 vision**[27] when it comes to the outrages of the past. As my friend the philosopher Anthony Appiah reminds us, "Once pretty much everywhere beating your wife and children was regarded as a father's duty. Homosexuality was a hanging offense. **Waterboarding**[28] was approved, in fact, invented by the Catholic Church. Through the middle of the 19th century the United States and other nations in the Americas condoned plantation slavery. Many of our grandparents were born in the states where women were forbidden to vote. And well into the twentieth century lynch mobs in this country tortured, hanged, and burned human beings at picnics." We look back on all this now with a self satisfied notion that we are beyond such cruelties. We are so far beyond them that we cannot imagine a moral sensibility that condoned and defended them. Because after all, we are so advanced, we are so good. But we are not so good. We are humans, and, as such, we are, without our quite knowing it, always living at least partly in the dark. What conditions do we tolerate now that require our, your, visionary capacity and effort? What will we look back on with incredulous shame and how will we begin to right it?

错误持续存在着，我们也依赖于你们用你们的双手、用你们的努力去纠正这些错误。

31　当谈到过去的暴行时，我们所有人都看得很清楚。我的哲学家朋友安东尼·阿皮亚提醒我们："曾几何时，几乎每个地方的人们都认为打老婆、孩子是做父亲的权利。同性恋是一种可以被判绞刑的罪行。水刑是被认可的逼供方式，事实上，该刑罚还是由天主教教会发明的。贯穿19世纪中叶，美国和美洲其他国家宽容了种植园奴隶制。我们的祖父母中有很多出生在妇女禁止投票的州。进入20世纪后，这个国家里滥用私刑的暴徒在野营地折磨、绞死、烧死同类。"现在我们回顾这一切，心里有一种沾沾自喜的感觉，因为我们远离了这样的残酷行为。我们离这些太远了，以至于我们意想不到我们的道德情感会宽容它们并为之辩护。因为毕竟我们是如此文明，我们是如此善良。但我们并非那么善良。我们是人，而且正因如此，我们总是生活在黑暗之中，至少是不那么光明的地方而对此我们并不自知。什么样的情况需

㉗ 20/20 vision 正常视力，即你在20英尺开外的地方能看清正常人在那个距离能看清的事物

㉘ waterboarding "水刑"，一种使犯人以为自己快被溺毙的刑讯方式，犯人被绑成脚比头高的姿势，脸部被毛巾盖住，然后把水倒在犯人脸上。

要你我的想象力和努力来予以容忍？什么情况让我们将带着难以置信的耻辱回顾它？我们将如何开始予以纠正呢？

32 是什么侵蚀了你的内心？你会如何处理呢？

32 What **gnaws at**[29] you? And what will you do about it?

33 Is it the way we treat and warehouse our elderly as our population grows older? Is it the way we isolate and underserve the physically and mentally disabled? Is it our absurd American fascination with guns and our insistence on valuing the so called rights of ownership over the clear and present danger of gun violence? What will we — what will you — do about the widening divides of class and opportunity in this country? You are, dear friends, about to enter an economy that is increasing **winner-take-all**[30]. Part of this is the result of globalization. But do we just throw up our hands and say that's the way it is? And what about our refusal to look **squarely**[31] at the degradation of the planet we inhabit? In the last election cycle many candidates refused even to acknowledge the hard science, irrefutable science, of climate change. The president, while readily accepting the facts, has done far too little to alter them. How long are we, are you, prepared to wait?

33 随着我国人口老龄化趋势的加快，我们对待和安置我们老人的正确方式是什么？我们应该孤立残疾人士和智障人士、让他们受到不应有的待遇？我们美国人应该在坚持所谓的所有权不可侵犯之下，荒谬地迷恋枪支而罔顾由枪支暴力泛滥带来的迫在眉睫的危险吗？对于这个国家中日益严重的阶级分化和机会不均等现象，我们应该做些什么——你们应该做些什么？亲爱的朋友们，你们即将进入一个赢家通吃的经济社会。全球化是造成这一结果的部分原因。但是，难道我们就只好摊开双手说事情原本就是这样吗？我们为何拒绝正视我们所居住的星球在退化这一事实？在上一次的选举中，许多候选人甚至拒绝承认硬科学，即不可驳倒的科学，所指出的气候变化。总统尽管痛快地接受了这个事实，但是他在改变气候变化方

㉙ gnaw at 啃，咬；侵蚀

㉚ winner-take-all 赢家通吃

㉛ squarely ['skweərlɪ] *adv.* 直角地；诚实地；正好；干脆地；正当地

34   No one is insisting you all become global politicians or selfless activists. Some of you will spend nearly all of your time pursuing private, professional, and personal comforts and rewards. But that does not rule out your spending at least some significant time in the service of all. Of all of us. Of seeing the world clear and taking part in some way large or small in making it better.

35   This is what comes with citizenship. This is what comes with a diploma. So while we all congratulate you today on in effect joining the world, we also ask that you help us see that world anew. See it more clearly. And then act. So that a generation from now when I'm gone and you're sitting at your own child's graduation, maybe here at Syracuse on Mother's Day, why not, you will know you've done your part for your son, for your daughter, and for everyone in this loud house and well beyond.

36   Thank you and congratulations!

面几乎无所作为。我们，还有你们，准备等待多久？

34   没有人要求你们成为全球政治家或无私的活动家。你们中的一些人将花费将近一辈子的时间去追求私人的、职业的和个人的舒适和回报。但这并不排除你们至少会拿出一些时间有效地为所有人服务，为我们所有的人服务，让世界变得干干净净，让我们以或大或小的参与方式使它变得更加美好。

35   这是伴随着公民身份而来的责任。这是伴随着文凭而来的责任。所以在我们都在祝贺你们今天正式踏入世界大门的同时，我们也请你们帮助我们看到一个全新的世界。让我们看得更清楚些。然后采取行动。所以，在我走后，你们这一代人正坐在你们自己孩子的毕业典礼上时，也许那天也是在母亲节当日，在雪城大学举行毕业典礼，何不让你们自己知道，你们已经为自己的儿女、为坐在这间喧哗之屋里以及远在别处的所有人尽了自己该尽的一份力呢？

36   谢谢你们，祝贺你们！

2.

Atul Gawande

阿图·葛文德
在北卡教堂山的演讲（2014年）

扫 一 扫

 人物档案

　　阿图·葛文德（Atul Gawande，1965 年 11 月 5 日—），是一位印裔美籍外科医生和作家，哈佛公共健康学院教授、哈佛医学院教授、世界卫生组织全球病患安全挑战项目负责人、美国麦克阿瑟奖获得者、2003 年美国最佳短篇奖得主、2002 及 2009 年美国最佳科学短篇奖得主，2004 年被《新闻周刊》评为"20 位最具影响力的南亚人物"，2010 年入选《时代周刊》评选的"100 位最具影响力人物"。

 场景介绍

　　北卡教堂山分校被公认为是美国 5 大公立大学之一（其他四所分别是加州大学伯克莱分校、加州大学洛杉矶分校、弗吉尼亚大学和密西根大学安娜堡分校），学校宗旨之一就是让所有人都上得起大学。

2 We All Have an Intrinsic Need to Pursue Purposes Larger than Ourselves
我们都有内在的需求去追求一个超越自我的目标

经典原文
Original Text

中文译文
Suggested Translation

1 Welcome graduates. Thank you for including all of us as honorees and including us as part of the University of the People. I even have a cousin, believe it or not, who is graduating this year among you, a North Carolina cousin — hello, Amelia, from my wife's side of the family.

2 I want to start by telling you a doctor story. I know, this is your graduation, and I'm gonna be talking to you about sick people? And I ask you to bear with me. I think you'll see why. And anyway, this is what you get when you put a doctor between you and your diploma.

3 Several years ago, I was having lunch with a colleague of mine, a pediatrician, and we got into a conversation about a project he was working on. He was trying to create a way of measuring the amount of suffering that children with cancer experienced as they went through chemotherapy, radiation and other treatments. (Sounds like such a great story, huh?)

1 欢迎各位应届毕业生。谢谢你们让我们这些荣誉学位获得者参加你们的毕业典礼，也谢谢你们让我们成为了民有大学的一分子。我今年还有一个表妹也在这里毕业呢，她来自北卡——你好啊，阿米莉亚。她是妻子的娘家人。

2 我想先讲一个医生的故事。我知道这是你们的毕业典礼，不过我打算跟你们谈谈病人的事。我请求你们忍受一下我的这种做法。我想你们过会儿会明白的。不管怎样，当一位医生阻挡在你们和你们的文凭之间的时候，你们就会明白了。

3 几年前，我和我的一个同事在吃午饭，他是一名儿科医生，我们谈起了他正在研究的一个项目。当时他正试图建立一种方法，去测量化疗、放射疗法和其他疗法给儿童癌症患者造成的痛苦程度。（听起来像是一个精

阿图·葛文德 *Atul Gawande*

He was thinking if he could design an objective way of measuring the overall well-being of these kids, doctors could make improvements that might reduce how much they had to endure.

4   The day we talked, however, he was incredibly frustrated. He had crafted a set of questions for the kids probing all kinds of aspects of their lives — how much pain they had, what kinda sports they could play or couldn't play, how happy they were. And he tested the questions in children treated for cancer and children who were healthy school kids. But the questionnaire didn't seem to work. That's why he was frustrated. The answers weirdly produced almost no difference between the two groups. Here he had sick kids in wheelchairs, oxygen tubing in their noses, hair gone, at threat of their lives. They'd report a bit more nausea and pain than a kid off the school playground. But that was about it. Overall, their responses suggested they had almost equal quality of life. Indeed, the sick kids sometimes reported a higher quality of life than the school kids.

5   One question asked kids, for example, can you play basketball? The kids in wheelchair, the

彩的故事，是吧？）他想，如果他能设计出来一种能测量这些孩子总体康乐状况的客观方法，医生们就可以改进治疗方案，从而有可能减少孩子们不得不忍受的痛苦。

4   那天我们谈起了这件事，但是，他感到非常沮丧。他为孩子们精心编制了一组问题，那些问题涉及到儿童生活的方方面面——他们感到有多痛苦，他们可以进行哪类体育运动或不可以进行哪类体育运动，他们感到有多快乐。他用这些问题对那些接受癌症治疗的儿童和那些在学校学习的健康儿童进行了测试。但问卷似乎并不奏效。这也是他感到沮丧的原因所在。因为非常奇怪的是两组儿童的答案几乎没有区别。他把问卷发给那些生病的孩子们，他们坐在轮椅里，鼻子里插着氧气管，头发都掉光了，他们面临着死亡的威胁。从他们回答上看，他们只比离开学校操场的孩子多感到一点恶心和疼痛。但那是自然的。总的来说，他们的回答显示他们的生活质量几乎和正常孩子的一样。事实上，报告显示，患病儿童们的生活质量有时会比学校里的孩子们更高。

5   比如，孩子们遇到这样一个问题：你会打篮球吗？坐在轮

wheelchair kids would say, "Yeah, I can play basketball." And the kid of playgound, he would say, "Nah, I can't play basketball." My colleague felt like he had to go back to the drawing board and come up with better questions.

6　But maybe not. Since we spoke, a pile of research has emerged showing similar results. And it has largely found that the social and emotional quality of life of these kids with cancer is as good as that of healthy children — and sometimes better. I have come to think that this puzzling research is telling us something useful about how people – all of us – flourish in life.

7　Powerful emotional strength

8　Earlier this spring, St. Jude's Children's Research Hospital in Memphis published results from studying 255 children after treatment for cancer. The average age was just 13. Half described their cancer battle as the most traumatic event of their life. And the only reason the other half didn't say so was they had gone on to face worse. One was injured in a drive-by shooting that killed their cousin. Another was displaced by Hurricane Katrina. A third was homeless. Others suffered the deaths of close family. Psychologists had said that most of them would likely have **post-traumatic stress disorder**[①]. Yet, when they were measured later, these kids had lower measures of post-traumatic stress than a matched group of children without cancer.

椅上的孩子会说："当然，我会打篮球。"但是，学校里的孩子们会说："噢不，我不会打篮球。"我的同事觉得，他必须得回到绘图板前面想出更好的问题。

6　但也许不必了。自从我们谈过之后，一大堆新出炉的研究显示出了类似的结果。那些研究主要还发现，患癌症的儿童在社会生活和情感生活方面的质量和健康儿童的一样高——有时比健康儿童更高。我开始认为，这项令人费解的研究告诉了我们一些关于人们——我们所有人——如何健康地生活下去的有用的东西。

7　强大的情感力量

8　今年早春时候，位于孟菲斯的圣裘德儿童研究医院发表了针对接受癌症治疗后的255个孩子的研究结果。他们的平均年龄只有13岁。其中一半的孩子说他们生活中最受伤的事情就是与癌症作战。而另一半的孩子没这么说的唯一原因是他们面临更糟糕的困境。一个孩子在一起驾车枪击案中受伤，而他们的堂兄弟被射杀。另一个孩子因为卡特丽娜飓风而流离失所。还有一个孩子无家可归。其他孩子刚遭受了亲人死亡的痛苦。心理学家们说，他们中的大多数都可能患有创伤后应激障碍症。然而，而后对他们

---

① post-traumatic stress disorder 创伤后紧张症；外伤性神经症

9　These researchers found that the experiences of these kids had paradoxically strengthened them. They'd developed social connections. They had a greater sense of empathy for others. They had increased emotional strength. They found them doing better, not worse, than the average child.

10　What was going on here? Normally, if you go through an extended period of suffering — pain, deprivation, violence — especially in childhood, it damages and weakens you. Something was different here.

11　Well, it appears the reason these children grew stronger was due to how the world around them led them to deal with their ordeal. The hospital created an environment full of people who cared about them, understood them and their difficulties, and helped them see beyond their disease to what was worth striving for. The children had their family all around and supporting them. They were connected with other children in similar straits and forged bonds of belonging and self-belief.

12　These were kids, in other words, who were helped to find their sense of meaning and purpose as well as find people who could share it with them. And the combination was so powerful it could carry them through terrible **travails**②. But for many of

的测试表明，这些孩子们创伤后的紧张情绪比对照组那些未患癌症儿童的创伤后紧张情绪要轻。

9　这些研究者们发现，这些孩子们的遭遇反而让他们变得更坚强。他们更加注重社会联系。他们对别人有更强烈的同情心。他们增强了情感力量。他们发现自己比一般的孩子做得更好，而不是更糟。

10　这到底是怎么一回事呢？通常，如果你经历了较长一段时间的痛苦——如疼痛、丧失、暴力——尤其是在童年时期，这段经历会损害你，会削弱你。但这里的情况有所不同。

11　嗯，看来这些孩子变得强大的原因，是由于他们周围的世界引导他们如何应对他们所遭受的苦难。医院创造了一个环境，让很多人关心他们，了解他们和他们的困难，帮助他们看到疾病之外值得为之奋斗的东西。孩子们的家人都在他们的身边支持着他们。他们与其他有着类似困境的孩子们有了联系，建立起了有归属感和自信感的感情纽带。

12　换句话说，这些孩子在人们的帮助下找到了生活的意义和目的，同时也找到了可以与他们分享这些的人。这种结合是如此强大，以至于可以让他们忍受住

② travail ['træveɪl] *n.* 分娩的痛苦；艰苦劳动

the healthy kids, it ironically remained an untapped source of strength and resilience.

13　Experiences of terrible adversity can sometimes bring out this kind of flourishing — for instance, when neighbors come together after a natural disaster and discover they feel more alive than they had. But it doesn't take suffering to find out how potent a feeling of purpose and connection to a community can be. And I suspect that you have experienced something very much like that feeling here in college and discovered how much it can make you grow.

14　"Find what you care about"

15　The aim of college is not complicated. It is to learn and try stuff so you can expand as a human being. Find what you care about. Maybe even figure out who you are and what you are here on this rock for.

16　I had by no means figured out who I was or what I was when I graduated from college. I would still have some years of wandering before I settled on medicine and writing and family and the other ways I would try to make my difference. But it was a special thing to be in a place like this with others who were also trying to figure out their spot in the world. I suspect you too had those late night dorm conversations, that random tutor or professor who took you under wing and believed in you, the encounters with people and ideas you never imagined.

可怕的阵痛。但对于很多健康的孩子们来说，很讽刺的是，他们的力量和韧性仍然有待于挖掘。

13　可怕的不幸经历有时可以带来这种繁荣的景象——例如，当邻居们经历一场自然灾害后走到了一起，他们发现他们感觉比以前更有活力。但我们无需经历痛苦才发现生活有目的以及与社区紧密相连可以焕发出多大的威力。我猜想你们在大学里已经有过了非常类似的经历，并发现了那种经历会使你们茁壮成长。

14　"找到你所关心的"

15　上大学的目的并不复杂，就是学习和尝试新东西以便让你实现一个人的成长。找到你所关心的东西。甚至还要弄清楚自己是谁，以及你来到这块"岩石"上是为了什么。

16　我从大学毕业的时候绝没有想明白我是谁或我是什么人。毕业后的几年我仍然徘徊不定，直到后来才决定尝试在医学、写作、家庭和其他方面让自己变得与众不同。但是和其他也想在找个世界上找到自己价值的人相聚在这样一个地方是一件很特别的事情。我估计你们也经历过那些发生在深夜宿舍里的卧谈会，也有某个导师或教授庇护着你们并看好你们，也要和你们意想不到的人相遇，与你们意想不到的想

法发生碰撞。

17　I arrived at college to find I was sharing a room with a long-haired, born-again Christian humanities major and an Air Force **ROTC**③ electrical engineer. We were, on paper, totally incompatible. But before you knew it, we'd joined together to put on a Wednesday 2 a.m. college radio show that was doomed within a month because none of us wanted to get out of bed for it. We ran what turned out to be an illegal business from our room supplying the dorm with **Twinkies**④, soda, and beer for pizza money. I joined a campus Amnesty International campaign for political prisoners and at one point nearly traveled to communist Poland on some **cockamamie**⑤ scheme we came up with to get illegal writings out from prisoners there, only to **chicken out**⑥.

17　我来到大学后发现，我跟一个留着长发、主修人文学科的虔诚基督徒以及一位来自空军后备军官训练队的电气工程师成为了室友。理论上我们完全是合不来的。但是不知不觉地，我们已经在一起参加星期三凌晨2点播放的学院广播节目了，不过我们的热情注定在一个月内消失，因为我们谁都不愿意为了那个节目而那么早就起床。我们做起了生意，后来发现这是违规的：我们利用我们的房间向整个宿舍楼售卖夹馅面包、苏打水、啤酒，目的是挣买披萨饼的钱。我加入了一个呼吁释放政治犯的校园国际特赦组织，还一度差点去了波兰人民共和国，因为我们想出了一个胡闹的方案：想从那里的囚犯手中得到非法作品，结果最后临阵退缩了。

18　And I think you've had your own inadvisable experiments, too. But because they gave you a sense of direction and connection to others, they are a big part of the reason why — despite the **slog**⑦ of coursework, the all-nighters, the sometime failures and personal setbacks — it's why most of you will long remember college, and Carolina, as among the best years of your lives.

18　我认为你们也有过失策的经历。但是因为这些经历给你们指明了方向，让你们和别人联系在了一起，正因为如此，尽管你们有大量的作业、有很多个不眠之夜、有时还有失败和挫折，你们中的大多数人还是会长久地记得这所大学，记得北卡罗来纳州，

③ ROTC *abbr.*（美）后备军官训练队（Reserve Officers' Training Corps）

④ Twinkies *n.* 夹馅面包

⑤ cockamamie [ˈkɒkəˌmeɪmɪ] *adj.* 繁琐的；假的

⑥ chicken out 临阵退缩；因害怕而停止做某事

⑦ slog [slɒg] *n.* 苦干；跋涉

19 Ultimately, it turns out, we all have an intrinsic need to pursue purposes larger than ourselves, purposes worth making sacrifices for. People often say: find your passion. But there's more to it than that. Not all passions are enough. Just existing for your desires feels empty and insufficient, because our desires are fleeting and insatiable. You need a loyalty.

20 The only way life is not meaningless is to see yourself as part of something greater: a family, a community, a society. And that is the best part of what college has allowed you to do. College made it easy. It gave you an automatic place in the world where you could feel part of something greater. The supposedly "real world" you are joining does not.

21 You face certain traps in moving on from here. One ugliness I think of the "real world" is its readiness to have you define your purpose in terms of an enemy — and I'm not talking about Duke. I'm talking about those we compete with or simply disagree with. The purpose for far too many is less to build something better than to destroy the other side. No tactic is too low as long as you can get away with it. More and more of public and private life seems defined by the strength of one's power rather than the strength of one's ideas.

将你们在这里的日子视为生命中最美好的几年时光。

19 最终事实证明，我们都有内在需求，需要去追求一个超越自我的目标、一个值得为之做出牺牲的目标。人们常说：找到你的激情。但只有激情还不够。不是所有的激情都可以满足要求。只为满足你的欲望而存在的激情让人感到空虚和不足，因为我们的欲望是转瞬即逝的、是贪得无厌的。你需要的是忠诚。

20 让生活过得有意义的唯一办法就是把自己视为某个更为重要的东西——家庭、社区、社会——的一部分。这是大学允许你们做的事中最好的部分。大学让这件事变得很容易。它自动为你在这个世界上找到一个位置，让你能感觉到某种东西比你更重要。你们即将进入的所谓"真实世界"没有这种功能。

21 你们从这里出发，一路上会面临某些的陷阱。我认为"真实世界"的一个丑陋之处就是它容易让你根据你的敌人来定义自己的意途——我说的不是杜克大学。我说的是那些与我们竞争的人，或只是和我们意见不一致的人。有太多人的目的不是建设更好的东西，而是摧毁对方的东西。为了摧毁敌方，人们可以不择手段。越来越多的公共生活和

私人生活似乎是由权力的力量而非思想的力量所决定。

22　And it is surprisingly seductive, you'll find when you get out there. We all find victories easier to come by when they are about knocking others down instead of winning them over. But we also eventually find that these are empty satisfactions.

22　这种诱惑的力量非常惊人，当你离开学校时你会发现这一点。我们都会发现，击倒别人的胜利比说服别人来得更加容易。但我们最终也会发现，这些胜利给我们留下的只是空虚的满足感。

23　A purpose larger than yourself

24　Our other tendency—especially when faced with this kind of nakedly adversarial world—is to narrow down, focus on just our own material needs and success. Why get involved in more when it so often involves dealing with the **antagonistic**[8] and the unkind? It's so much simpler and less messy to hold ourselves back and stay removed in our own private realm.

25　The trouble is, you will wake up one day asking yourself why it is so unfulfilling to simply exist. You cannot flourish without a larger purpose. And that's lucky in a way because our society cannot flourish without your reaching for a larger purpose, either.

26　But what purpose? People and their experiences again offer a clue. And what people find is that they have no more **transcendent**[9] experience than getting to see and help others find their own purpose, to achieve their own potential. And your parents and teachers today can tell you a little about that

23　树立一个超越自己的目标

24　我们的其他偏好——特别是当面对这个赤裸裸的充满敌手的世界时——在减少，我们只专注于自己的物质需求和成功。当人们疲于应付对手和异己的时候，为什么还要卷入其它事情中呢？待在小楼成一统要简单得多，也省去了很多麻烦事。

25　问题是，你会有一天醒来问自己：为什么简单地存活于世让人感到如此空虚？没有一个更远大的目标，你就无法活得精彩。在某种程度上这是幸运的，因为你若不去实现一个更远大的目标，我们的社会也不能繁荣。

26　但是你要设定一个什么样的目标呢？人类及其经验再次为我们提供了线索。人们发现，没有什么经验比通过观察来帮助其他人找到他们自己的目标并挖掘他们自己的潜力更让人感到光荣

⑧ antagonistic [æn͵tægəˈnɪstɪk] *adj.* 敌对的；对抗性的；反对的
⑨ transcendent [trænˈsɛndənt] *adj.* 卓越的；超常的；出类拔萃的

incredible feeling. The lasting wonder and beauty of places like this is their commitment to building people up rather than beating them down. And our great hope is that you carry that ethos with you into the rest of your life.

27   One thing I came to realize after college was that the search for purpose is really a search for a place, not an idea. It is a search for a location in the world where you want to be part of making things better for others in your own small way. It could be a classroom where you teach, a business where you work, a neighborhood where you live.

28   The key is, if you find yourself in a place where if you stop caring — where if your greatest concern becomes only you — you get out of there. You want to put yourself in a place that suits who you are, links you to others, and gives you something beyond yourself worth making sacrifices for.

29   For me, that place happened to be a hospital. I found great satisfaction in learning how to do difficult things that were so valued by others. I liked having the privilege of getting to know people so intimately as a doctor and learning skills they need and could depend on me for. I also liked being the kind of person a hospital forced me to be. Things in a hospital don't always work. The people you take care of aren't

的了。对于这不可思议的感觉，今天你们的父母和老师可以告诉你们一二。像大学这样的地方，它们永恒的奇迹和美就在于它们致力于造就人，而不是打败人。我们最大的希望就是你们在你们的余生中传承这一精神。

27   大学毕业后我逐渐明白了一件事，就是搜寻人生目标其实就是搜寻人生的位置，而不是搜寻一个想法。也就是在这个世界上搜寻一个位置，在那个位置上，你希望通过自己的小小努力成人之美。你的位置可能就在你教书的教室里，可能就在你工作的商业领域中，可能就在你住的附近一带。

28   关键是，如果你为自己找到了一个位置，而在那个位置上如果你不再关心别人——在那里如果你最关心的就只有你自己——那么你就失去了那个位置。你要把自己放在一个适合自己、让自己和别人建立联系并且让你为了某个目标而甘愿做出牺牲来超越自己的地方。

29   对我来说，那个地方恰巧就在医院。我发现我在学习如何克服那些被别人无比看重的困难时，得到了极大满足。我喜欢作为一名医生拥有亲密接触病人的特权，我喜欢学习让他们需要且可以依赖于我的技巧。我也喜欢成为医院迫使我成为的那类人。

always pleasant or, certainly, happy. But everyone has to matter. Everyone deserves respect and our effort to understand them and help them achieve whatever well-being is possible for them. After all, isn't that what we want for ourselves? If so, then that has to be what we seek for others — whether they are a 90-year-old with **dementia**⑩ or a 13-year-old with cancer.

30　Nobody here knows where the place for you will be. But graduates, we do know there is a place for you. In fact, there are likely many of them. You are going to even create some of those places yourselves, and the world is going to benefit from that. That is the reason why we are all excited for you today — and the reason you too can be glad to move on from here.

31　Congratulations to you all. Thank you for all you're going to do, and thank you for making me a **Tar Heel**⑪!

医院里的事并不总是那么顺利。你照顾的人并不总是和蔼可亲，当然也并不总是幸福快乐。但是每个人都必须受到重视。每个人都应该得到尊重，都应该值得我们努力去理解并帮助他们得到一切可能得到的康乐。这毕竟也是我们自己想要得到的东西。如果是这样的话，那无疑就是我们该为别人寻找的东西——无论他们是 90 岁的痴呆症患者，还是 13 岁的癌症患者。

30　这里没人知道你们的位置会在哪里。但毕业生们，我们确实知道会有一个适合你们的位置。事实上，可能有很多适合你们的位置。你们自己甚至将要创造出一些这样的位置，而世界将从中受益。这是我们今天都为你们感到激动的原因——也是你们可以很高兴地离开这里、继续前行的原因。

31　祝贺你们所有人。谢谢你们即将做的一切，感谢你们让我成为了一名"焦油脚人"！

---

⑩ dementia [dɪ'menʃə] *n.* [内科] 痴呆

⑪ Tar Heel ['tɑːhiːl] [美国英语] 焦油脚人 [美国北卡罗来纳州 (Tar Heel State) 人的绰号]

3.

Joss Whedon

乔斯·韦登

在卫斯理公会大学的演讲（2013年）

扫一扫

人物档案

　　乔斯·韦登（Joss Whedon，1964 年 6 月 23 日），美国著名作家、导演、演员，代表作有《复仇者联盟》、《捉鬼者巴菲》、《天使》和《萤火虫》。乔斯·韦登生在一个编剧之家，乔斯·韦登的祖父和父亲都是著名的电视编剧，他从小便展露出类拔萃的写作才能。16 岁时，他来到英国，就读于温切斯特公学并以全优成绩毕业，后回美在卫斯理大学进修电影，1987 年毕业后到洛杉矶发展。

场景介绍

　　卫斯理公会大学（Wesleyan University），又译卫斯理大学、卫斯廉大学、卫斯理安大学，位于美国东北部康涅狄格州的米德尔敦，于 1831 年由卫理公会派教徒所建立，其名称是来自于卫理公会派的建立者 John Wesley（目前该校与卫理公会派无任何联系），是一所私立四年制文理学院。

You Are the Future
你们就是未来

乔斯 · 韦登 *Joss Whedon*

经典原文
Original Text

1　Commencement address. It's going well, it's going well.

2　OK, no, this is going to be great. This is going to be a good one. It's going to go really well.

3　"**Two roads diverged in a wood and**① …" No, I'm not that lazy.

4　I actually sat through many graduations. When I was sitting where you guys are sitting, the speaker was **Bill Cosby**②. He was very funny and he was very brief and I thank him for that. But he gave us a message that I really took with me, and that a lot of us never forgot, about changing the world. He said, "You're not gonna change the world, so don't try."

中文译文
Suggested Translation

1　毕业典礼演讲——很好，很好。

2　好吧，没事，这会是一场精彩的演讲。这会是一场很好的演讲。会非常顺利地进行下去。

3　"两条道路在一片森林里交汇，而……"不引用别人的名言了。我可没有那么懒。

4　实际上我参加过很多次毕业典礼。当我还坐在你们现在坐的那个位置的时候，演讲嘉宾是比尔·科斯比——一个风趣幽默的男人，他的演讲很简短，就这一点我要感谢他。不过，关于改变世界，他给了我们一条建议，让我受益匪浅，也让我们很多人难以忘怀。他说："你们无法改变世界，所以就不要尝试去改变世界了。"

① 这一句引自著名美国诗人 Robert Lee Frost（1874—1963）的自传诗 "The Road Not Taken"。该诗的最后两句常常被人们引用："I took the one less traveled by / And that has made all the difference"
② 关于比尔·科斯比的简历和演讲参见本丛书之《明星篇》

5　That was it! Like, he didn't buy that back at all. And then he complained about buying his daughter a car, and then we left. And I remember thinking, "You know, I think I can do better. I think I can be a little more inspiring than that."

6　So, what I'd like to say to all of you is that you are all going to die.

7　This is a good commencement speech! Because I'm figuring, it's got to go up from here, right? It can only get better, so this is good. It can't get more depressing. You have, in fact, already begun to die.

8　You look great. Don't get me wrong. And you are youth and beauty, you are at your physical peak. Your bodies have just gotten off the ski slope at the peak of growth and potential! And now comes **the black diamond mogul run**③ to the grave.And the weird thing is — your body wants to die. On a cellular level, that's what it wants. And that's probably not what you want.

9　I'm confronted by a great deal of grand and worthy ambition from this **student body**④. You want to be politicians, social workers, you want to be an artist. Your body's ambition? Mulch. Your body wants to make some babies and then go in the ground and

5　就那么简单。他根本没有详细解释。然后他抱怨起自己给女儿买了一辆车的事，再然后我们就离开了。我记得我是这么想的："我想我可以做得更好。我想我可以发表一篇更加鼓舞人心的演讲。"

6　所以，我想对大家说的是，你们所有人都会死掉。

7　这是一场很好的毕业演讲，因为我在想，从现在开始只会一路向上。后面只能越来越好，所以这是好事。没有什么（比刚才我说的话）更让人沮丧的了。事实上，你们已经开始迈向死亡。

8　你们看起来很不错。不要误会我的意思。你们尚青春年少，男生帅女生美。你们正处于身体条件的黄金时期。你们的身体刚刚越过了成长和潜能的峰值，现在迎来了奔向坟墓的颠簸不平的下坡滑道。奇怪的是你们的身体渴望死亡。站在细胞水平的角度上，你们的身体想要死亡。但你们可能并不想死。

9　我在各位那里看到了不少的雄心壮志。你们想成为政治家、社会工作者。你们想成为艺术家。但你们身体的野心却只是枯枝烂叶。你们的身体想生出

③ the black diamond mogul run 滑雪运动术语，指的是坑坑洼洼的下坡滑行
④ student body 全体学生；学生的总称

fertilize things. That's it! And that seems like a bit of a contradiction. That doesn't seem fair. For one thing, we're telling you, "Go out into the world!" exactly when your body is saying, "Hey, let's **bring it down a notch**⑤.Let's take it down."

10   And it is a contradiction, and that's actually what I'd like to talk to you about: the contradictions between your body and your mind, between your mind and itself. I believe these contradictions and these tensions are the greatest gift that we have and hopefully, I can explain that.

11   But first let me say when I talk about contradiction, I'm talking about something that is a constant in your life and in your identity. Not just in your body, but in your own mind in ways you may recognize and you may not.

12   Let's just say, hypothetically, that two roads diverged in a wood and you took the path less traveled. Part of you is just going, "Look at that path! Over there! It's much better! Everybody's traveling on it and it's — it's paved and there's, like, a Starbucks every 50 yards. This is wrong. This path's got nettles and Robert Frost's body and — somebody should have moved that, Ithink. It feels weird."

一些孩子，然后归于尘土，变成养料。就是这样。这似乎有点矛盾。这似乎不公平。一方面，我们要告诉各位"走出象牙塔走进这个世界"；但另一方面，你们的身体正在告诉自己："嘿，让我们悠着点。让我们慢慢来。"

10   这是一个矛盾。这也正是我想和你们谈的事情——存在于你们的身体和你们的内心之间的矛盾以及存在于你们的内心深处的矛盾。我相信这些矛盾和张力是我们所拥有的最好的礼物，我希望可以解释清楚这个问题。

11   但首先让我说明一点：我所说的矛盾，指的是永久存在于你们的生命和你们的身份之中的东西，它不只是存在于你们的身体之内，它还存在于你们的内心深处，你们或许以某种方式意识到了，或许没有意识到。

12   让我们假设森林里有一道分岔路，而你踏上了其中少有人问津的那一条路。你身体的一部分对你说："看看那条路吧！那条路要比这条好走得多。每个人都走那条路。那条马路铺得很平坦，好像每隔 50 码就有一家星巴克。你走这条路是错的。这条路上荆棘密布，还有罗伯特·弗罗斯特的尸体——应该有人把他

⑤ take (bring/let) someone down a notch (two) 灭某人的威风，挫某人的锐气，压下某人的气焰

13 Not only is your mind telling you this, it is on that other path. It is behaving as though it is on that path; it is doing the opposite of what you are doing. And for your entire life you will be doing, on some level, the opposite not only of what you are doing but of what you think you are. That is just going to go on. What you do with all your heart, you will do the opposite of. And what you need to do is to honor that. To understand it. To unearth it. To listen to this other voice.

14 All right, I'm losing this now because otherwise it's coming off in a dramatic fashion at the wrong time. [Takes off his cap] I know, I've worked on this hair for a long time, so I had to **bust it out**⑥.

15 You have, which is a rare thing, the ability and the responsibility to listen to the dissent in yourself, to at least **give it the floor**⑦. Because it is the key, not only to consciousness, but to real growth.

16 To accept duality is to earn identity, and identity is something that you are constantly earning. It is not just "who you are," it is a process that you must be active in, and it's not parroting your parents

13 你的内心不仅仅是这么说的，它还踏上了另外那条路，它的表现就好像它走在那条路上一样。它所做的和你正在做的正相反。你一生中在某种程度上都会做完全相反的事——不仅仅和你所做的完全相反——也和你自认为的你是个什么样的人完全相反。你如今所全力以赴做的事情，将来你会做相反的事。你需要做的就是尊重这一事实，去理解它，发掘它，并倾听另外一种声音。

14 好吧，我现在要摘下帽子，因为不然它会在错误的时间以夸张的方式掉下去（他摘掉博士帽）。我知道头发问题困扰了我很久，因此我不得不豁出去了。

15 极为珍贵的是，你们拥有倾听来自你们心中那个不同声音的能力和责任，至少给它一个表达的机会，因为它不仅在意识觉醒方面起到关键作用，它对于一个人的真正成长也至关重要。

16 接受这种二元性就等于为自己赢得了身份，而你的身份是你一直在赢取的东西。这不仅表明"你是谁"，这还是一个你必

的尸体移开才对啊——走这条路让人感到莫名其妙。"

---

⑥ bust out 相当于 burst out，意思是"闯出来；突发；摆脱"
⑦ give it the floor 给予发言权

or even the thoughts of your learned teachers. It is, now more than ever, about understanding yourself so you can become yourself.

17   I talk about this contradiction and this tension — there's two things I want to say about it. One, it never goes away. And if you think that achieving something, if you think that solving something, if you think a career or a relationship will quiet that voice, it will not. If you think that happiness means total peace, you will never be happy. Peace comes from the acceptance of the part of you that can never be at peace. They will always be in conflict and if you accept that, everything gets a lot better!

18   The other reason is that because you are establishing your identities and beliefs, you need to **argue yourself down**[8], because somebody else will. Somebody's going to **come at**[9] you. Whatever your belief, your idea, your ambition — somebody's going to question it. And unless you have first, you won't be able to **answer back**[10]. You won't be able to hold your ground. You don't believe me, try taking a stand on just one leg. You need to see both sides.

须积极参与的过程；这不是机械地模仿你的父母，甚至也不是继承你那些博学的老师们的思想。而是以往任何时候都要更多地了解你自己以便让你可以成为真正的自己。

17   我谈到了这种矛盾和张力——有两件事情我想说一说。第一，它永远不会消失。如果你认为你取得的成就，如果你认为你解决的问题，如果你认为拥有某个职业或是建立某种关系就会平息那种声音，那你就错了。如果你认为幸福就意味着全然的平静，那你就永远不会幸福。平静的前提是你接受这样一个事实：你的某一部分可能永远无法安宁。这部分将永远处于张力之中。如果你接受这一事实，那么一切就会变得好多了。

18   另一个原因是，正因为你们在建立自己的身份和信仰，你们就要学会驳倒自己因为别人将会那么做。有人会攻击你。不管你的信仰、你的想法、你的雄心是什么，总会有人质疑你。除非你首先自我质疑，否则你将无法予以回击。你无法坚持立场。你若不相信我，那就试试金鸡独立这种姿势吧。你需要看清事物的

---

⑧ argue yourself down 驳倒自己

⑨ come at 攻击，袭击；达到；得到

⑩ answer back [通信] 应答，回复；顶嘴

19 Now, if you do, does this mean you get to change the world? Well, I'm getting to that, so just chill.

20 All I can say, at this point, is that I think we can all agree that the world could use a little changing. I don't know if your parents have explained this to you about the world but — we broke it? Ah, we're sorry? It's a bit of a mess. It's a hard time to go out into it. And it's a weird time in our country. And the thing about our country is — oh, it's nice. I like it. It's not long on contradiction or ambiguity. It's not long on these kind of things. It likes things to be simple. It likes things to be **pigeonholed**⑪. Good or bad. Black or white. Blue or red. And we're not that. We're more interesting than that.

21 The way that we go into the world understanding is to have these contradictions in ourselves and to see them in other people and not judge them for it. To know that — in a world where debate has kind of fallen away, given away to shouting and bullying — the best thing is not just the idea of honest debate, the best thing is losing a debate. Because it means that you learned something, you changed your position.

两面。

19 那么，如果你这样做了，这是否意味着你可以改变世界了呢？好吧，我马上就讲到这个话题了，所以别着急。

20 关于这一点，我只能说，我认为我们都同意世界需要一点点改变。关于这个世界，我不知道你们的父母是否向你们作了解释，但……是我们搞坏了它？噢，对不起，世界是有点乱糟糟。现在离开校园步入社会是很艰难。我们国家现在正处于一个奇怪的历史时期。关于我们国家的情形——噢，还不错。我喜欢。它不过多地纠缠于矛盾或歧义。它不过多地纠缠于这些事情。它喜欢将事情简单化，它喜欢把事情进行分门别类：好或坏，黑或白，蓝或红。不过我们不是那样。我们可更有趣。

21 若我们进入这个世界时想要能够了解它，就需要我们看到自身的这些矛盾，也看到其他人身上的这些矛盾，但并不因此而评价他们。要知道——在一个辩论已似乎没落，而叫嚣和恃强凌弱最为有效的世界上——最好的做法不只是拥有诚实辩论的想法，最好的做法是输掉辩论，因为那就意味着你学到了东西，你

---

⑪ pigeonhole ['pɪdʒɪnhəʊl] vt. 分类；把……留在记忆中；缓办；把……隔成小格

22 The only way, really, to understand your position and its worth is to understand the opposite. That doesn't mean the crazy guy on the radio who's spewing hate, it means the decent human truths of all the people who feel the need to listen to that guy. You are connected to those people. They're connected to him. You can't get away from it.

23 This connection is part of contradiction. It is the tension I was talking about. Because tension isn't about two opposite points, it's about the line in between them and it's being stretched by them. We need to acknowledge and honor that tension and the connection that that tension is a part of. Our connection, not just to the people we love, but to everybody, including people we can't stand and wish weren't around. The connection we have is part of what defines us on such a basic level.

24 Freedom is not freedom from connection. Serial killing is freedom from connection. Certain large investment firms have established freedom from connection. But we as people never do, and we're not supposed to. We shouldn't want to. We are individuals, obviously, but we are more than that.

25 So here's the thing about changing the world. It turns out that's not even the question, because

改变了自己的观点。

22 真正了解你的立场及其价值的唯一方法就是了解它的对立面。我指的不是那个在收音机里发泄仇恨的疯子，我指的是所有觉得有必要去听听那个家伙在说什么人所表现出的人类宽容的真实面。你们和那些人关联在一起。他们和那个疯子关联在一起。你不能逃避这个事实。

23 这种关联是矛盾的一部分。这就是我所谈论过的张力。因为张力并不是两种观点的对立，而是两种对立观点之间的那条线，那条线被双方拉得很紧。我们必须承认并尊重这种张力，以及包含这种张力的的关联。我们不只是和我们所爱的人有关联，我们和每个人都有关联，包括那些我们无法忍受、不希望有任何接触的人。我们拥有的关联是从根本上定义我们是怎样的人的一部分。

24 自由不是远离关联。连环杀人犯脱离了关联。某些大型投资公司脱离了关联。但我们作为正常人从来没不与关联脱节，我们也不应该那么做。我们也不想那样，虽然我们很明显是不同的个体，但我们不仅仅是单独的个体。

25 因此，下面是关于改变世界的话。事实证明，改变世界根

you don't have a choice. You are going to change the world because that is actually what the world is. You do not pass through this life, it passes through you. You experience it, you interpret it, you act and then it is different. That happens constantly. You are changing the world. You always have been.

26   And now it becomes real on a level that it hasn't been before. And that's why I've been talking only about you and the tension within you. Because you are, not in a cliched sense but in a weirdly literal sense, the future. And after you walk up here and walk back down you're going to be the present. You will be the broken world and the act of changing it in a way that you haven't been before.

27   You will be so many things and the one thing that I wish I'd known and want to say, is: don't just be yourself, be all of your selves. Don't just live, be that other thing connected to death. Be life. Live all of your life. Understand it, see it, appreciate it, and have fun. Thank you.

本就不是个问题，因为你们别无选择。你们就是要改变世界，因为这是世界的真实面目。你不是历练今生，而是今生历练你。你体验它，解释它，你行动起来，然后它就会变得不同。这种事情一直在发生。你们正在改变世界。你们一直都在改变着世界。

26   现在，改变世界对你们来说变得空前得真实。这就是为什么我一直只谈论你们和你们内在的张力。因为你们就是未来，这不是陈词滥调，而是一个奢侈的字面意义。当你们走上讲台拿到学位然后走下讲台后，你们将成为当下的主人。你们将踏入这个支离破碎的世界并采取行动，用以前所未有的方式改变它。

27   你们将有很多作为，有一种作为我真希望自己早点知道，而我现在想告诉你们，那就是：你们不只是要成就你自己，你们要成就你的方方面面。你们不要单纯地活着，你们还要想到死亡。你们要成就生命。你们要成就生命里的每一天。你们要理解它，明白它，欣赏它并享受它。谢谢大家。

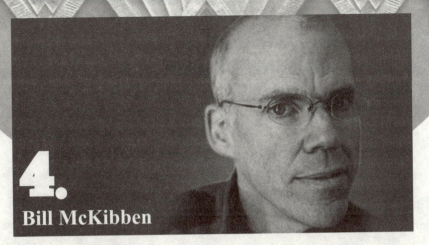

4.

Bill McKibben

比尔·麦克基本

在埃克德学院的演讲（2013年）

扫 一 扫

 人物档案

比尔·麦克基本（Bill Mckibben），1960年出生在美国加利福尼亚，毕业于哈佛大学，后在纽约工作成为自由撰稿人。他是美国著名的环境保护主义理论家，在《纽约人》《纽约时报》等国家级报刊发表的数百篇有关自然的文论在美国引起了巨大的反响，他广博的知识以及在哲学、自然科学方面的造诣，确立了他在环境科学领域的重要地位，被认为是与梭罗、卡逊齐名的环保作家。20世纪80年代以来，他先后出版了《信息遗失的时代》《可能是一个：关于小家庭的个人与环境讨论》等论著多部。《自然的终结》是其中最具影响力的代表作。

 场景介绍

埃克德学院（Eckerd College）是一所私立非营利大学，在2013年的美国文理院校排名中位列第141名，学院位于佛罗里达州，邻接坦帕湾和墨西哥湾。

4 It Requires Active Citizenship
我们需要的是积极主动的公民

1 Good morning, everyone. Thank you so much for that greeting and thank you so much for the privilege of getting to be here with you on this most important of days. There is no place that I would rather be right now than right here. My good fortune may not be your good fortune, quite, you know. This is an incredibly cheerful and celebratory day, and you've picked as your speaker someone whose most famous book has the title *The End of Nature*. There are moments when I think my role in the world is essentially to be a professional bummer-outer of other human beings. So I will try to avoid that as much as possible. It's also always, when I give a talk at Commencement, a sort of reminder that I'm the last obstacle standing between you and a diploma. Many, many years ago you started in kindergarten, and you've been forced for all those years to sort of listen to people stand at the front of a room and **talk at**[①] you, over and over and over again, and I'm the last one. If you can make it through this, then you're on your own.

1 大家早上好。非常感谢你们的掌声，也非常感谢你们给我这个机会，让我在这个最重要的日子里与你们在一起。此时此刻，这里是我最想待的地方。我的好运气可不一定就能成为你们的好运气，这一点你们非常清楚。今天是值得大声欢呼和大肆庆祝的一天，而你们选择的演讲嘉宾，他最有名的一本书的书名却是《自然的终结》。有时我会觉得我在这个世界上的角色基本上就是一个让别人感到沮丧的专业人士。所以我将会尽量避免让你们沮丧。当我在毕业典礼上演讲时，我也总会觉得我是立在你们和你们的文凭之间的最后一道障碍。许多许多年以前，你们从幼儿园开始就被迫听别人站在房间的前面对你们滔滔不绝地训话，这些年来这种情形重复了一

---

① talk at 影射；对……不停地说

4

比尔·麦克基本 *Bill McKibben*

2　What I want to talk to you about today for a moment, a short moment, is citizenship. You enter a lot of things today. You enter the ranks of the alumni of this college, and with any luck, you enter the ranks of the employed. But, just as important, you enter completely and fully into the ranks of citizens of this country and this world. You're already there in many ways, in fact; you've served as good citizens already. But now you're needed as you've never been needed before. It is a great cliché at events like this to talk about the unprecedented challenges that face our time and one, dare say, that commencement speakers for a very long time have been making that claim. But in this case, I'm afraid, it's really true. We're here at the 50th Eckerd Commencement — if we don't get it right, the 100th Commencement won't be right here because this will be underwater.

3　The burden of my work has been to watch as what scientists told us about the future would happen, happens. Now this is a college that graduates an enormous number of students in environmental studies and in marine science, and so you know all

遍一遍又一遍，我是最后一个对你们训话的人。如果你们能够顺利听完这场演讲，那以后你们就得自己听自己的了。

2　今天我想跟你们谈的——就谈一会，时间很短——是公民身份的问题。今天你们的身份发生了很多变化。你们进入了这所大学的校友行列，而且如果运气好的话，你们也迈上了工作岗位。但是，同样重要的是，你们完全加入了这个国家和这个世界的公民行列。事实上，你们在许多方面早已经步入了公民行列；你们已经做了好公民该做的事情。但现在你们被需要的程度是以前所不及的。在这样的活动上谈我们这个时代所面临的空前挑战是一个非常不错的老套做法，我敢说，很长时间以来，毕业典礼演讲嘉宾们一直都是谈那个问题的。但在今天这种情况下，恐怕这种挑战是真实的。我们今天在这里庆祝的是埃克德学院第50届毕业典礼——如果我们不拨乱反正的话，第100届毕业典礼将不会在这里举行，因为这里将会被淹没于水下。

3　我的工作带给我的负担是目睹着科学家们曾告诉我们的未来会发生的事情正在发生。这所大学的毕业生中有很多很多的人是学习环境研究和海洋科学的，

37

that I'm telling you already. But you know it with real depth and power. You know what it means when we say that the ocean is 30% more **acidic**② than it was 40 years ago. That's a change on an almost **epic**③ scale. You know what it means when we say that last summer while you were in college the Arctic melted. That 80% of the sea ice in the Arctic that was there 40 years ago is now gone. That we've taken one of the largest physical features on earth, and in your lifetime on this planet, we've broken that physical feature and the rest following close behind.

4 Every generation has its challenges, but no generation has had a challenge like the one before you. And it requires that we do not let the world operate on autopilot, that we don't let it just keep heading in the same direction. We've told ourselves now for some years in this country that most of what needs accomplishing will be accomplished if we simply get out of the way and let markets do their thing. And markets are very powerful. But clearly they are not saving the Arctic, preventing the acidification of the ocean, keeping the atmosphere from becoming wetter **at every turn**④. Global warming in some sense is a profound **market failure**⑤. Since we don't price carbon there's no reason for markets to do anything about it and, hence, the biggest problem we've ever

所以你们清楚我所告诉过你们的一切，而且你们是真正地了解，深入地了解。当我们说海洋的酸度比40年前增加了30%时，你们知道这是什么意思。这几乎是翻天覆地的变化。如果我们说，去年夏天当你们还在大学里的时候，北极圈融化了，你们知道这意味着什么。40年前还存在的80%的北极海冰现在已经消失了。我们已经耗费了地球上最大的地貌特征之一，而在你们居住于这个星球上的这一生中，我们已经破坏了那个地貌特征，其他的地貌特征也紧随其后。

4 每一代人都面临着自己的挑战，但没有哪一代人面临过你们现在所面临的挑战。这一挑战要求我们不要让世界放任自流，我们不要让它继续沿着原来的方向前进。在这个国家里，我们多年来都告诉自己，如果我们只是袖手旁观，就让市场发挥作用，那么最需要实现的事情点会实现。市场的力量是非常强大的。但显然市场拯救不了北极、防止不了海洋的酸化、阻止不了全球大气层变得越来越潮湿。从某种意义上说，全球变暖完全是市场失效。因为我们没有给碳制订价

---

② acidic [ə'sɪdɪk] *adj.* 酸的，酸性的；产生酸的
③ epic ['epɪk] *adj.* 史诗的，叙事诗的
④ at every turn 事事；到处
⑤ market failure 市场失灵；市场失效

4

比尔·麦克基本 *Bill McKibben*

faced. But that market failure can only be stopped by all of us engaging as citizens to do the sort of political work necessary to make sure that something changes. The good news is that's beginning to happen, even on campuses. Yours is not the only campus where this is starting to happen in profound ways.

5　A year ago, we launched a campaign to try to get colleges to **divest**⑥ their holdings in the fossil fuel industry to send a message to those companies. Now on 340 college campuses, students are involved in that fight, and five of those campuses have already divested. As *The New York Times* said not long ago, "This is the fastest-growing student movement in generations." So you're part of a wave that's beginning to build. But it has to build very quickly. Unlike the other challenges that we've faced, this one comes with an absolute time limit. If we don't get it right quickly, we will not get it right. And so it requires not passive spectator citizenship, but active citizenship.

6　**As it happens**⑦, I grew up in, went to high school in, the town of Lexington, Massachusetts,

格，我们就没有理由让市场来发挥作用，因此，这是我们所面临的最大问题。但要想制止市场失效，只能通过我们大家以公民的身份参与一些政治活动，以便确保事情有所变化。好消息是，这种事情已经开始发生了，甚至在校园里就有。你们的校园也并非是已经开始发生这一深刻变化的唯一校园。

5　一年前，我们发起了一场运动，旨在争取让大学放弃其在化石燃料公司的股份，以向那些公司传递一个信息。现在已有340所大学的学生参与了那场运动，其中有5所大学已经放弃了它们在那类公司的股份。正如《纽约时报》不久前所说："这是几代人中成长最快的学生运动。"所以你们现在融入了这开始聚集的潮流之中。但这个潮流必须要很快集聚起来。不同于我们所面临过的其他挑战，伴随这次挑战而来的是一个绝对的时间底限。如果我们不能快速地拨乱反正，我们将不会再有拨乱反正的机会。因此，我们需要的不是被动的只会旁观的公民，我们需要的是积极主动的公民。

6　巧合的是，我在美国自由的诞生地马萨诸塞州的列克星敦

---

⑥ divest [daɪ'vest] *vt.* 剥夺；使脱去，迫使放弃
⑦ as it happens 碰巧；偶然发生
⑧ tricorn ['traɪˌkɔːn] *adj.* 有三只角的
⑨ give sb. a tour 带某人参观某地

39

which was the birthplace of American liberty. For my summer employment, I wore a **tricorn**[8] hat and **gave tours of**[9] the Battle Green every day telling people the story of the first battle of the American Revolution. One of the things that was good about that was a reminder to me, all the time, that patriotism and dissent often go hand-in-hand. Now we do not need to be active citizens in quite the way that the **Minutemen**[10] were. We don't need you shooting anybody, but we do need standing up to the biggest empires of our time. We need you standing up to them quickly and powerfully.

7　The fossil fuel industry — the most powerful and richest industry that the world has ever seen — has, so far, dominated this debate. And they've done it in all kinds of ways. The largest corporate campaign donation that was ever given came two weeks before the last election, from Chevron, and it was designed to make sure that the House of Representatives would stay in the hands of people who would do nothing about this biggest of challenges, and it was successful, and since we will never outspend the Chevrons and the Exxons of the world, then our only hope is to find the other currencies we can spend. The currencies of movement, passion, spirit, creativity — the kinds of things that you guys have demonstrated **in spades**[11] for the last four years. As you go ahead now into the next part of your life, we'll need you to do some of

小镇上长大并在那里读了高中。到了夏天勤工俭学的时候，我就戴着三角帽，每天都到绿野之战发生的地方，告诉人们在美国独立战争第一场战役中发生的故事。这件事有一点好处，就是它总是在提醒着我，爱国主义和政见分歧常常是携手并进的。我们现在不需要成为像当年那些民兵一样行事的积极公民。我们不需要你们开枪打人，但是我们需要你们勇敢地站起来面对我们时代最大的"帝国"。我们需要你们迅速而有力地站起来。

7　化石燃料行业——世界上有史以来最强大、最富有的行业——到目前为止已经主导了这次辩论。它们以各种方式进行这件事。最大规模的企业捐赠行为发生在上次选举的两周前，由雪佛龙公司举办，其目的是确保众议院还是控制在那些面对最大挑战而无所作为的人们手中，而这次活动也取得了成功，因为我们所花费的永远不会超过世界顶尖的雪佛龙公司和埃克森美孚公司，于是我们把唯一的希望寄托在找到其他可以消费的"货币"形式上。运动、激情、精神和创新就是这些货币——在过去四年里，你们无所保留地向人们展示

---

⑩ Minutemen ['mɪnɪtmen] *n.* 美国独立战争时期招之即来的民兵（Minuteman 的复数）

⑪ in spades 坦率地；肯定；非常

your good work at the office. Those of you who are going into careers that have something to do with any of this, we need you very, very badly.

8　But the work of citizenship, as opposed to the work for which you'll be paid, the work of citizenship is done mostly **after hours**⑫, and it's done on weekends. It's the work of engaging with the world around you. It is, in some sense, a burden — that work. It would be nicer to live in one of those ages, I suppose, when there is no great need of you. When all your responsibility would be to yourself and to your family. But we don't live in an age like that. And it's not just a burden; it's also, in certain ways, a great privilege and a great honor to get to be part of that fight. And to do it knowing that you're among the relatively few people situated in this world who have the **leverage**⑬ to be effective citizens.

9　At 350.org, we organize all over the world. We've organized about 20,000 demonstrations in every country in the world, except North Korea. As I look at the pictures in the Flickr account of what those rallies have looked like, one of the things that strikes me always is how wonderful it is that people

了这些东西。随着你们现在开始迈入生命里的下一阶段，我们需要你们在职场中做一些有益的事情。你们当中那些即将从事和这类事有关的工作的人们，我们非常非常需要你们。

8　但以公民身份进行的工作和你为了得到报酬而从事的工作不同，公民身份的工作主要是在下班之后以及周末的时间里进行的。它是一项与你周围的世界相融合的工作。从某种意义上说，这项工作是一个负担。我想，如果我们生活在一个你们不是特别被需要的时代，我们过得会更滋润。在那样一个时代里，你负责的对象只有你自己和你的家庭。但我们并没有生活在那样的一个时代。那项工作不仅仅是一个负担；从某种意义上说，能够参加那场战斗也是一项了不起的特权和巨大的荣耀，尤其当你在做这件事的时候，你发现你是这世界上有能力成为有影响力公民的相对少数人之一。

9　我们在 350.org 网站上向全世界发起组织。我们从全世界除朝鲜之外的各个国家组织了 2 万次游行。每当我看着存在 Flickr 帐户里的这些集会照片的时候，我总是觉得有些东西在触动着

---

⑫ after hours *adv.* 下班；工作完毕后

⑬ leverage [ˈlevərɪdʒ] *n.* 手段，影响力；杠杆作用；杠杆效率

around the world who have done nothing to cause the problems that we face are willing to join with us in trying to solve them, but of course there are limits to what can be done.

10　Last year in Haiti, at a rally, there were students holding a big sign, and their sign said, "Your actions affect us." And they were right. We watched in horror as Hurricane Sandy came up the east coast of the United States. We watched the devastation it did in New York City where it filled the subway system with seawater. But it killed more people in Haiti than it did in New York. In fact, there's still a **cholera**[14] outbreak underway there in its wake. And there is nothing that people there can do to solve this problem. They do not have the world's sole superpower close to hand. They do not have the headquarters of the most important corporations on earth. They don't have the leverage; you do have the leverage.

11　This is not an end, Commencement. It's an opening. Your minds have been brought alive, and hopefully your hearts have been brought alive as well by the education for the last many years. Do not let those hearts and those minds go back to sleep. I know that you won't. I won't soon forget, standing outside the White House in Washington a year ago, as we were trying to gather enough people to circle that White House in what was the largest, to date, demonstration about climate that this country has ever seen. And we didn't know when we asked

我，其中之一就是世界各地的那些和引起我们所面临的问题一点关系都没有的人们愿意和我们一起去解决问题，这是多么美妙的一件事啊，但当然，我们可以做的事还有限制。

10　去年在海地的一次集会上，有学生举着一个大牌子，牌子上写着：“你们的行为影响了我们。”他们说的是对的。我们惊恐地目睹了飓风桑迪横扫美国东海岸。我们看到了它对纽约市造成的破坏——它把海水灌进了地铁里。但它令海地的死亡人数比纽约更多。事实上，飓风过后那里还爆发了霍乱。那里没有什么人能解决这个问题。他们没有世界上唯一的超级大国在身边。他们没有地球上最重要的公司总部。他们没有能力；你们却有此能力。

11　毕业典礼不是结束。它是开始。过去几年的教育激活了你们的大脑，也希望激活了你们的心。不要让你们的心灵和头脑回去睡大觉。我知道你们不会的。我久久难忘的是一年前发生在华盛顿白宫外面的一件事，当时我们发动了这个国家有史以来最大规模的关于气候问题的示威活动，我们努力召集足够多的人把白宫团团围住。当我们邀请人们

⑭ cholera [ˈkɒlərə] n. [内科] 霍乱

people to come whether people really would. And to watch bus after bus roll up from Eckerd College from a long, long bus ride away — to know that this college had sent, per **capita**⑮, more students off to that demonstration, and many other demonstrations, than any college in this country — was to understand that this is a key place for the future, and you are key players for the future.

12 I cannot promise you that we are going to win this fight or many of the other fights that we face. We don't know if we're going to win. The physics of climate change are daunting. Now that the Arctic has melted, things are progressing at a rapid rate. I don't know whether 50 years from now, we'll be able to gather here for this kind of ceremony or whether this will be soggy ground. But I do know now that we're going to fight this fight, and I will consider it one of the great privileges of my life to get to fight shoulder to shoulder with you all.

13 Congratulations and so many thanks.

前来参加游行时，我们不知道他们是否真的愿意来。当我们看到大巴车一辆接一辆从很远很远的埃克德学院开过来——知道了该学院组织参加本次示威和许多其他示威活动的学生人数按照比例计算超过了我们国家的其他任何一所高校——就明白了这是未来的一个关键的地方，而你们是未来的核心队员。

12 我不能承诺你们我们会赢得这场战斗或我们所面对的许多其他战斗。我们不知道我们是否会胜利。气候变化的物理现象是可怕的。既然北极已经融化，事情在以一个极快的速度发展着。我不知道从现在起的50年以后，我们能否像今天这样聚集在这里举行这种仪式，我也不知道50年以后的这里是否水漫金山。但现在我确实知道，我们将要搏此一搏，而且我会认为能和你们并肩作战是我一生中巨大荣耀之一。

13 祝贺你们，非常感谢。

---

⑮ per capita [统计] 人均；(拉丁) 每人；按人口计算

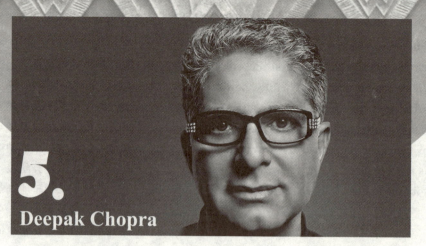

5.
Deepak Chopra

狄巴克·乔布拉

在哈特威克学院的演讲（2013年）

扫 一 扫

 ## 人物档案

　　狄巴克·乔布拉（Deepak Chopra，1947 年 10 月 22 日—），被誉为当代最具原创力及最有深度的思想家和作家之一，是主张身心调和、心灵意志至上的医学博士，出生于印度，他运用古印度的智慧来解决现代文明的疑难杂症，现居于美国。畅销作品包括《不老的身心》及《成功的七项灵性法则（生命的七大精神法则）》、《欢喜活力》、《做自己的心灵帝王》等书。

 ## 场景介绍

　　哈特威克学院（Hartwick College）是一所位于纽约州的无宗派、私立、4 年制的文理科大学，在美国大学排名里属中等。

Reflect on the Gift of Life Itself
对生命之礼的反思

经典原文
Original Text

1　President Margaret Drugovich, Trustees of Hartwick College, Guests, Teachers, Faculty members, Parents and most importantly the Students of the Class 2013. It is to you that I address my remarks.

2　Dear graduating class, today, as you celebrate this major milestone in your life and commence a new stage of your life journey, I ask you to reflect on the gift of life itself. And life, in essence, is nothing but awareness. Furthermore, human life, considered the **pinnacle**① of **biological evolution**②, is not just awareness, but self-awareness. Amongst creatures on this planet, we human beings are not only aware; we have the capacity to be aware that we are aware, to be conscious of our own consciousness. In that self-awareness lies our potential and power to direct our own future evolution and the future evolution of civilization.

中文译文
Suggested Translation

1　玛格丽特德拉格维奇校长、哈特威克大学的校董们、来宾们、老师们、教职员工们、学生家长们以及最重要的2013届毕业班的同学们（我的演讲是对你们发表的）：

2　亲爱的毕业班的同学们，今天在你们庆祝人生的这一重要里程碑事件以及开启人生旅程的新阶段之际，我恳求你们反思一下生命本身这个恩赐之物。生命在本质上不过就是意识存在。此外，被认为是生物进化顶峰的人类生命不仅仅是意识存在，而且还是自我意识存在。在这个星球上的生物之中，我们人类不仅是有意识的；我们还有能力意识到我们是有意识的，我们有能力意识到我们是有自我意识的。我们引导我们自己的未来进化方向和文明未来的进化方向的潜能就存

---

① pinnacle ['pɪnəkl] *n.* 高峰；小尖塔；尖峰；极点
② biological evolution 生物进化

3 Biological evolution has been summed up in the phrase of "survival of the fittest," but with overpopulation and overconsumption of resources, the future belongs to "survival of the wisest." It is imperative for the future of humanity that wisdom becomes the new criterion for sustainable life on this planet. And wisdom becomes that knowledge that nurtures life in all its dimensions — not only for us, but also for the generations that follow us.

4 Today's age is frequently referred to as the Information Age. The hallmarks of this age are the gifts of science and technology that have created the miracles of molecular medicine, real-time imaging of cellular function, instant accessibility of global knowledge, and social networks. Yet despite this emerging global brain, paradoxically we are **beset**③ with the same **scourges**④ of war and terrorism, of radical poverty in 50% of the world's population, **irreversible**⑤ climate change, along with deepening social and economic injustice! Furthermore, humanity suffers from massive malnutrition in which half the world suffers from hunger and the other half from obesity, leading to **inflammatory**⑥ disorders, increasing the risk of chronic illnesses including many types of cancer and **cardiovascular diseases**⑦ while the hungry die from compromised immune function and infectious diseases. The information revolution has not led to the wisdom needed to solve our world

在于这种自我意识之中。

3 "适者生存"这句话概括总结了生物进化理论，但是随着人口过剩和资源过度消耗，未来的口号将是"最聪明的人生存"。对人类的未来而言，智慧成为这个星球上可持续生存方式的新标准已经势在必行。智慧变成了全方位滋养生命的知识——不仅对我们是如此，对我们的后代也是如此。

4 今天的时代常被称为"信息时代"。这个时代的特点是科学技术人才已经创造了分子医学、细胞功能实时成像、全球知识即时可得以及社交网络这些奇迹。尽管出现了全球大脑，奇怪的是我们还是遭受着同样的苦难：战争和恐怖主义、全球50%人口的生活极端贫困、不可逆转的气候变化、还有日益恶化的社会和经济上的不公！此外，人类遭受了大范围的营养不良：世界上一半的人忍饥挨饿，而另一半人则深受肥胖症的困扰，而肥胖又导致炎症性疾病、致使患慢性疾病的风险增加，其包括许多类型的癌症和心血管疾病；而挨饿的人们则死于免疫功能受损和各种传染病。信息革命没有导致为

③ beset [bɪ'set] vt. 困扰；镶嵌；围绕

④ scourge [skɜːdʒ] n. 鞭；灾祸；鞭子；苦难的根源

⑤ irreversible [ˌɪrɪ'vɜːsəbl] adj. 不可逆的；不能

取消的；不能翻转的

⑥ inflammatory [ɪn'flæmə'tɔrɪ] adj. 炎症性的；煽动性的；激动的

⑦ Cardiovascular Diseases 心血管疾病

5 狄巴克 · 乔布拉 *Deepak Chopra*

crisis in health and well-being.

5　If ever humanity had the power of mass self-extinction on planet earth, it is today. And if it happens, it will be because we allowed our emotional and spiritual evolution to be outpaced by the evolution of our science and technology. Nuclear proliferation, biological warfare, eco-destruction, the extinction of species and the poisoning of our atmosphere, our rivers and waters and the very food that sustains our life and all life loom before us as imminent threats. But just as in other critical phases of transformation, while there is disaster looming on one hand, there is on the other hand the potential to create a radical reorganization into something much greater than was ever conceived of before.

6　Today, I ask you my young friends, you who are the future hope of humanity, you who represent the future leaders of the world; today, I ask you what Mahatma Gandhi once asked, "Can you be the change you want to see in the world?"

7　In fact, there can be no social or world transformation unless there is your own inner transformation. Today, I ask you to face a fundamental truth. Today, I ask you to consider that there is no "you" that is separate from the world. The gift of life, your own self-consciousness, is your key to inner transformation and wisdom, and that in turn is how you will transform the world. Today, I ask you to acknowledge that you are the world and that your transformation of consciousness will be the future of the world. This self-transformation is the wisdom that we need for our planet's survival.

解决危及我们健康和幸福的世界危机所需要的智慧的出现。

5　如果说人类曾经在地球上拥有大规模地自我毁灭的力量，那就是今天。如果那种事情发生了，那是因为我们允许我们的情感和灵性的进化赶不上我们的科学技术的发展。核扩散、生物战、生态破坏、物种灭绝以及维持我们人类生命和一切生命的大气层、河流、水和食物的污染都是摆在我们面前的威胁。但就像在其他改革的关键阶段一样，虽然一方面灾难正在降临，但另一方面我们有潜力彻底重建一个远远超过之前设想的东西。

6　今天，我年轻的朋友们，你们是人类未来的希望，你们是这个世界的未来领袖，我问你们；今天，我问你们一个圣雄甘地曾经问过的一个问题："欲变世界，先变其身"

7　事实上，除非你的内心发生了转变，否则这个社会或整个世界就不可能发生转变。今天，我请你们面对一个基本真理。今天，我请你们考虑一下这个命题：世界上不存在一个与世隔绝的"你"。你自己的自我意识是生命给予你的礼物，它是你内心转变和智慧的关键，从而它又是你将如何改变世界的关键。今天，我恳请你们承认你们就是世界，承认你们的意识转变就将是世界的未来。这种自我的转变就是我们所需要的让我们星球生存的智慧。

8 As I enter the autumn of my life and you the springtime of yours, I want to leave you with seven skills in self-awareness that I have learned and that I hope will serve you no matter what profession you choose, or where your life and destiny take you as a future leader of humanity.

8 当我进入生命的秋天时，你们正处于生命的春天，我想留给你们我所学到的在自我意识方面的七个技巧，我希望这七个技巧能好好地为你们服务，不管你们选择什么职业，也不管你们作为人类的未来领袖被你们的人生和命运带往哪里。

9 Skill 1: Become the best listener you can be. Learn to listen with the instruments of the body, the feelings of the heart, the logic of the mind and the stillness of your soul. As you listen deeply, reflect on the following questions: What am I observing? What am I feeling? What is the need of the moment? What is the best way to fulfill this need?

9 技巧1：尽可能成为最好的倾听者。学会用身体的表现、心灵的感觉、头脑的逻辑和灵魂的宁静去倾听。当你用心聆听时，请思考以下问题：我观察到了什么？我感觉到了什么？眼下需要的是什么？满足这一需要的最好方法是什么？

10 Skill 2: Bond emotionally with friends, professional colleagues and those you interact with daily. Understand that each of us is part of a web of relationships that is nurtured through love, kindness, compassion, empathy and joy. Emotional bonds create effective teamwork where nothing is impossible because you have a shared vision for service, contribution and success and because you complement each other's strengths and talents.

10 技巧2：和朋友、工作上的同事以及那些每日与你交流的人建立感情纽带。要明白，我们每个人都是关系网中的一部分，而关系网是通过爱、仁慈、怜悯、同情和欢乐来培育的。情感纽带会建立有效的团队，而对于有效的团队而言，没有什么是不可能的，因为你们对服务、贡献和成功拥有一个共同的愿景，因为你们会弥补彼此的优势和天赋。

11 Skill 3: Expand your awareness by knowing that all human beings have a **hierarchy of needs**[8] that start with survival and safety and progressively expand

11 技巧3：扩展你的意识，要知道所有人的需求都是有层次的，从生存需求、安全需求开始

⑧ hierarchy of needs 需要层次；需求层次理论

48

through stages that include love and belonging, true self esteem, success as in the progressive realization of worthy goals, creative expression, higher consciousness and self-actualization. As you expand your awareness, learn to harness your spiritual gifts that come in the form of the powers of intention, intuition, creativity, imagination and conscious choice making.

12　Skill 4: Remember the importance of action. Learn to be action oriented and know that there is no power higher than love in action. Remember that love without action is meaningless and action without love is irrelevant.

13　Skill 5: Assume responsibility for your own well being in all its various facets. Your well being encompasses every aspect of your life — your career, your social interactions, your personal relationships, your community and your financial success. Take time to rest and play, to be with your family and friends, to exercise and nourish your body with healthy food.

14　Skill 6: Empower yourself with true self-esteem. Learn to be independent of the good and bad opinion of others. Recognize the power of your presence alone. Do not allow yourself to be distracted. Know your life purpose and the contribution you want to make to society.

15　Skill 7: Know your true self. Your true self is not your self-image that is dependent on the labels you and others have given yourself. Your true self is the innermost core of your being that is beyond all labels, definitions and limitations. All the wisdom

逐步延伸到需求的其他阶段，包括对爱与归属感的需求、对真正的自尊的需求、对逐步实现有价值的目标方面的成功需求、对创造性的表达的需求、对更高意识的需求和自我实现的需求。当你扩展你的意识的时候，你学会了驾驭你的意念、直觉、创造力、想象力和有意识的选择，这些都是强大的精神恩赐。

12　技巧4：记住行动的重要性。学会成为一个行动导向型的人，要知道没有什么东西比付诸行动的爱更有力量。记住，没有行动的爱是没有意义的，而没有爱的行动是毫无目的的。

13　技巧5：从各个方面为自己的福祉承担责任。你的福祉包括你生活里的各个方面——你的职业，你的社会交往，你的人际关系，你的社会和经济成就。抽出时间来休息和娱乐，和家人与朋友待在一起，锻炼你的身体并用健康的食物保养你的身体。

14　技巧6：用真正的自尊武装自己。学会不受别人意见的左右，不论好坏。要认识到你独立个体的威力。不要让自己分心。要认清你的人生目标以及想为社会做出的贡献。

15　技巧7：了解你的真实自我。你的真实自我并不是你的自我形象，自我形象是依赖于你和其他人给自己贴的标签的。你的真正自我则是你存在的最内在的

traditions tell us that the human spirit is a field of infinite possibilities, a field of infinite creativity, love, compassion, joy and profound **equanimity**⑨. Know you can only give to the world that which you possess in that innermost core of your own being. Remember that you will create peace only when you are peaceful and create a loving world only when you have learned to love.

16　I entreat you today not to lose your idealism with the passage of years. That idealism is connected to your knowingness of the good that can be created and the power to manifest it. In you lies the potential for a more peaceful, just, sustainable, healthier and happier world. I am reminded today of an assignment that **John Lennon**⑩ was given by his elementary school teacher when he was seven years old. He and his classmates were asked to write a short description of who they wanted to be when they grew up. John Lennon wrote down that he wanted to be "always happy." When his teacher complained that John did not understand the assignment, John's mother told him to tell the teacher that he did not understand life.

核心，它超越了所有的标签、定义和限制。所有充满智慧的传统都告诉我们，人类的精神家园是一个充满无限可能性的地方，是一个充满无限创意、爱意、同情心、喜悦之情和深刻平静的地方。要知道你们给予世界的只能是你们所拥有的属于你自己的最核心的东西。要记住你们只有当自己心平气和的时候才能创造和平，只有当你学会了如何去爱的时候你才能创造出一个充满爱的世界。

16　今天我请求你们不要随着岁月的流逝而失去你们的理想主义。理想主义让你知道好东西是可以被创造出来的，并赋予你彰显它的力量。你身上具备建设一个更和平、更公正、更可持续、更健康、更幸福的世界的潜力。我今天想起了约翰·列侬七岁的时候发生在他身上的一个故事，当时约翰·列侬的小学老师给他布置了一道作业。老师要求他和他的同学们写一篇简短的文章，描述他们长大后希望成为什么样的人。约翰·列侬写的是他想"永远快乐"。当他的老师抱怨说约翰没有弄明白作业内容的时候，约翰的母亲要约翰告诉老

⑨ equanimity [ˌɛkwəˈnɪmətɪ] *n.* 平静；镇定
⑩ John Lennon 约翰·列侬（1940—1980），英国著名摇滚乐队"披头士"成员，摇滚史上最伟大的音乐家之一，披头士乐队的灵魂人物，诗人，社会活动家，反战者，以身为披头士乐队创团团员扬名全球。

17　But what do we really know about happiness? Recently there has been a lot of research on the dynamics of happiness. Most people think that if they are successful in achieving their goals or have good relationships or if they are healthy, they will be happy. In fact it is **the other way around**[11]. If you are a happy person you are likely to have healthy habits, and nurturing relationships and great success in life. Social scientists today describe what they call Happiness formula. And here is my opportunity to give you today the Happiness formula. The Happiness formula is: H = S + C + V

18　H stands for happiness
　　S stands for set point in the brain
　　C stands for conditions of living
　　V stands for voluntary choices

19　"S" stands for the set point in the brain and refers to our mechanisms of perception. We all have a semi-fixed place on the happiness spectrum based on our outlook of life. Happier people see the opportunities, whereas unhappy people see problems. The set point for happiness can be upregulated, or shifted toward greater happiness, through self-reflection on limiting beliefs. The set point determines 50% of our happiness experience on a daily basis. The "C" in the formula is for conditions of living and refers mainly to material success and personal wealth. It determines about 12% of your daily

师，就说他不懂生活。

17　但是我们真的了解幸福吗？最近有很多关于幸福动力学的研究。大多数人认为，如果他们成功地实现了自己的目标，或者拥有良好的人际关系，或者如果他们的身体健康，他们就是幸福的。事实上，幸福完全不是这么回事。如果你是一个幸福的人，你可能拥有健康的习惯和良好的人际关系，你可能在生活中取得了巨大的成功。社会科学家们如今给出了一套所谓的"幸福公式"。今天我有机会把这个公式拿出来与诸位分享。"幸福公式"就是：H = S + C + V

18　其中H代表幸福；S代表大脑中的设定点；C代表生活条件；V代表自愿选择。

19　"S"代表大脑中的设定点，指的是我们机械的观点。关于我们的人生幸福观我们都有一个基于人生哲学的半固定的看法。比较幸福的人看到的是机会，而不幸福的人看到的是问题。幸福的设定点可以上调，也就是说可以通过对限制性信念的自我反思而转向更大的幸福点。在我们的日常生活中，幸福设定点决定了我们50%的幸福感。公式中的"C"代表的是生活条件，主要是指物质上的成功和个人财富。它决定了你每天12%的

⑪ the other way around 倒过来；从相反方向

happiness experience. If you win the lottery, you will be extremely happy for a few months, but after one year, you will return to your set point. Voluntary choices represent choices that we make on a daily basis. Choices for personal pleasure bring **transient**[12] happiness, while selfless choices bring inner fulfillment through purpose and meaning, e.g. by making other people happy, meaningful relationships bring more permanent happiness than any other thing. So to be happy, it's fine to have material comforts around you, but that will only account for 12% of your happiness experience. To really be happy you need to expand awareness and overcome your self-limiting beliefs and then choose selfless actions, or ways to be of service to others happy. This leads to true and lasting happiness and wisdom.

20　Finally today, more than any other day, remember to be grateful. Gratitude will open the door to abundant consciousness. Express your gratitude today particularly to your parents, teachers and fellow students, all who have helped bring you to this threshold of life.

21　You are now ready to **embark on**[13] the hero's journey, the hero's quest. Good luck and **God speed**[14].

幸福感。如果你中了彩票，你会在未来的几个月里感到非常幸福，但一年后，你又会回到你的幸福设定点。自愿选择代表着我们每天都要做出的选择。为个人快乐做出的选择带来的是短暂的快乐，而有目的、有意识的无私选择——例如让其他人幸福——带来的则是内心的满足，有意义的人际关系带来的是更为长久的幸福。所以要想幸福，你得到物质享受是没问题的，但这仅占你幸福感的 12%。要想真正幸福，你就需要扩展你的意识，克服你自我限制的信念，然后选择无私的行动，也就是说选择让他人幸福的方式。这会让你得到真正的、持久的快乐和智慧。

20　最后，比起其他任何一天，你们今天都更应该记得要感恩。感恩之心将会为你们打开丰富的意识之门。今天表达你们的感激之情吧，特别要感激你们的父母、老师和同学们，他们都是帮助你们走到今天的人。

21　现在你们已经准备好了，你们就要踏上英雄之旅，去追求英雄的梦想。祝你们好运，祝你们一路平安。

---

⑫ transient ['trænzɪənt] *adj.* 短暂的；路过的
⑬ embark on 从事，着手；登上船

⑭ God speed "may God cause you to succeed" 的意思

6.
George Saunders

乔治·桑德斯

在雪城大学毕业典礼上的演讲（2013年）

扫一扫

 人物档案

乔治·桑德斯（George Saunders，1958年12月2日—），美国著名小说家，曾三次获得美国文学大奖——欧·亨利奖，代表作有《小魔怪黏巴达》《天堂主题公园》《12月10日：短篇小说集》等。

 场景介绍

雪城大学（Syracuse University），是一所享誉世界的私立研究型大学。该校成立于1870年，坐落于美国纽约州雪城（Syracuse），其建筑学院、信息学院、计算机科学与工程学院、Maxwell公民与公共事务学院、Newhouse公共传播学院、视觉与表演艺术学院、教育学院均在美国名列前茅，在各学科领域中成就卓著并影响巨大。

6 Try to Be Kinder
努力向善

经典原文
Original Text

1 Down through the ages, a traditional form has evolved for this type of speech, which is: Some old fart, his best years behind him, who, over the course of his life, has made a series of dreadful mistakes (that would be me), gives heartfelt advice to a group of shining, energetic young people, with all of their best years ahead of them (that would be you).

2 And I intend to respect that tradition.

3 Now, one useful thing you can do with an old person, in addition to borrowing money from them, or asking them to do one of their old-time "dances," so you can watch, while laughing, is ask, "Looking back, what do you regret?" And they'll tell you. Sometimes, as you know, they'll tell you even if you haven't asked. Sometimes, even when you've specifically requested they not tell you, they'll tell you.

4 So: What do I regret? Being poor from time to time? Not really. Working terrible jobs, like "knuckle-puller in a slaughterhouse?" (And don't even ASK

中文译文
Suggested Translation

1 长年以来，一种传统形式的演讲已发展至此：某个老家伙早已度过了他人生中最美好的时光，而在他的一生中，他犯下了一系列可怕的错误（那人就是我），他给一群神采奕奕、精力充沛、所有最美好岁月就在眼前的年轻人（那就是你们）提出衷心的建议。

2 我打算尊重这一传统。

3 对付一位老人的一个有效方法（除了向他们借钱或请他们跳一支他们那个年代的"舞蹈"然后你边看边笑之外）是问一句："回首往事，你有什么遗憾？"他们会告诉你的。有时，如你们所知，他们会告诉你的，即使你没有问他们。有时候，就算你已经明确要求他们不用告诉你了，他们也会告诉你的。

4 那么，我的憾事是什么？一直贫穷吗？不尽然。做了一些可怕的工作，比如像"在屠宰场

what that entails.) No. I don't regret that. **Skinny-dipping**[①] in a river in Sumatra, a little **buzzed**[②], and looking up and seeing like 300 monkeys sitting on a pipeline, **pooping**[③] down into the river, the river in which I was swimming, with my mouth open, naked? And getting deathly ill afterwards, and staying sick for the next seven months? Not so much. Do I regret the occasional humiliation? Like once, playing hockey in front of a big crowd, including this girl I really liked, I somehow managed, while falling and emitting this weird whooping noise, to score on my own goalie, while also sending my stick flying into the crowd, nearly hitting that girl? No. I don't even regret that.

5   But here's something I do regret:

6   In seventh grade, this new kid joined our class. In the interest of confidentiality, her Convocation Speech name will be "Ellen." Ellen was small, shy. She wore these blue cat's-eye glasses that, at the time, only old ladies wore. When nervous, which was pretty much always, she had a habit of taking a strand of hair into her mouth and chewing on it.

7   So she came to our school and our neighborhood, and was mostly ignored, occasionally teased ("Your hair taste good?" — that sort of thing). I could see this hurt

抠关节"（别问我这是什么工作）吗？不是。我不后悔。在苏门答腊岛的一条河流里裸泳，有点自我陶醉，抬头一看，发现大概有 300 只猴子坐在一个管道上面向河里排便，而我正在那这条河里张着嘴裸泳，后悔吗？此后我得了重症，一直病了七个月，后悔吗？没有那么后悔。我对偶尔受到的羞辱感到遗憾吗？比如有一次，我在一大群人面前打曲棍球，人群里有一个我很喜欢的女孩，不知怎的，当我摔倒发出这种奇怪的呼喊声时，我竟然设法将球打进了自家的球门，同时也让我手中的曲棍飞向了人群，差点砸到那个女孩子！不，我甚至对这件事都不感到遗憾。

5   但下面这件事让我感到遗憾：

6   上七年级的时候，我们班里来了位新生。为保密起见，她在本次演讲的名字将是"艾伦"。艾伦矮小又害羞。她戴着蓝色的猫眼眼镜，当时只有老太太戴那种眼镜。当她紧张的时候（她几乎总是紧张），会习惯性地把一缕头发放在嘴里咀嚼。

7   于是她来到了我们学校，成了我们的邻居，但几乎没人理她，偶尔会有人嘲弄她（比

---

① skinny-dipping [ˈskɪnɪˈdɪpɪŋ] *n.* 裸泳

② buzzed [bʌzd] *adj.* 陶醉的；茂密的

③ poop [pʊp] *vi.* 疲乏；排便

her. I still remember the way she'd look after such an insult: eyes cast down, a little **gut-kicked**④, as if, having just been reminded of her place in things, she was trying, as much as possible, to disappear. After awhile she'd drift away, hair-strand still in her mouth. At home, I imagined, after school, her mother would say, you know, "How was your day, sweetie?" and she'd say, "Oh, fine." And her mother would say, "Making any friends?" and she'd go, "Sure, lots."

8　Sometimes I'd see her hanging around alone in her front yard, as if afraid to leave it.

9　And then — they moved. That was it. No tragedy, no big final **hazing**⑤.

10　One day she was there, next day she wasn't.

11　End of story.

12　Now, why do I regret that? Why, forty-two years later, am I still thinking about it? Relative to most of the other kids, I was actually pretty nice to her. I never said an unkind word to her. In fact, I sometimes even (mildly) defended her.

13　But still. It bothers me.

如 "你的头发好吃吗？"，诸如此类）。我可以看出来这让她伤心。我还记得她受到这种侮辱后的样子：低头垂目，身体有点摇晃，她尽可能想在我们面前消失，好像意识到了她在班级中的位置。没一会儿她就溜走了，嘴里仍有一绺头发。回到家里，我想象着如下的情形：放学后，她妈妈会问她："亲爱的，你今天过得怎么样？"她回答说："哦，挺好的。"妈妈继续问道："交到朋友了吗？"她答道："当然了，交了很多朋友呢。"

8　有时我会看到她独自一人在她家的前院里闲晃，仿佛害怕离开它。

9　后来，她们搬走了。事情就那样结束。没有悲剧，也没有最后一次严重的侮辱。

10　前一天她还在那里，第二天她就不在了。

11　故事结束了。

12　那么我为什么要感到遗憾呢？为什么四十二年以后我仍然想着那件事？相对于其他大多数孩子而言，我实际上对她很好。我从来没有对她说过一句难听的话。事实上，我甚至（略微地）保护着她。

13　但这件事仍然困扰着我。

④ gut-kicked 源自成语 kick in the guts，意思是对某人身体或精神予以沉重打击
⑤ hazing ['heɪzɪŋ] n. 被欺侮；罚做苦工

14   So here's something I know to be true, although it's a little **corny**[6], and I don't quite know what to do with it:

15   What I regret most in my life are failures of kindness.

16   Those moments when another human being was there, in front of me, suffering, and I responded... sensibly. Reservedly. Mildly.

17   Or, to look at it from the other end of the telescope: Who, in your life, do you remember most fondly, with the most undeniable feelings of warmth?

18   Those who were kindest to you, I bet.

19   It's a little **facile**[7], maybe, and certainly hard to implement, but I'd say, as a goal in life, **you could do worse than**[8]: Try to be kinder.

20   Now, **the million-dollar question**[9]: What's our problem? Why aren't we kinder?

21   Here's what I think:

22   Each of us **is born with**[10] a series of built-in confusions that are probably somehow Darwinian. These are: (1) we're central to the universe (that is, our personal story is the main and most interesting

14   我知道接下来的解释是事实，虽然有点陈词滥调，我也不太知道怎么改进：

15   我一生中最大的遗憾就是不能扬善。

16   在某些时候，当别人在我面前遭受痛苦的时候，我的反应是……明哲保身、温文尔雅以及提供些微的帮助。

17   或者从"望远镜"的另一端看这个问题：在你的生命中，谁会无可争议地出现在你最温馨的记忆里，让你心里充满爱意？

18   我敢打赌是那些曾经对你最友善的人。

19   尽量友善一些——也许说得容易但无疑是很难做到的，不过我想说的是，将其作为生活的目标，你可以做得更好。

20   现在，最重要的疑问是：我们的问题出在哪里？我们为什么不可以更友善一些？

21   我是这样思索的：

22   我们每个人天生就是个矛盾体，这可能就是某种达尔文现象吧。矛盾之处在于：（1）我们是宇宙的中心（即我们个人的故

---

⑥ corny ['kɔːnɪ] *adj.* 谷类的；粗野的；陈腐的；乡下味的

⑦ facile ['fæsl] *adj.* 温和的；灵巧的；易做到的

⑧ you could do worse than 倒不如做某事；你可以做，你能的。是一种间接肯定法，即用否定形式表示肯定意义。意思就是：做某事并不是个坏的选择，因为做其它事可能更糟糕。

⑨ the million-dollar question 最最重要的问题

⑩ be born with 天生具有

story, the only story, really); (2) we're separate from the universe (there's US and then, out there, all that other junk — dogs and swing-sets, and the State of Nebraska and low-hanging clouds and, you know, other people), and (3) we're permanent (death is real, O.K., sure — for you, but not for me).

23   Now, we don't really believe these things — intellectually we know better — but we believe them **viscerally**[11], and live by them, and they cause us to prioritize our own needs over the needs of others, even though what we really want, in our hearts, is to be less selfish, more aware of what's actually happening in the present moment, more open, and more loving.

24   So, the second million-dollar question: How might we DO this? How might we become more loving, more open, less selfish, more present, less delusional, etc., etc?

25   Well, yes, good question.

26   Unfortunately, I only have three minutes left.

27   So let me just say this. There are ways. You already know that because, in your life, there have been High Kindness periods and Low Kindness periods, and you know what inclined you toward the former and away from the latter. Education is good;

事是主要的和最有趣的故事，而且是唯一的故事，真的）；（2）我们与宇宙是分离的（这里有我们，而除此外的地方都是其他的垃圾——狗狗、秋千、内布拉斯加州和低垂的云彩以及其他人）；（3）我们是永恒的（死亡是真实的，当然——对你而言是这样，对我则不然）。

23   我们并不真正相信这些东西——从智力上判断，我们更清楚——但我们发自内心地相信这些，并靠它们活着，它们使我们优先考虑自己的需要，而不是别人的需要，即使我们心中真正想要的是别那么自私、更多地了解当下发生的事情、多些包容、多点爱心。

24   所以，第二个最重要的问题是：我们应该怎么做呢？我们如何变得更有爱心、更加包容、少些自私、多点现实、少点妄想等等等等呢？

25   嗯，是的，这是个好问题。

26   遗憾的是，我只剩下三分钟的时间了。

27   所以我只想说一点：有办法。你们已经知道了这个道理，因为在你们的生命中，曾出现过大善时期和小善时期，你们知道是什么让你们奔向前者而远离

---

⑪ viscerally ['vɪsərəlɪ] *adv.* 肺腑地；出自内心地；本能地；粗俗地；低级地

immersing ourselves in a work of art: good; prayer is good; meditation's good; a frank talk with a dear friend; establishing ourselves in some kind of spiritual tradition — recognizing that there have been countless really smart people before us who have asked these same questions and left behind answers for us.

28   Because kindness, it turns out, is hard — it starts out all rainbows and puppy dogs, and expands to include... well, everything.

29   One thing **in our favor**⑫: some of this "becoming kinder" happens naturally, with age. It might be a simple matter of **attrition**⑬: as we get older, we come to see how useless it is to be selfish — how illogical, really. We come to love other people and are thereby counter-instructed in our own centrality. We get our butts kicked by real life, and people come to our defense, and help us, and we learn that we're not separate, and don't want to be. We see people **near and dear**⑭ to us dropping away, and are gradually convinced that maybe we too will drop away (someday, a long time from now). Most people, as they age, become less selfish and more loving. I think this is true. The great Syracuse poet, Hayden Carruth, said, in a poem written near the end of his life, that he was "mostly Love, now."

后者。教育是好事；沉浸在艺术作品中是好事；祷告是好事；冥想是好事；和挚友坦诚交谈是好事；让我们自己皈依某种精神传统是好事——我们认识到，在我们中前有无数真正聪明的人问了这些同样的问题，并给我们留下了答案。

28   因为事实证明友善很难——从对彩虹和小狗到对一切事物。

29   有一件事对我们是有利的：随着年龄的增长，"变得更加友善"自然就会发生。这可能仅仅是因为岁月的侵蚀：随着我们年龄的增长，我们发现自私是多么得无用——是多么不合乎逻辑，真的。我们逐渐去爱别人，从而反对我们那些以自我为中心的想法。当现实生活给了我们当头一棒时，会有人过来保护我们，帮助我们，我们知道，我们是不分开的，我们也不想分开。我们看到身边的亲人离我们而去，我们逐渐相信，也许我们也会离去（有一天会离去，不过离现在还很遥远）。大多数人会随着年龄的增长而变得不那么自私，会变得更有爱心。我认为这是真的。伟大诗人海登·卡鲁斯在临终时写过一首诗，诗中写道，他"现在的

---

⑫ in one's favor 对……有利；支持某人

⑬ attrition [ə'trɪʃən] *n.* 摩擦；磨损；消耗

⑭ near and dear 极为亲密

30 And so, a prediction, and my heartfelt wish for you: as you get older, your self will diminish and you will grow in love. You will gradually be replaced by love. If you have kids, that will be a huge moment in your process of self-diminishment. You really won't care what happens to You, as long as they benefit. That's one reason your parents are so proud and happy today. One of their fondest dreams has come true: you have accomplished something difficult and tangible that has enlarged you as a person and will make your life better, from here on in, forever.

31 Congratulations, by the way.

32 When young, we're anxious — understandably — to find out if we've got what it takes. Can we succeed? Can we build a viable life for ourselves? But you — in particular you, of this generation — may have noticed a certain cyclical quality to ambition. You do well in high-school, in hopes of getting into a good college, so you can do well in the good college, in the hopes of getting a good job, so you can do well in the good job so you can . . .

33 And this is actually OK. If we're going to become kinder, that process has to include taking ourselves seriously — as doers, as accomplishers, as dreamers. We have to do that, to be our best selves.

主要任务是去爱人"。

30 因此，我预测，其实也是我对你们的衷心祝愿：随着你们的年龄渐长，你们的私心将会减少，你们的爱心将会增多。自我将逐渐被爱心取代。如果你们有了孩子，那将是你们自我丧失进程中的重要时刻。只要是对他们有益，你们真的不在乎自己到底怎样。这是你们父母今天感到非常自豪和高兴的一个原因。他们最热切的梦想之一已经实现：你们完成了一件困难重重却又实实在在的事，一件让你们变得更强大并从此开始让你们的生活永远变得更美好的事。

31 顺便祝贺你们。

32 年轻的时候，我们急切地想知道，我们是否得到了回报，这是可以理解的。我们能成功吗？我们可以安身立命吗？但是你们——尤其是你们这一代人——可能已经注意到了野心是有一定的良性循环特征的。你在高中成绩很好，你就希望进入一所好的大学，然后你就可以在好大学里学得好，从而你希望找到一份好工作，从而你就可以在好的工作岗位上干得好，从而你就可以……

33 这实际上没什么问题。如果我们想成为更友善之人，这一过程就必须包括认真对待自己——无论我们作为实干家、践

行者还是作为梦想家。我们必须成就最好的自己。

34   Still, accomplishment is unreliable. "Succeeding," whatever that might mean to you, is hard, and the need to do so constantly renews itself (success is like a mountain that keeps growing ahead of you as you hike it), and there's the very real danger that "succeeding" will take up your whole life, while the big questions go untended.

34   不过，成就是不可靠的。不管"取得成功"对你而言可能意味着什么，它都是很难的，并且成功的意味会不断更新（成功就像一座大山，当你攀爬时，它会在你眼前不断增长），而且还有一个非常现实的危险摆在你面前，就是"取得成功"将占据你的整个人生，而你却会忽略一些重要的问题。

35   So, quick, end-of-speech advice: Since, according to me, your life is going to be a gradual process of becoming kinder and more loving: Hurry up. Speed it along. Start right now. There's a confusion in each of us, a sickness, really: selfishness. But there's also a cure. So be a good and proactive and even somewhat desperate patient on your own behalf — seek out the most **efficacious**[15] anti-selfishness medicines, energetically, for the rest of your life.

35   因此，我要在演讲即将结束的时候快速地给你们提出建议：根据我的经验，既然你们的生命将是一个逐渐变得更友善和更具爱心的过程，那么就赶快行动、加速前进吧。现在就开始。在我们每个人身上都存在着矛盾的另一面——自私，这是一种病态，真的。但也有治疗方法。所以你就代表你自己成为一个好的、主动的甚至有点迫切的病人吧——在你的余生中努力寻找最有效的药物对抗自私。

36   Do all the other things, the ambitious things — travel, get rich, get famous, innovate, lead, fall in love, make and lose fortunes, swim naked in wild jungle rivers (after first having it tested for monkey poop) — but as you do, to the extent that you can, err in the direction of kindness. Do those things that incline you toward the big questions, and avoid the things

36   雄心勃勃地做所有其他的事吧——旅行、发财、成名、创新、领先、恋爱、攫取和失去财富、在丛林的河流里裸泳（先调查一下有没有猴子的粪便）——但你们在做这些事情的时候，你们会在某种程度上犯下善良方面

⑮ efficacious [ˌefɪ'keɪʃəs] *adj.* 有效的；灵验的

that would reduce you and make you trivial. That **luminous**[16] part of you that exists beyond personality — your soul, if you will — is as bright and shining as any that has ever been. Bright as Shakespeare's, bright as Gandhi's, bright as Mother Teresa's. Clear away everything that keeps you separate from this secret luminous place. Believe it exists, come to know it better, nurture it, share its fruits tirelessly.

37　And someday, in 80 years, when you're 100, and I'm 134, and we're both so kind and loving we're nearly unbearable, **drop me a line**[17], let me know how your life has been. I hope you will say: It has been so wonderful.

38　Congratulations, Class of 2013.

39　I wish you great happiness, all the luck in the world, and a beautiful summer.

的错误。做那些会引导你思考大问题的事情，避免做那些降低你人格、让你变得渺小的事情。那存在于你人格之外的闪闪发光的部分——你的灵魂，如果你愿意这么说的话——和任何曾经闪闪发光的灵魂一样明亮。和莎士比亚的灵魂一样明亮，和甘地的灵魂一样明亮，和特蕾莎修女的灵魂一样明亮。扫除一切让你从这个闪闪发光的秘密之处分离的东西。相信它的存在，更好地了解它，培育它，并不知疲倦地分享它的成果。

37　在 80 年后的某一天，当你 100 岁的时候，我 134 岁，那个时候我们都是如此得善良和具有爱心以至于我们几乎无法忍受，到那时写信给我，让我知道你们生活得怎么样。我希望你们会说：生活是如此美妙。

38　祝贺你们，2013 届毕业生。

39　我祝愿你们生活幸福，祝愿你们得到世界上的所有好运，并祝愿你们度过一个美丽愉快的夏天。

---

⑯ luminous ['luːmɪnəs] *adj.* 发光的；明亮的；清楚的

⑰ drop me a line 写信给我；写封信给我

7.

Jonathan Safran Foer

乔纳森·萨福兰·弗尔

在米德尔布里学院毕业典礼上的演讲（2013年）

扫 一 扫

 人物档案

乔纳森·萨福兰·弗尔（Jonathan Safran Foer），1977 年出生于华盛顿，在普林斯顿大学求学期间学习写作，获得高级创意写作论文奖。他的短篇小说曾在《巴黎评论》和《纽约客》上发表，2000 年获得西洋镜小说奖。毕业之后，弗尔完成首部长篇小说《了了》，该书为他赢得全美犹太人图书奖和《卫报》首作奖。2005 年，《了了》被导演列维·施瑞博尔搬上银幕。同年，《特别响，非常近》出版，为他带来更大的荣誉和更广泛的认知度，并被《朗读者》导演斯蒂芬·戴德利看中，改编成电影。2009 年，弗尔出版了非虚构作品《吃动物》，书探讨了素食主义。2007 年，弗尔入选《格兰塔》杂志"美国最优秀青年作家"，2010 年，入选《纽约客》"四十岁以下二十位最佳作家"。目前，弗尔担任纽约大学创意写作课程教授，与同是小说家的妻子妮可·克劳斯住在布鲁克林。

 场景介绍

米德尔布里学院（Middlebury College）是全美国的顶级文理学院之一，位于美国佛蒙特州，2008 年学校在全美国文理学院中排名第五。

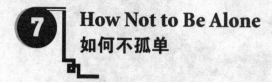

How Not to Be Alone
如何不孤单

1　A couple of weeks ago, I saw a stranger crying in public. I was in Brooklyn's Fort Greene neighborhood, waiting to meet a friend for breakfast. I arrived at the restaurant a few minutes early and was sitting on the bench outside, scrolling through my contact list. A girl, maybe 15 years old, was sitting on the bench opposite me, crying into her phone. I heard her say, "I know, I know, I know" over and over.

2　What did she know? Had she done something wrong? Was she being comforted? And then she said, "Mama, I know," and the tears came harder.

3　What was her mother telling her? Never to stay out all night again? That everybody fails? Is it possible that no one was on the other end of the call, and that the girl was merely rehearsing a difficult conversation?

4　"Mama, I know," she said, and hung up, placing her phone on her lap.

1　几周前，我看见一个陌生人在公共场所哭泣。我当时正在布鲁克林的格林尼堡附近等朋友一起吃早餐。我提前几分钟到达餐厅，坐在餐厅外的板凳上，翻阅手机上的联系人列表。此时一个15岁左右大的女孩坐在我对面的长椅上，对着她的手机哭泣。我听见她一遍又一遍地说着："我知道，我知道，我知道。"

2　她知道些什么？她又做错了什么？她得到安慰了吗？后来她说："妈妈，我知道。"随后她哭得更加厉害了。

3　她妈妈告诉了她什么？是叮嘱她别再彻夜不归？还是安慰她说，每个人都会不及格？有没有可能电话那头根本没人接听，只是那个女孩在练习和妈妈进行一次艰难的对话？

4　"妈妈，我知道，"她说完后就挂断了电话，把手机放在她的膝上。

5   I was faced with a choice: I could **interject**[①]
myself into her life, or I could respect the boundaries
between us. Intervening might make her feel worse,
or be inappropriate. But then, it might ease her pain,
or be helpful in some straightforward logistical way.
An affluent neighborhood at the beginning of the day
is not the same as a dangerous one as night is falling.
And I was me, and not someone else. There was a lot
of human computing to be done.

6   It is harder to intervene than not to, but it is
vastly harder to choose to do either than to retreat into
the scrolling names of one's contact list, or whatever
one's favorite iDistraction happens to be. Technology
celebrates connectedness, but encourages retreat. The
phone didn't make me avoid the human connection,
but it did make ignoring her easier in that moment,
and more likely, by comfortably encouraging
me to forget my choice to do so. My daily use of
technological communication has been shaping me
into someone more likely to forget others. The flow
of water carves rock, a little bit at a time. And our
personhood is carved, too, by the flow of our habits.

7   Psychologists who study empathy and
compassion are finding that unlike our almost
instantaneous responses to physical pain, it takes time
for the brain to comprehend the psychological and
moral dimensions of a situation. The more distracted

5   我面临着一个选择：我可以走进她的生活；或者我可以恪守我们之间的界限。干涉她的生活可能会使她感觉更糟糕，或者感觉不当。但是，若以一种直接了当又符合逻辑的方式进行干预，也可能会缓解她的痛苦，或对她有所帮助。清晨时的富裕居民区不同于夜幕降临时的危险居民区。我是我，而不是其他人。我要算计很多事情。

6   放手不易，干预更难，但在二者之间进行决择比退回到翻阅手机联系人名单的状态或回头玩自己喜欢的手机应用里的随便什么游戏以分散注意力要困难得多得多。科学技术促进人们互联互通，却又鼓励人们退缩。手机虽然没有让我避免与人们之间的联系，但在那一刻它确实让我对她痛苦的无视变得更容易，更可能让我舒舒服服地忘记我这样做的选择。通信技术的日常使用已经把我塑造成了一个更容易忘记别人的人。滴水可以穿石。我们的人格也是被我们那些习惯的细流雕琢而成。

7   研究同情和怜悯的心理学家发现，和我们对身体疼痛的几乎瞬间反应不同，大脑对某一情况的心理和道德维度的理解是需要一些时间的。我们越是分心，

① interject [ˌɪntəˈdʒekt] *vt.* 突然插入；插嘴

we become, and the more emphasis we place on speed at the expense of depth, the less likely and able we are to care.

8　Everyone wants his parent's, or friend's, or partner's undivided attention — even if many of us, especially children, are getting used to far less. **Simone Weil**[2] wrote, "Attention is the rarest and purest form of generosity." By this definition, our relationships to the world, and to one another, and to ourselves, are becoming increasingly miserly.

9　Most of our communication technologies began as diminished substitutes for an impossible activity. We couldn't always see one another face to face, so the telephone made it possible to keep in touch at a distance. One is not always home, so the answering machine made a kind of interaction possible without the person being near his phone. Online communication originated as a substitute for telephonic communication, which was considered, for whatever reasons, too burdensome or inconvenient. And then texting, which facilitated yet faster, and more mobile, messaging. These inventions were not created to be improvements upon face-to-face communication, but a **declension**[3] of acceptable, if diminished, substitutes for it.

10　But then a funny thing happened: we began to prefer the diminished substitutes. It's easier to make a

我们越注重速度并以牺牲深思的能力为代价，而我们就越不太可能也越无法在乎他人。

8　每个人都希望得到自己父母或朋友或伴侣的全部关注——尽管我们中的许多人，尤其是孩子们，已经习惯于被予以较少的关注。西蒙娜·韦伊写过："关注是表现慷慨的最稀有和最纯粹的形式。"根据这个定义，我们与世界、与他人和与自己的关系变得越来越冷漠。

9　我们大多数的通信技术最开始是作为一种无法实现的人类活动的替代品出现的。我们并不能总是面对面看到彼此，所以电话让我们远距离的也能保持联系。一个人并不总是在家，所以录音电话让人们能够不用守在电话旁边也可互动。网上在线交流是作为电话通信的替代品被发明出来的，不知什么原因，电话通信被认为过于繁琐或不太方便。后来人们发明了发短信，使得消息发送得更快、更机动。这些发明的产生不是为了改进人们面对面的交流，而是作为可接受的退化型替代品出现的。

10　但后来发生了一件有趣的事：我们开始喜欢这些退化的

---

② Simone Weil 西蒙娜·韦伊（1909.2.3—1943.8.23），犹太人，神秘主义者、宗教思想家和社会活动家，深刻地影响着战后的欧洲思潮。

③ declension [dɪˈklenʃən] n. 词尾变化；变格；倾斜；衰退

乔纳森 · 萨福兰 · 弗尔 *Jonathan Safran Foer*

phone call than to **schlep**④ to see someone in person. Leaving a message on someone's machine is easier than having a phone conversation — you can say what you need to say without a response; **hard news**⑤ is easier to leave; it's easier to check in without becoming entangled. So we began calling when we knew no one would pick up.

11　Shooting off an e-mail is easier, still, because one can hide behind the absence of vocal **inflection**⑥, and of course there's no chance of accidentally catching someone. And texting is even easier, as the expectation for articulateness is further reduced, and another shell is offered to hide in. Each step "forward" has made it easier, just a little, to avoid the emotional work of being present, to convey information rather than humanity.

12　THE problem with accepting — with preferring — diminished substitutes is that over time, we, too, become diminished substitutes. People who become used to saying little become used to feeling little.

13　With each generation, it becomes harder to imagine a future that resembles the present. My grandparents hoped I would have a better life than they did: free of war and hunger, comfortably situated in a place that felt like home. But what futures would

替代品。打个电话比爬山涉水地亲自去看一个人要容易。在某人的留言机上留言比电话交谈更容易——你可以说你需要说的话，而一端无需有反应；重大事件更容易以留言的形式说出来；也更容易在不受纠缠的情况下挂断电话。所以我们开始在明知道没有人会接电话时打电话。

11　发送电子邮件仍然是比较容易的，因为人们可以掩盖语调变化的缺失，当然也就没有机会意外地听到某人说话。发短信更容易了，因为人们对表达能力的期望进一步降低了，因此人们可以躲进另外一个壳子里。每一次技术的"大跃进"都使得人们避免表现出情绪的工作而容易，让传达信息而非人情味变得更容易，哪怕只是一点点。

12　接受——乃至喜欢——退化型替代品的问题在于，随着时间的推移，我们也成为了退化的替代品。习惯少说话的人们也习惯了少接触。

13　对于每一代人而言，越来越难想象未来会像当前那个样子一样。我的爷爷奶奶希望我比他们生活得更好：没有战争和饥饿，可以舒适地置身于一个感觉

④ schlep [ʃlep] *vi.* 拖曳；缓慢费力地行进

⑤ hard news（关于政治、国际问题的）硬新闻，重大新闻，重大事件报道，真实事件报道

⑥ inflection [ɪnˈflekʃən] *n.* 弯曲，变形；音调变化

I dismiss out of hand for my grandchildren? That their clothes will be fabricated every morning on 3-D printers? That they will communicate without speaking or moving?

14　Only those with no imagination, and no grounding in reality, would deny the possibility that they will live forever. It's possible that many reading these words will never die. Let's assume, though, that we all have a set number of days to **indent**⑦ the world with our beliefs, to find and create the beauty that only a finite existence allows for, to **wrestle with the question**⑧ of purpose and wrestle with our answers.

15　We often use technology to save time, but increasingly, it either takes the saved time along with it, or makes the saved time less present, intimate and rich. I worry that the closer the world gets to our fingertips, the further it gets from our hearts. It's not an either/or — being "anti-technology" is perhaps the only thing more foolish than being unquestioningly "pro-technology" — but a question of balance that our lives hang upon.

16　Most of the time, most people are not crying in public, but everyone is always in need of something that another person can give, be it undivided attention, a kind word or deep empathy. There is no better use

像家的地方。但我会交给我的子孙一个什么样的未来？他们的衣服会是每天早上由 3D 打印机打印出来的吗？他们能够不用说话或移动即可交流吗？

14　只有那些没有想象力、没有根植于现实的人才会否认他们会永生的可能性。很多现在阅读这些文字的人可能将会长生不老。不过让我们假设，我们都有一定的时间用我们的信仰去投入到这个世界，去发现和创造只有有限的生命才顾及的美，去苦思冥想人生目的这样的问题并寻找答案。

15　我们经常利用技术节省时间，但越来越多的情况则是，要么技术本身花掉了节省下来的时间，要么让节省下来的时间变得不那么有用、私人和宝贵。我担心世界离我们的指尖越近，它离我们的心就越远。这不是一个非此即彼的问题——"反对技术"也许是唯一一个比毫无条件地"赞成技术"更为愚蠢的做法——但它是一个决定我们的生命如何达到平衡的问题。

16　大多时候多数人都不会在公共场合哭泣，但每个人总是需要某种东西，而另一个人又能够提供那种东西，它要么是全部的

---

⑦ indent [ɪn'dent] vt. 定货；缩排；印凹痕
⑧ wrestle with the question 遇到难题而左思右想

乔纳森·萨福兰·弗尔 *Jonathan Safran Foer*

of a life than to **be attentive to**[9] such needs. There are as many ways to do this as there are kinds of loneliness, but all of them require attentiveness, all of them require the hard work of emotional computation and corporeal compassion. All of them require the human processing of the only animal who risks "getting it wrong" and whose dreams provide shelters and vaccines and words to crying strangers.

17   We live in a world made up more of story than stuff. We are creatures of memory more than reminders, of love more than likes. Being attentive to the needs of others might not be the point of life, but it is the work of life. It can be messy, and painful, and almost impossibly difficult. But it is not something we give. It is what we get **in exchange for**[10] having to die.

关注，要么是一句善意的话语，要么是深深的同理心。最好地利用利用生命的方法莫过于关注这些需求。有多少种孤独，就有多少方法可以做到这一点，但所有方法都需要关注，都需要我们在情感上尽心考量、在物质上表现怜悯。所有这些方法都要求那个动物必须有人性，让其愿冒"犯错"之险，并梦想为哭泣的陌生人提供庇护所和安慰的话。

17   在我们生活的世界里，无形的故事多过有形的物质。我们依靠的是记忆，而非提醒；我们寻求的是爱，而非喜欢。关心别人的需求或许不是生命的重点，却是生命的责任。这也许棘手、痛苦、无比困难。但这并不是我们的奉献。这是我们用必须逝去的生命交换得来的。

---

⑨ be attentive to 注意；照应   ⑩ in exchange for 作为……的交换

8.

Neil Gaiman

尼尔·盖曼

在费城艺术大学的演讲（2012年）

扫一扫

 人物档案

尼尔·盖曼（Neil Gaiman，1960 年 11 月 10 日—），出生于英格兰，是一名移居美国的英国作家，犹太人。其创作的领域横跨了幻想小说、科幻小说、恐怖小说、儿童小说、漫画以及歌词。《睡神》系列《仲夏夜之梦》1991 年获世界奇幻奖。尼尔·盖曼被视为新一代幻想文学的代表，他曾凭借代表作《美国众神》收获获雨果奖、星云奖等文学大奖。他的作品《星尘》和《鬼妈妈》也被搬上电影荧幕，成为经典。

 场景介绍

费城艺术大学（University of the Arts（Philadelphia））是全美最古老的致力于艺术教育的学校，位于宾夕法尼亚州中心城市费城的艺术大道。费城艺术大学于 1985 年由费城表演艺术学院（PCPA）和费城艺术学院（PCA）合并而成，两所学校的历史可以追溯到 19 世纪 70 年代。

8 Make Good Art
创作优秀的艺术作品

经典原文
Original Text

1　Thank you.

2　I never really expected to find myself giving advice to people graduating from an **establishment**① of higher education. I never graduated from any such establishment. I never even started at one. I escaped from school as soon as I could, when the prospect of four more years of enforced learning before I'd become the writer I wanted to be was **stifling**②.

3　I got out into the world, I wrote, and I became a better writer the more I wrote, and I wrote some more, and nobody ever seemed to mind that I was making it up as I went along, they just read what I wrote and they paid for it, or they didn't, and often they **commissioned**③ me to write something else for them.

4　Which has left me with a healthy respect and fondness for higher education that those of my friends

中文译文
Suggested Translation

1　谢谢诸位。

2　我从来没有真正想到自己会给高校毕业生们提出忠告。我从来没有从任何高校毕业。我甚至从来没有进过高校。当我意识到实现成为作家这个梦想前，还要先完成四年多的沉闷的强制教育时，我就尽快地逃离了学校。

3　我踏进社会，开始写作，而我写得越多，我就成了更加优秀的作家，于是我就写得越来越多，人们似乎从来不在意这些故事全是我编造出来的，他们只是阅读我写的东西，他们花钱买我的作品，或者他们不花钱就白看，还经常有人委托我为他们写点别的东西。

4　这让我对高等教育产生了尊重和喜爱，而我那些上过大学

---

① establishment [ɪ'stæblɪʃmənt] *n.* 确立，制定；公司；设施
② stifling ['staɪflɪŋ] *adj.* 令人窒息的；沉闷的
③ commission [kə'mɪʃən] *vt.* 委任；使服役；委托制作

and family, who attended Universities, **were cured of**[④] long ago.

5   Looking back, I've had a remarkable ride. I'm not sure I can call it a career, because a career implies that I had some kind of career plan, and I never did. The nearest thing I had was a list I made when I was 15 of everything I wanted to do: to write an adult novel, a children's book, a comic, a movie, record an audiobook, write an **episode**[⑤] of *Doctor Who*, and so on. I didn't have a career. I just did the next thing on the list.

6   So I thought I'd tell you everything I wish I'd known starting out, and a few things that, looking back on it, I suppose that I did know. And that I would also give you the best piece of advice I'd ever got, which I completely failed to follow.

7   First of all: When you start out on a career in the arts you have no idea what you are doing.

8   This is great. People who know what they are doing know the rules, and know what is possible and impossible. You do not. And you should not. The rules on what is possible and impossible in the arts were made by people who had not tested the bounds of the possible by going beyond them. And you can.

的朋友和家人们很久以前才从高等教育中复原过来。

5   回顾过去，我拥有过一段精彩的人生旅程。我不确定是否能称之为职业，因为所谓职业，意味着我曾经做过某种职业规划，而我却不曾做过。我做过最接近职业规划的事情是，我15岁时列了一张清单，写下了我想做的每一件事：写一部成人小说、一本儿童读物、一本漫画、一部电影、录制一本有声读物，为科幻电视剧《神秘博士》撰写一集剧本等等。我没有自己的职业。我只是完成了清单上列出的下一件事。

6   所以，我想跟大家聊聊所有我希望自己一开始就了解的事，还有一些现在回想起来我认为当初确实就了解的事。我也想提供给大家我所知道的最好的忠告，不过这些建议我本人却完全没有遵循。

7   首先：当你开始迈向艺术生涯时，你并不知道自己在做什么。

8   这是一件好事。那些知道自己在做什么的人懂得其中的规则，知道什么可行、什么不可行。但你们不知道。你们最好也不要知道。在艺术领域中，那些什么可行、什么不可行的规则是由那些不曾尝试跨越可能性边界的人所

④ be cured of 复原
⑤ episode ['epɪsəʊd] *n.* 插曲；一段情节；插话；有趣的事件

9 If you don't know it's impossible it's easier to do. And because nobody's done it before, they haven't made up rules to stop anyone doing that again, yet.

10 Secondly, if you have an idea of what you want to make, what you were put here to do, then just go and do that.

11 And that's much harder than it sounds and, sometimes in the end, so much easier than you might imagine. Because normally, there are things you have to do before you can get to the place you want to be. I wanted to write comics and novels and stories and films, so I became a journalist, because journalists are allowed to ask questions, and to simply go and find out how the world works, and besides, to do those things I needed to write and to write well, and I was being paid to learn how to write economically, **crisply**[6], sometimes under adverse conditions, and on time.

12 Sometimes the way to do what you hope to do will be **clear cut**[7], and sometimes it will be almost impossible to decide whether or not you are doing the correct thing, because you'll have to balance your goals and hopes with feeding yourself, paying debts, finding work, **settling for**[8] what you can get.

制定的。但你们可以尝试。

9 如果你们不知道一件事是否可行，那你们做起来会更容易。因为之前不曾有人尝试过，所以还没人制定不让谁再次做那件事的规定。

10 第二，如果你对自己想做什么已经有了想法，知道自己来这里做什么，那么尽管放手去做就好了。

11 说起来简单做起来难，但有时最终的情况或许比你想像的要容易得多。因为通常情况下，你在实现梦想之前必须先做一些尝试。我想创作漫画、小说、故事和电影，所以我先成为了一名记者，因为记者能不断地提问题，可以用最直接的方式了解世界是如何运转的。此外，要做这些事，我就必须写东西，而且要写得好，我在拿工资的情况下学习如何多快好省地写作，有时写作环境非常恶劣，那也要按时交稿。

12 有时做你希望做的事情的途径十分明确，有时则很难确定自己是否在做正确的事情，因为你必须在目标和希望之间取得平衡，你得养活自己、偿还债务、找工作、勉强接受你所能得到的东西。

---

⑥ crisply ['krɪsplɪ] *adv.* 清楚地；易碎地

⑦ clear cut 清楚的，明确的；轮廓鲜明的

⑧ settle for something 勉强接受某事物；退而求其次

13　Something that worked for me was imagining that where I wanted to be — an author, primarily of **fiction**⁹, making good books, making good comics, making good drama and supporting myself through my words — was a mountain. A distant mountain. My goal.

14　And I knew that as long as I kept walking towards the mountain I would be all right. And when I truly was not sure what to do, I could stop, and think about whether it was taking me towards or away from the mountain. I said no to editorial jobs on magazines, proper jobs that would have paid proper money, because I knew that, attractive though they were, for me they would have been walking away from the mountain. And if those job offers had come along earlier I might have taken them, because they still would have been closer to the mountain than I was at the time.

15　I learned to write by writing. I tended to do anything as long as it felt like an adventure, and to stop when it felt like work, which meant that life did not feel like work.

16　Thirdly, When you start out, you have to deal with the problems of failure. You need to be **thickskinned**⁰, to learn that not every project will survive. A **freelance**⁰ life, a life in the arts,

13　我的办法是对我想要实现的目标展开想像——我要成为一名作家，主要是写小说、写好书、创作好的漫画、创作好的剧本并通过我的文字养活自己——并想像我的目标是一座山，一座远山。那就是我的目标。

14　我知道，只要我一直朝那座山迈进，我就能达成目标。当我真的不确定该怎么做时，就停下脚步，思考这么做会使我朝着那座山迈进，还是会让我远离那座山。我拒绝了一些杂志社的编辑工作——我本可以拿到合理报酬的正式工作——因为我知道，虽然那些工作很吸引人，但对我来说，它会使我与那座山渐行渐远。如果那些工作机会早一些来到我身边的话，我或许会接受，因为对当时的我来说，那些工作还是会让我离那座山近一点的。

15　我通过写作学习写作。我愿意尝试做任何能让我感觉如冒险一般的事，而当某件事让我感觉仅像是一份工作时，我就罢手，也就是说，生活和工作不一样。

16　第三，当你展开人生旅程时，你必须认真地对待失败。你的内心必须要坚强，你需要知道并非所有计划都能落实。一个自

⑨ fiction ['fɪkʃən] *n.* 小说；虚构，编造；谎言

⑩ thickskinned ['θɪk'skɪnd] *adj.* 感觉迟钝的；脸皮厚的

⑪ freelance ['friːlæns] *n.* 自由作家；自由记者 *adj.* 自由投稿的

is sometimes like putting messages in bottles, on a desert island, and hoping that someone will find one of your bottles and open it and read it, and put something in a bottle that will wash its way back to you: appreciation, or a commission, or money, or love. And you have to accept that you may put out a hundred things for every bottle that **winds up**⑫ coming back.

17　The problems of failure are problems of discouragement, of hopelessness, of hunger. You want everything to happen and you want it now, and things go wrong. My first book — a piece of journalism I had done for the money, and which had already bought me an electric typewriter from the advance — should have been a bestseller. It should have paid me a lot of money. If the publisher hadn't gone into involuntary **liquidation**⑬ between the first print run selling out and the second printing never happening, and before any **royalties**⑭ could be paid, it would have done.

18　And I shrugged, and I still had my electric typewriter and enough money to pay the rent for a couple of months, and I decided that I would do my best in future not to write books just for the money. If you didn't get the money, then you didn't have

由作家的生活、一个艺术工作者的生活有时就像在荒岛上把信装进漂流瓶里，你希望有人会发现其中的一个瓶子，打开它并阅读瓶中的信件，然后把某个东西装回瓶子中，让瓶子冲回到你身边，让你看到那个人的回应：或是欣赏，或是委托，或是金钱，或是爱慕。你必须接受的事实是，你要为每一个最终回到身边的瓶子付出成百个瓶子的代价。

17　失败带来的苦恼包括沮丧、失望和渴望；你希望一切事情马上如愿以偿地发生，但偏偏出错。我的第一本书——一本为了钱而出的杂志，我用它赚的预付版税买了一台电动打字机——本应该是一本畅销书。出版商应该付我很多钱。如果出版商在第一次印刷卖完之后，在永远也没来得及的第二次印刷也没来得及给我支付版税之前，没有被强制清算的话，我应该大赚一笔的。

18　对此我一笑置之，毕竟我还拥有我的电动打字机和足够支付两个月租金的钱，因此我下定决心，往后我会尽最大努力不要仅是为了钱而写书。如果你没有钱，你便什么都没有。如果我做

---

⑫ wind up 结束；使紧张；卷起；(非正式) 忽悠某人（wind sb. up）

⑬ liquidation [ˌlɪkwɪˈdeɪʃən] *n.* 清算；偿还；液化；清除

⑭ royalty [ˈrɔɪəltɪ] *n.* 皇室；版税；王权；专利税

anything. If I did work I was proud of, and I didn't get the money, at least I'd have the work.

19　**Every now and again**⑮, I forget that rule, and whenever I do, the universe kicks me hard and reminds me. I don't know that it's an issue for anybody but me, but it's true that nothing I did where the only reason for doing it was the money was ever worth it, except as bitter experience. Usually I didn't wind up getting the money, either. The things I did because I was excited, and wanted to see them exist in reality have never let me down, and I've never regretted the time I spent on any of them.

20　The problems of failure are hard.

21　The problems of success can be harder, because nobody warns you about them.

22　The first problem of any kind of even limited success is the unshakable conviction that you are getting away with something, and that any moment now they will discover you. It's **Imposter Syndrome**⑯, something my wife Amanda **christened**⑰ the Fraud Police.

23　In my case, I was convinced that there would

的工作是让我感到自豪的工作，那么即使我没挣到钱，至少我还拥有那份工作。

19　有时候我会忘了这一原则，而每当我忘了的时候，上天就会狠狠地教训我一顿，让我想起它来。我不知道别人是否也存在这样的问题，但于我而言真真切切的一件事就是，无论我做什么，只要是我单纯为了钱而去做那件事，那么除了痛苦的经历之外，就永远不会留下有价值的东西。通常那种情况下我也拿不到钱。那些我很兴奋地去做、并希望看到它们存在于现实中的事从来没让我失望过，而我也从不后悔在那类事情上花费时间。

20　失败带来的问题让人难以接受。

21　但成功带来的问题可能更让人难以接受，因为没有人向你提出警告。

22　任何成功、哪怕是小小的成功产生的第一个问题都是：你坚信你正在投机取巧，而人们随时会发现你。这是"冒名顶替综合征"，我妻子阿曼达称其为"冒牌警察"。

23　以我为例，我曾确信有人

---

⑮ every now and again 偶尔，有时

⑯ imposter syndrome 这是一种特殊的妄想观念，也可称之为冒充者综合症。这种妄想观念多涉及与本人关系密切的人

⑰ christen ['krɪsn] *vt.* 为……命名；为……施洗礼

be a knock on the door, and a man with a clipboard (I don't know why he had a clipboard, but in my head, he always had a clipboard) would be there, to tell me it was all over, and they had caught up with me, and now I would have to go and get a real job, one that didn't consist of making things up and writing them down, and reading books I wanted to read. And then I would go away quietly and get the kind of job where I would have to get up early in the morning for, and wear a tie, and not make things up anymore.

24   The problems of success, they're real, and with luck you'll experience them. The point where you stop saying yes to everything, because now the bottles you threw in the ocean are all coming back, and you have to learn to say no.

25   I watched my peers, and my friends, and the ones who were older than me and watch how miserable some of them were: I'd listen to them telling me that they couldn't **envisage**[18] a world where they did what they had always wanted to do any more, because now they had to earn a certain amount every month just to keep where they were. They couldn't go and do the things that mattered, and that they had really wanted to do; and that seemed as a big a tragedy as any problem of failure.

26   And after that, the biggest problem of success is that the world conspires to stop you doing the thing that you do, because you are successful. There was a

会敲我的门，门外会站着一个手拿写字板的男人（我不知道他为什么拿着写字板，在我的脑海里他就是拿着那玩意），他告诉我说一切都结束了，他们已经抓到了我的把柄，现在我不得不出门找一份真正的工作，一份不包括编造故事并把它们写下来还能想读什么书就读什么书的工作。然后我会安静地出门找一份我必须起大早、打领带、不再胡编乱造的工作。

24   成功带来的问题是真实的，运气好的话，你会体验这些问题。到那时你不再对任何事情都说"是"，因为你扔进大海里的瓶子现在都回来了，因此你要学会说"不"。

25   我看着我的同龄人、我的朋友们以及那些比我年长的人，看看他们中的一些人是多么得可怜：我常常听他们说他们无法再想象一个他们总是可以做自己喜欢做的事的世界，因为为了让自己维持现状，他们现在必须每月挣够一定数目的钱。他们无法去做重要的事情，去做他们真正想做的事情；这个悲剧似乎一点不亚于失败带来的任何悲剧。

26   接下来，成功带来的最大问题是，世界上所有人都齐心协力阻止你做事，因为你成功了。

---

⑱ envisage [ɪnˈvɪzɪdʒ] *vt.* 正视，面对；想像

day when I looked up and realised that I had become someone who professionally replied to email, and who wrote as a hobby. I started answering fewer emails, and was relieved to find I was writing much more.

27　Fourthly, I hope you'll make mistakes. If you make mistakes, it means you're out there doing something. And the mistakes in themselves can be useful. I once misspelled Caroline, in a letter, **transposing**[19] the A and the O, and I thought, "Coraline looks almost like a real name…"

28　And remember that whatever discipline you are in, whether you are a musician or a photographer, a fine artist or a cartoonist, a writer, a dancer, a singer, a designer, whatever you do you have one thing that's unique. You have the ability to make art.

29　And for me, and for so many of the people I have known, that's been a **lifesaver**[20]. The ultimate lifesaver. It gets you through good times and it gets you through the other ones.

30　Sometimes life is hard. Things go wrong, in life and in love and in business and in friendship and in health and in all the other ways that life can go

有一天当我仔细回想时，我发现自己已经沦为了一个专业回复电子邮件的人，而且把写电子邮件当成了一种业余爱好。我开始减少回复电子邮件的次数，我很欣喜地发现，我写的东西比以前多多了。

27　第四，我希望你犯错误。如果你犯了错误，这就意味着你在做着什么事情。错误本身也可以变得有用。我曾经在一封信中拼错了"卡洛琳"这个名字，我把字母"A"和"O"写颠倒了，我想："考拉林看上去差不多就是一个真正的名字……"

28　请记住无论你学的是哪一科，不管你是音乐家还是摄影师，不论你是位优秀的艺术家还是一位漫画家、作家、舞者、歌唱家、设计师，无论你是做什么的，你都拥有一种独一无二的能力。你具备艺术创作的能力。

29　对我来说，对我所认识的很多人来说，这是一根救命稻草，而且是一根终极的救命稻草。它能让你度过美好的时光，同时也能让你度过不那么美好的时光。

30　生活有时是很艰难的。事情出了差错，生命中哪个方面都可能出差错，在生活上，在爱情

⑲ transpose [træn'spəuz] vt. 调换；移项；颠倒顺序

⑳ lifesaver ['laɪf'sevə] n. 济急的人；水难救生员；救命者；救命稻草

wrong. And when things get tough, this is what you should do. Make good art.

31　I'm serious. Husband **runs off with**[21] a politician? Make good art. Leg crushed and then eaten by mutated **boa constrictor**[22]? Make good art. **IRS**[23] on your trail? Make good art. Cat exploded? Make good art. Someone on the Internet thinks what you do is stupid or evil or it's all been done before? Make good art. Probably things will work out somehow, and eventually time will take the sting away, but that doesn't even matter. Do what only you do best. Make good art.

32　Make it on the bad days, and make it on the good days too.

33　And Fifthly, while you are at it, make your art. Do the stuff that only you can do.

34　The urge, starting out, is to copy. And that's not a bad thing. Most of us only find our own voices after we've sounded like a lot of other people. But the one thing that you have that nobody else has is you. Your voice, your mind, your story, your vision. So write and draw and build and play and dance and live as only you can.

上，在生意上，在友情上，在健康上以及在其他所有方面。当事情变得艰难时，你应该做的就是创作优秀的艺术作品。

31　我是认真的。丈夫和一个政客私奔了？那就创作好的艺术作品。腿被突变的蟒蛇压碎并吃掉了？那就创作好的艺术作品。国税局调查你？那就创作好的艺术作品。家猫爆发了？那就创作好的艺术作品。有人在网上说你的所作所为是蠢事的或败坏的或是拾人牙慧的事？那就创作好的艺术作品。也许事情会得到圆满解决，而时间终会带走痛楚，但那都不重要。做你最擅长做的事。创作好的艺术作品。

32　在阴云密布的日子里你要这么做，在阳光灿烂的日子里你也要这么做。

33　第五，当你进行创作时，创作你自己的艺术作品。创作只有你能创作的东西。

34　这份冲动始于模仿。这不是一件坏事。我们大多数人只有在模仿很多人之后才找到了自己的声音。但是，你拥有其他人所没有的东西，那就是你自己，你的声音，你的思想，你的故事，你的愿景。所以，以你独特的方式去写作，去绘画，去建造，去

㉑ run off with 携……私奔

㉒ boa constrictor 蟒蛇；王蛇

㉓ IRS *abbr.* 美国国税局（Internal Revenue Service）

35 The moment that you feel that, just possibly, you're walking down the street naked, exposing too much of your heart and your mind and what exists on the inside, showing too much of yourself. That's the moment you may be starting to get it right.

36 The things I've done that worked the best were the things I was the least certain about, the stories where I was sure they would either work, or more likely be the kinds of embarrassing[24] failures people would gather together and talk about until the end of time. They always had that in common: looking back at them, people explain why they were inevitable successes. While I was doing them, I had no idea.

37 I still don't. And where would be the fun in making something you knew was going to work?

38 And sometimes the things I did really didn't work. There are stories of mine that have never been reprinted. Some of them never even left the house. But I learned as much from them as I did from the things that worked.

39 Sixthly. I will pass on some secret freelancer knowledge. Secret knowledge is always good. And it is useful for anyone who ever plans to create art for other people, to enter a freelance world of any kind. I learned it in comics, but it applies to other fields too. And it's this:

表演，去舞蹈，去生活吧。

35 假设在某个时刻，你觉得应该赤身裸体地走在大街上，将心灵、思想、存在于内心的一切都暴露在外，尽情展现自我。在那一刻，你或许才开始步入正轨。

36 我写过的最好的作品是我最没把握的作品，是那些我确信要么成功但更有可能会遭受尴尬的失败、直到世界末日人们还聚在一起评头论足的故事。这些故事基本上都有一个共同点：回头看看它们，人们会解释为什么它们必然大获成功。而当我创作这些故事时，我压根没想到它们会取得成功。

37 现在我依然没弄明白。创作你知道会成功的作品还有什么乐趣可言？

38 有时，我创作的作品确实不好。我写的一些小说从来没有重印过。其中一些甚至从来没有与读者见面过。但我从它们那里学到的就跟我从那些成功作品那里学到的一样多。

39 第六点，我想传授一些从事自由写作方面的秘诀。秘诀总是有好处的。它对任何打算为大众创作艺术作品、或想进入任何一类自由写作领域的人来说都有用。这些秘诀是我从漫画创作生涯中获得的，但同时也适用于其

㉔ embarrassing [ɪmˈbærəsɪŋ] adj. 使人尴尬的；令人为难的

他领域。秘诀如下：

40　People get hired because, somehow, they get hired. In my case I did something which these days would be easy to check, and would get me into trouble, and when I started out, in those pre-internet days, seemed like a sensible career strategy: when I was asked by editors who I'd worked for, I lied. I listed a handful of magazines that sounded likely, and I sounded confident, and I got jobs. I then **made it a point of honour**[25] to have written something for each of the magazines I'd listed to get that first job, so that I hadn't actually lied, I'd just been **chronologically**[26] challenged… You get work however you get work.

40　人们之所以被雇用，是因为他们莫名其妙地就被雇用了。就我本身的情况来说，我曾经做过一些在如今这个年代很容易查出来并会让我惹上麻烦的事。当我开始找工作时，互联网还没出现，我采取的是一种貌似合理的求职策略：当编辑们问我曾经在什么地方工作过时，我说了谎。我列出几个听上去像那么回事而我说出来又很自信的杂志社，于是我得到了那份工作。后来为了保住面子，我为每一家自己为了得到这第一份工作而列出来的杂志社写了些文章，所以实际上我并没有撒谎，我只是颠倒了时间顺序而已……总之，为了找到工作，你可以不择手段。

41　But people keep working, in a freelance world, and more and more of today's world is freelance, because their work is good, and because they are easy to get along with, and because they deliver the work on time. And you don't even need all three. Two out of three is fine. People will tolerate how unpleasant you are if your work is good and you deliver it on time. People'll forgive the lateness of the work if it's good, and if they like you. And you don't have to be as good as the others if you're on time and it's always a pleasure to hear from you.

41　但人们不断地进行创作，在当今世界里，从事自由写作职业的人也越来越多，因为他们的作品优秀，因为他们容易相处，因为他们能准时交稿。你甚至不需要同时拥有这三项优点，只要你拥有其中两项就可以了。人们会容忍你的不好相处，如果你的作品优秀且能准时交稿的话。人们会原谅你延期交稿，如果你的作品优秀而且人们喜欢你的话。你不必和别人一样优秀，如果你

㉕ made it a point of honou 为维护脸面必须做的事

㉖ chronologically [krɒnə'lɒdʒɪklɪ] *adv.* 按年代地

能准时交稿且人们收到你的消息总是感到心情舒畅的话。

42　So when I agreed to give this address, I thought what the best piece of advice I was ever given, and I realized that it was actually a piece of advice that I had failed to follow.

42　当我同意发表这篇演讲的时候，我想到了我这一辈子得到的最好的建议是什么，而我也意识到我自己实际上没有按照那个建议去做。

43　And it came from **Stephen King**[27] twenty years ago, **at the height of**[28] the success, the initial success, of *Sandman*[29], the comic I was writing. I was writing a comic that people loved and they were taking it seriously. And Stephen King liked *Sandman* and my novel with **Terry Pratchett**[30], Good Omens, and he saw the madness that was going on, the long signing lines, all of that stuff and his advice to me was this:

43　那个建议是二十年前史提芬·金给我的，那时我创作的漫画书《睡魔》获得了初步成功。我创作了一本漫画书，人们爱不释手，认真对待。史提芬·金喜欢《睡魔》以及我和特里·普拉切特合写的小说《好兆头》，他也看到人们对我的书表现出的狂热，要求我签名的人排成了长龙，如此等等，而他给我的建议是这样的：

44　He said, "This is really great, you should enjoy it." And I didn't. Best advice I ever got that I ignored. Instead, I worried about it. I worried about the next deadline, the next idea, the next story. There wasn't a moment for the next fourteen or fifteen years, that I wasn't writing something in my head or wondering about it. And I didn't stop and look around and go, "This is really fun." I wish I'd enjoyed it more. It's been an amazing ride but there were parts of the ride I

44　他说："这真是太棒了。你应该好好享受这时刻。"可是我没有。这是我得到的最好的建议，但我忽略了它。相反，我忧心忡忡起来。我担心下一个截稿日期，担心下一个想法，担心下一个故事。在接下来的十四五年里，我无时无刻不在我的脑海里写东西或者在思考要写什么，我

㉗ Stephen King 史蒂芬·金（美国恐怖小说家）

㉘ at the height of 在……顶点；在……的顶峰或鼎盛时期

㉙ Sandman 尼尔·盖曼的《睡魔》漫画由 DC-VERTIGO 出版，从 1989 年连载至 1996 年共 75 集。该系列由数篇互相独立的故事构成。盖曼负责整个系列的编剧，而不同的主题都由不同的漫画家参与绘制。所以，《睡魔》漫画充满了多元化的个人风格，画面的语言如梦境般多姿多彩。

㉚ Terry Pratchett 科学幻想小说作家特里·普拉切特（Terry Pratchett）

missed because I was too worried about things going wrong, about what came next, to enjoy the **bit**[31] that I was on. That was the hardest lesson for me, I think — to let go and enjoy the ride. Because the ride takes you to some remarkable and unexpected places.

45 And here, on this platform, today for me, is one of those places. I am enjoying myself immensely. I'd actually put that in brackets just in case I wasn't; I wouldn't say.

46 To all today's graduates: I wish you luck. Luck is useful. Often you will discover that the harder you work, and the more wisely you work, the luckier you get. But there is luck, and it helps.

47 We're in a transitional world right now, if you're in any kind of artistic field, because the nature of distribution is changing, the models by which creators got their work out into the world, and got to **keep a roof over their heads**[32] and buy sandwiches while they did that, are all changing. I've talked to

没有停下脚步看看四周，说："这真是有趣。"我倒是希望我尽情地享受了那次的成功。这是一次奇妙的人生旅程，但是我错过了其中的某些部分，因为我过于担心事情会出错，太担心接下来会发生什么，结果没有享受到成功的喜悦。对我来说，那是最难学的一课：关于如何放下心事去享受人生之旅，而它会把你带到一些精彩而又意想不到的地方。

45 对我来说，今天我站在了这个讲台上，因此这里正是那些意想不到的地方之一。我十分享受这个过程。老实说，我得把刚才那句话放在括号里，以防万一我没有享受这个过程；对此我就不想再多说了。

46 所有今天毕业的同学们：我祝你们好运。好运气是有用的。通常你们会发现，你越努力工作，你越巧妙地工作，你就会越幸运。但运气成份确实存在，而且它会助你一臂之力。

47 我们现在正处于一个变迁中的世界，如果你身处艺术领域（无论是哪类艺术领域）的话，你便倍感如此，因为作品发行的性质正在发生变化，作者将作品公布于世的模式也在发生着

---

③ bit [bɪt] *n.* 一点，一些；小片，小块；小段，片段；部分

③ we had a roof over our heads 这句话该如何翻译？我的理解是我们的头上有屋顶，引申为"有房子"

people at the top of the food chain in publishing, in bookselling, in music, in all those areas, and no one knows what the landscape will look like two years from now, let alone a decade away. The distribution channels that people had built over the last century or so are **in flux**[33] for print, for visual artists, for musicians, for creative people of all kinds.

48　Which is, on the one hand, intimidating, and on the other, immensely liberating. The rules, the assumptions, the now-we're-supposed-to's of how you get your work seen, and what you do then, are breaking down. The gatekeepers are leaving their gates. You can be as creative as you need to be to get your work seen. YouTube and the web (and whatever comes after YouTube and the web) can give you more people watching than television ever did. The old rules are crumbling and nobody knows what the new rules are.

49　So make up your own rules.

50　Someone asked me recently how to do something she thought was going to be difficult, in this case recording an audio book, and I suggested she pretend that she was someone who could do it. Not pretend to do it, but pretend she was someone who

变化，过去作者靠出卖作品让自己过上住食无忧的生活这一情况也发生了变化。我和身后出版界、图书销售界、音乐界以及所有那些领域的食物链顶端的人物交谈过，他们中没有人知道两年后业界将是怎样一番景象，更别说十年之后了。人们在过去差不多一个世纪左右的时间里建立起来的销售渠道正处于变化之中，对印刷业是如此，对视觉艺术家、音乐家和各种有创意的人也是如此。

48　这一方面着实令人心惊肉跳，但另一方面它又是极大的解放。我们现在所认为的关于应该如何让你的作品呈现给大众以及接下来你要如何做的规则和假设都已被打破。守门人正在离开大门。为了让人们看见你的作品，你能够尽可以地发挥创意。视频网站和互联网（以及任何在视频网站和互联网之后出现的渠道）可以让观看你作品的人数超过看电视的人数。旧规则正在崩蹋，而没人知道新规则是什么。

49　所以，请建立你自己的规则。

50　最近有位女士问我怎么处理她认为会很困难的事，就她本人而言，那件事是录制音频书，我建议她假装她是行家里手。不要假装要去做那件事，而要假装

㉝ be in flux 处于不断变化中

could. She put up a notice to this effect on the studio wall, and she said it helped.

51   So be wise, because the world needs more wisdom, and if you cannot be wise, pretend to be someone who is wise, and then just behave like they would.

52   And now go, and make interesting mistakes, make amazing mistakes, make glorious and fantastic mistakes. Break rules. Leave the world more interesting for your being here. Make good art. Thank you.

她是能干那件事的人。她把我的建议贴在录音室的墙壁上,她说这的确有帮助。

51   因此,要成为一位智者,因为这个世界需要更多的智慧;如果你不能成为一位智者的话,那就假装自己是智者,那么你的言行举止就会像智者了。

52   现在出发吧,犯下一些有趣的错误,犯下一些奇妙的错误,犯下一些辉煌又美妙的错误。打破规则吧。让世界因为你的存在而变得更有趣。创作优秀的艺术作品吧。感谢诸位。

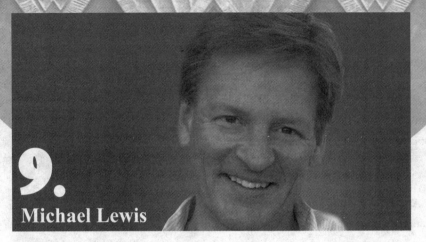

9.
Michael Lewis

迈克尔·刘易斯

在普林斯顿大学毕业典礼上的演讲（2012年）

扫一扫

 **人物档案**

迈克尔·刘易斯（Michael Lewis，1960年10月15日—），美国当代报告文学作家、财经记者，毕业于普林斯顿大学和伦敦经济学院。大学主修艺术史。他所写的畅销书包括《说谎者的扑克牌》、《将世界甩在身后》、《魔球：逆境中制胜的智慧》和《弱点：比赛进程》等。其中《说谎者的扑克牌》和《将世界甩在身后》同被《福布斯》评为"20世纪最具影响力的20部商业书籍"。目前他是《名利场》的特约编辑。

 场景介绍

普林斯顿大学（Princeton University），位于美国新泽西州的普林斯顿，是美国一所著名的私立研究型大学，八所常春藤盟校之一。学校于1746年在新泽西州伊丽莎白镇创立，是美国殖民时期第四所成立的高等教育学院，当时名为"新泽西学院"，1747年迁至新泽西州，1756年迁至普林斯顿，并于1896年正式改名为普林斯顿大学。普林斯顿保有浓厚的欧式教育学风，非常重视本科生教育，创立宗旨方面则强调训练学生具有人文及科学的综合素养。

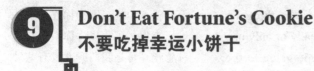

9 | Don't Eat Fortune's Cookie
不要吃掉幸运小饼干

经典原文
Original Text

中文译文
Suggested Translation

1　I've never been **up here**①. Thank you. President Tilghman.

2　Trustees and friends. Parents of the Class of 2012, wherever they put you. Members of the Class of 2012. Why don't you give yourself a round of applause? So the next time you look around a church and see everyone dressed in black, it'll be awkward to do that. But enjoy the moment, enjoy the moment.

3　Thirty years ago, I sat where you sat. I must have listened to some older person share his life experiences. But I don't remember a word. I couldn't even tell you who spoke. And you won't be able to, either. What I do remember, vividly, is graduation. I'm told you're meant to be excited, maybe even a little relieved that you are getting out of here. And maybe all of you are. I was not. I was totally outraged. Here I'd gone and given them four of the best years of my

1　我以前从来没登到这上面来过。谢谢你，迪尔曼校长。

2　校理事会成员和朋友们；2012 届毕业生的家长们；不论你们被学校安排在什么地方；2012 届的毕业生们，何不给你们自己送上一轮热烈的掌声呢？下一次你们在教堂里看到每个人都穿着黑衣服的时候，如果你们鼓掌的话，恐怕就会有点尴尬了。但是现在你们可以尽情享受，享受此刻。

3　30 年前，我就坐在你们现在坐着的位置上。我当时一定听过某个比我岁数大的人分享着他的人生经验。但是我现在一个字都不记得了。我甚至都无法告诉你们演讲者是谁。你们将来也不会记得的。不过让我记忆犹新的是毕业本身。别人告诉我说，你们应该会感到激动，或许你们甚

---

① up here 普林斯顿大学非常奇特，毕业典礼是在教堂举行，而在毕业典礼上发表演讲的人要登上一个高约 2 米的台子上去演讲。

life and this is how they rewarded me by throwing me out. At that moment I was sure really of only one thing: I was of no possible economic value to the outside world. I'd majored in art history, **for a start**②. Even then majoring in art history was regarded as an act of insanity. I was almost certainly less well prepared than you are for the marketplace.

4   Yet somehow I've wound up rich and famous. Sort of. I'm going to explain, briefly, how that happened. I want you to understand just how mysterious careers can be, before you go out and have one for yourself. So I graduated from Princeton without ever having published a word of anything, anywhere. I didn't write for *The Prince*, or for anyone else. But at Princeton, studying art history, I felt really the first **twinge**③ of literary ambition. It happened while I was working on my senior thesis. My adviser was a really gifted man, an archaeologist named William Childs. The thesis I wrote for him tried to explain how the Italian sculptor Donatello used Greek and Roman sources, which is actually totally beside the point, but I've always wanted to tell someone. God knows what Professor Childs thought of it, but

至会松一口气，因为你终于要从这里走出去了。也许你们都有这种感觉。可是我当时就没有这种感觉。我当时非常愤怒。我来到了这里，把我生命里最美好的4年光阴给了他们，他们就这样一下子把我甩掉了，这就是他们对我的回报吗？那时我能够确定的唯有一件事：我对外面的世界而言没有任何经济价值。首先，我主修的是艺术史。即便在那个时候，主修艺术史也被认为是个疯狂的行为。我当时几乎和你们现在一样没有做好踏入职场的心理准备。

4   不过不管怎么说，我最终变得既有钱又有名。有那么一点点吧。我将会简单地解释一下那是如何发生的。我只是想让你们在走出校门迈入职业生涯之前明白，一个人的职业生涯是多么难以预测。就这样，我在没有发表过任何文章的情况下从普林斯顿毕业了。我没有给《普林斯顿日报》写过东西，也没有给其它什么报纸写过东西。但是当我在普林斯顿学习艺术史时，我第一次真切地体会到了文学抱负带给人的刺痛。那件事是在我写本科毕业论文时发生的。我的指导老师确实是一位具有天赋的人，他

---

② for a start 首先；作为开始　　　　　③ twinge [twɪndʒ] *n.* 阵痛；悔恨

he helped me to become **engrossed**④. Actually more than engrossed: totally obsessed. When I handed it in, I knew what I wanted to do for the rest of my life: I want to write senior theses. Or, to put it differently: to write books. Then I went to my **thesis defense**⑤. It was just a few yards from here, over in McCormick Hall. I listened and waited for Professor Childs to tell how well written my thesis was. He didn't. So after about 45 minutes I finally said, "So... What did you think of the writing?" "**Put it this way**⑥," he said, "Never try to **make a living**⑦ at it." And I didn't — not really. I did what everyone does who has no idea what to do with themselves: I went to graduate school. I wrote at nights, without much effect, mainly because I hadn't the first clue what I should write about.

5   One night I was invited to a dinner, where I sat next to the wife of **a big shot**⑧ at a big Wall Street

是位考古学家，名叫威廉·蔡尔兹。我写给他的论文试图解释意大利雕刻家多纳泰罗如何利用了希腊和罗马的素材，这实际上和今天的主题完全无关，但是我一直想把这件事跟别人分享一下。天晓得蔡尔兹教授当时对我那篇论文有何想法，但是他帮助我全神贯注地写论文。实际上不止是全神贯注；我完全痴迷于此了。当我提交我的论文时，我就知道我的下半生想做的事情是什么：我想写毕业论文。或者，换一个说法：我想写书。然后我参加了论文答辩。答辩的地方离这里不远，就在麦考米克大厅。我聆听并期待着蔡尔兹教授称赞我的论文写得有多棒。他并没有。因此大约45分钟之后，我终于忍不住问道："那么，你认为我写得怎么样？""这么说吧，"他说，"千万别尝试靠写作谋生。"我确实也没有靠写作谋生——也不尽然。我做了一件和所有不知道自己该干什么的人所做的一样的事情：我去读了研究生。我晚上写作，但没多大效果，主要是因为我不知道应该写些什么。

5   有天晚上，我被邀请参加一个晚宴，坐在了一位夫人旁

---

④ engrossed [ɪnˈgrəʊst] *adj.* 全神贯注的；专心致志的
⑤ thesis defense 论文答辩

⑥ put it this way 这样说；这样做
⑦ make a living 谋生，维持生活
⑧ a big shot 大人物；大亨

investment bank, called Salomon Brothers. She more or less forced her husband to give me a job. I knew **next to nothing**[9] about Salomon Brothers. But Salomon Brothers happened to be where Wall Street was being reinvented — into the Wall Street we have all come to know and love today. When I got there I was assigned, almost arbitrarily, to the very best job in the place to observe the growing madness: they turned me into the in-house **derivatives**[10] expert. A year and a half later, Salomon Brothers was handing me a check for hundreds of thousands of dollars to give advice about derivatives to professional investors. Now I had something to write about: Salomon Brothers.

6　Wall Street had become so unhinged[11] that it was paying recent Princeton graduates who knew nothing about money **small fortunes**[12] to pretend they were experts about money. I'd stumbled into my next senior thesis. At that point, I called up my father. I told him I was gonna quit this job that promised me millions of dollars to write a book for **an advance**[13] of 40 **grand**[14]. There was this long pause on the other end of the line. "You might just want to think about that one," he said. "Why?" I asked. "You can stay at Salomon Brothers for 10 years, you can make your

边，她的丈夫是一家叫做所罗门兄弟公司的华尔街投资银行的大亨。她差不多是逼着她老公给我安排了一份工作。当时我对所罗门兄弟几乎一无所知。但碰巧的是那时所罗门兄弟公司正赶上华尔街整改的当口——它被改造成了如今我们大家都十分了解和热爱的华尔街。当我进入那家公司时，我几乎是被随意地分派到了一个可以观察那段疯狂发展历史的最佳岗位：他们把我培养成了金融衍生产品专家。一年半后，所罗门兄弟公司开始付给我好几十万美金的工资支票，让我给职业投资人提供关于金融衍生品方面的建议。现在我就有东西可写了：所罗门兄弟公司。

6　当时的华尔街已经变得无比疯狂，以至于能给那些对金钱毫无概念的刚从普林斯顿大学出来的毕业生支付可观的薪水，让他们假装自己是金融方面的专家。就这样，我误打误撞地找到了我的下一篇论文素材。就在那个时候，我给我父亲打了电话。我告诉他我打算辞掉这份能保证给我带来数百万美元收入的工作，去写一本只有 4 万美元预付

---

⑨ next to nothing *adv.* 几乎没有

⑩ derivative [dəˈrɪvətɪv] *n.* [化学] 衍生物，派生物

⑪ unhinged [ʌnˈhɪndʒd] *adj.* 精神错乱的

⑫ small fortune 大量的钱

⑬ an advance 预付款

⑭ grand [grænd] *n.* 一千美元

fortune, and then you can write your books," he said. But I didn't need to think about it. I knew what intellectual passion felt like — because I'd felt it here, at Princeton — and I wanted to feel it again. I was 26 years old. Had I waited until I was 36, I would never have done it. I would have forgotten the feeling. I would have felt it too risky. The book I wrote was called *Liar's Poker*. It sold a million copies. I was 28 years old. I had a career, a little fame, a small fortune and a new life narrative.

7　All of a sudden people were telling me I was a born writer. This was absurd. Even I could see there was another, more true narrative, with luck as its theme. What were the odds of being seated at that dinner next to that Salomon Brothers lady? Of landing inside the best Wall Street firm to write the story of the age? Of landing in the seat with the best view of the business? Of having parents who didn't disinherit me but instead sighed and said "do it if you must"? Of having had that sense of "must" kindled inside me by a professor of art history at Princeton? Of having been let into Princeton in the first place? This isn't just false humility. It's false humility with a point. My case illustrates how success is always rationalized. People really don't like to hear success explained away as luck! Especially successful people. As they age, and

稿酬的书。电话另一头沉默了很长一段时间。"你或许该好好想想，"他说。"为什么？"我问。他回答："你可以先在所罗门干 10 年，赚够了钱，然后再去写你的书。"但是我不需要考虑。我清楚那种当你对知识产生热情时会有的感受——因为我在普林斯顿这里已经感受过了——而且我想再感受一次。当时我 26 岁。如果我等到 36 岁的时候再去写，我就永远都写不成了。我会忘记那种感受。我会觉得那样做太冒险了。我写的那本书叫作《说谎者的扑克牌》。它的销量达 100 万册。我那时 28 岁。我有了一份事业，一点名气，一大笔钱和一个崭新的人生故事。

7　突然之间，人们对我说我是个天才作家。实在可笑。就连我自己都知道还有一个更加真实的故事，而它的主题是运气。晚宴时被安排坐在那个所罗门兄弟公司大亨夫人旁边的机率有多大？进入华尔街最好的公司从而可以写一本描写时代风云变幻的书的机率有多大？被安排到了能以最佳视角观察行业变化的职位的机率有多大？拥有没有和我断绝关系而只是叹口气说一句"如果你一定要怎么做，那就去做吧"的父母的机率有多大？遇上一位能激发我内心那种"非做不可"的热情的普林斯顿艺术史教

succeed, people feel their success was somehow inevitable. They don't want to acknowledge the role played by accident in their lives. There is a reason for this: the world doesn't want to acknowledge it either.

8   I actually wrote a book about this, called *Moneyball*. It was **ostensibly**⑮ about baseball but was in fact about something else. There are poor teams and rich teams in professional baseball, and they spend radically different sums of money on their players. When I wrote my book the richest team, the New York Yankees, was then spending about $120 million on its 25 players. The poorest team was the Oakland A's. They were spending about $30 million. And yet the Oakland team was winning more games, or as many games as the New York Yankees. And more games than every other team, all of them were richer than they were. This isn't supposed to happen. In theory, the rich teams should buy the best players and win all the time. But the Oakland team had figured something out that no one else has figured out: the rich teams didn't really understand who the best baseball players were. The players were misvalued. And the biggest single reason they were misvalued

授的机率有多大？而最初能进入普林斯顿大学的机率有多大？这不是假谦虚。这是有道理的假谦虚。我的例子说明了成功是如何总被认为是理所当然的事情的。人们确实不喜欢听到"成功是运气带来的"这类话！成功人士尤为不喜欢听。随着他们年龄增长，逐步取得成功时，人们会觉得他们的成功在所难免。他们不愿意承认运气在他们的生命中所起的作用。这其中有一个原因：全世界的人也不愿意承认这一点。

8   关于这一点，我还真写了本书，书名叫《滚钱球》。它表面上是写棒球的，但实际上说的是另外一件事。在职业棒球领域里有富队和穷队之分，它们花在球员身上的钱可谓是有着天壤之别。就在我写那本书的时候，最有钱的球队是纽约洋基队，这个队当时在25个球员身上的花费大约是1.2亿美元。而最穷的球队是奥克兰运动家队。他们的花费大约只有3000万美元。可是奥克兰运动家队赢球的场次一点也不比纽约洋基队少，甚至比纽约洋基队还要多。奥克兰运动家队赢球的场次更比除了纽约洋基队外的其它所有球队都多，而这些球队个个都比奥克兰运动家队有钱。这种事情本不应该发生。

---

⑮ ostensibly [ɒsˈtensəblɪ] *adv.* 表面上；外表。

迈克尔 · 刘易斯 *Michael Lewis*

was that the experts did not pay sufficient attention to the role of luck in baseball success. Players got given credit for things they did that depended on the performance of others: pitchers got paid for winning games, hitters got paid for knocking in runners on base. Players got blamed and credited for events totally beyond their control. Where balls that got hit happened to land on the field, for example.

9 Forget baseball, forget the game of sports. Here you had these corporate employees, being paid millions of dollars a year. They were doing exactly the same job that people in their business had done for more than a century. In front of millions of people, each of them think they are an expert on what a good baseball player is. They had statistics attached to every move they made on their job. And yet they were misvalued! Because the wider world was blind to their luck. So I think you have to ask: if a professional athlete paid millions of dollars a year can be misvalued, who can't be? If the supposedly pure **meritocracy**⑯ of professional sports can't distinguish between the lucky and good, who can?

理论上讲，有钱的球队应该签约到最佳球员并赢得所有比赛。但是奥克兰运动家队悟出了一个别人都没有悟出的道理：有钱的球队并不真正了解谁是最好的球员。球员的价值被误估了。球员之所以被误估，其最大的原因就是运气在棒球中所起的作用没有引起专家们足够的重视。有些球员因为自己的表现而得到了赞扬，但他们的表现依赖于其他球员的表现：投球手因为赢球而获得报酬，而击球手则因为送队友上垒而获得报酬。球员们因为一些完全不受自己控制的事件而受到指责或者表扬。比如，被击中的球恰好落在场地上的某个位置。

9 且按下棒球或者体育运动不表。看看这些年薪数百万美元的公司员工吧。他们做的工作和100多年来业内人士已经做过的工作完全一样。在数百万人面前，他们个个都认为自己在研究"什么样的棒球选手是一名优秀的棒球手"方面是专家。他们对自己在工作中的一举一动都进行统计分析。可是他们的身价仍然会被估错！因为外面更为广阔的世界对他们的运气视而不见。因此我想你们必须问这样一个问题：如果一个年薪数百万美元的职业运动员其身价可能被估错的话，谁的

⑯ meritocracy ['merɪ'tɒkrəsɪ] *n.* 英才教育（制度）；精英管理的社会

身价又不会被误估呢？如果被认为是纯粹精英制度的职业体育运动界都无法区分运气和实力，那么谁又会有这个能力呢？

10　The *Moneyball* story has practical implications. If you use better data, you can find better values; there are always **market inefficiencies**[17] to exploit, and so on. But, to me, it has a broader and less practical message: don't be deceived by life's outcomes. Life's outcomes, while not entirely random, have a huge amount of luck baked into them. Above all, recognize that if you have had success, you have also had luck! And with luck comes obligation. You owe a debt, and not just to your Gods. You owe a debt to the unlucky. I make this point because along with this speech, it is something that will be easy for you to forget.

10　《滚钱球》的故事有现实的启发意义。如果你使用更好的数据，那么你就能够发现更好的价值；市场总有失灵的地方可以加以利用，如此等等。不过对我而言，它具有一个更为广范却不太实用的信息：不要被生活的结果所欺骗。生活的结果尽管不完全是随机的，却也蕴含着大量的偶然因素。最重要的是，你要认识到，如果你成功了，那么运气也在陪伴着你！伴随运气而来便是责任。你欠下了一份情，不仅欠上帝的。你欠那些不走运的人一份情。我指出这一点是因为，这个道理和我的这个演讲一样，很容易就被你们遗忘了。

11　I now live in Berkeley, California. A few years ago, just a few blocks from my home, a pair of researchers in the Cal psychology department staged an experiment. They began by grabbing students like you, to use as his lab rats. Then they broke the students into teams, segregated by sex. Three men, or three women, on a team. Then they put these teams of three into a room, and arbitrarily assigned one member of the team to be the leader. Then they gave them some complicated moral problem to solve: say what should be done about academic cheating, or how

11　目前我住在加州伯克利市。几年前，就在离我家几个街区远的地方，两个加州大学心理系的研究人员设计了一项实验。他们找了一些像你们一样的学生作为他们的实验对象。然后他们按性别对学生们进行分组。三个男生一组，或者三个女生一组。随后他们把这些3人小组带进一个房间，并随意指派一名小组成员担任组长。然后他们向这些小

⑰ market inefficiency 市场无效率

to regulate drinking on campus. Exactly 30 minutes into the problem-solving the researchers interrupted each group. They entered the room bearing a plate of cookies. Four cookies. The team consisted of three people, but there were these four cookies. Every team member obviously got one cookie, but that left a fourth cookie, just sitting there. It should have been awkward. But it wasn't.

12　With incredible consistency the person arbitrarily appointed leader of the group grabbed the fourth cookie, and ate it. Not only ate it, but ate it with **gusto**[18]: lips **smacking**[19], mouth open, **drool**[20] pooling at the corners of their mouths. In the end all that was left of the extra cookie were the crumbs on the leader's shirt. So this leader had performed no special task. He had no special virtue. He'd been chosen at random, 30 minutes earlier. His status was nothing but luck. But it left him with a sense that this cookie, the 4th cookie, should be his.

13　This experiment helps to explain Wall Street bonuses, CEO pay, and I'm sure lots of other human behavior. This is how people behave, when they are

组提出一个复杂的伦理问题让他们解决：比如应该如何处理学术作弊问题，或如何管控校园饮酒问题等。在他们开始解决问题整整 30 分钟后，研究人员打断了他们。研究人员端着一盘饼干走进房间。盘子里一共有四块饼干。每个小组由三人组成，而饼干却有四块。很显然，每个小组成员都拿了一块饼干，但这样就剩下了第四块饼干，静静地躺在那里。这本该是个尴尬的场面。但其实不然。

12　结果出奇得一致：那个被随意指定为组长的人抓起了那第四块饼干并且吃了下去。不仅仅是吃了下去，而且是有滋有味地吃了下去：嘴巴咂咂作响、大口张开、口水从嘴角直流而下。最后，那块多余的饼干剩下的就只有留在组长衬衫上的饼干渣。这个组长并没有承担任何特别的任务。他也没有任何特殊的优点。他只是在 30 分钟前被随机选定的。他得到的地位只不过是靠运气而已。然而这让他觉得多出来的第四块饼干就应该是他的。

13　这个实验可以帮助我们解释华尔街的奖金和 CEO 的高薪现象，我相信也可以解释很多人类

⑱ gusto ['gʌstəʊ] *n.* 爱好；由衷的高兴；嗜好；有滋有味

⑲ smack [smæk] *vi.*（尤指嘴馋或回味而）咂嘴

⑳ drool [dru:l] *n.* 口水；梦话

blind in their own luck. But it's also relevant to you, to new graduates of Princeton University. Because in a general sort of way, you have been appointed the leader of the group. Your appointment may not be entirely arbitrary. But you must sense right now its arbitrary aspect: you are the lucky few. Lucky in your parents, lucky in your country, lucky that a place like Princeton exists that can take in lucky people, introduce them to other lucky people, and increase their chances of becoming even luckier. Lucky that you live in the richest society the world has ever seen, in a time when no one actually expects you to sacrifice your interests to anything. All of you have been faced with the extra cookie. All of you will be faced with many more of them. In time you will find it easy to assume that you deserve the extra cookie. For all I know[21], you may deserve the extra cookie. But you'll be happier, and you will be better off, if you at least pretend that you don't.

14　So never forget: In the nation's service. **In the service of**[22] all nations.

15　Thank you.

16　And good luck.

的其它行为。当人们无视自己的好运时，人们就是这样行事的。但这和你们也有关系，和作为普林斯顿大学新一届毕业生的你们有关系。因为从广泛的意义上说，你们已经被指定成为了小组的领导者。你们的任命也许并不是完全随机的。但是你现在必须意识到到这里面是存在随意成份的：你属于那些少数的幸运者。你的好运在于有你的父母，你的好运在于有你的国家，你的好运在于有像普林斯顿大学这样的地方吸收了幸运的人并把他们介绍给其他幸运的人，从而增加了他们变得更幸运的机会。为生活在这个世界上最富有的社会里而感到幸运吧，为生活在一个没人指望你为什么而牺牲兴趣的时代而感到幸运吧。你们所有人都面对过这样"一块多余的饼干"。你们所有人都将面临很多这样的"饼干"。将来有一天，你们会发现，自认为自己应该得到这块"多余的饼干"是一件多么容易的事。就我所知，你可能确实有资格拥有那块"多余的饼干"。但是，如果你至少装作不知道的话，你就会更快乐、更富有。

14　因此，我们永远不要忘记：为祖国服务。为所有国家服务。

15　谢谢你们。

16　祝各位好运！

㉑ for all I know 就我所知　　　　　　㉒ in the service of 为……服务；造福于

10.
Aaron Sorkin

阿伦 · 索尔金

在雪城大学的演讲（2012年）

扫一扫

 人物档案

　　阿伦 · 索尔金（Aaron Sorkin，1961 年 6 月 9 日—），美国著名剧作家，1983 年毕业于雪城大学，主修音乐舞台剧。早期著名影视作品有《义海雄风》及《白宫奇缘》、《白宫风云》等。近作有《查理 · 威尔逊的战争》、《社交网络》等。《社交网络》更获得第 83 届奥斯卡最佳改编剧本奖。

 场景介绍

　　雪城大学（Syracuse University），是一所享誉世界的私立研究型大学。该校成立于 1870 年，坐落于美国纽约州雪城（Syracuse），其建筑学院、信息学院、计算机科学与工程学院、Maxwell公民与公共事务学院、Newhouse 公共传播学院、视觉与表演艺术学院、教育学院均在美国名列前茅，在各学科领域中成就卓著并影响巨大。

10 Don't Ever Forget That You're a Citizen of This World
永远不要忘了你们是世界公民

Original Text

Suggested Translation

1 Thank guys. Madam Chancellor, members of the Board of Trustees, members of the faculty and administration, parents and friends, honored guests and graduates, thank you for inviting me to speak today at this magnificent commencement ceremony.

2 There's a story about a man and a woman who have been married for 40 years. One evening at dinner the woman turns to her husband and says, "You know, 40 years ago on our wedding day you told me that you loved me and you haven't said those words since." They sit in silence for a long moment before the husband says, "If I change my mind, I'll let you know."

3 Well, it's been a long time since I sat where you sit, and I can remember looking up at my teachers with great admiration, with fondness, with gratitude and with love. Some of the teachers who were there that day are here this day and I wanted to let them know that I haven't changed my mind.

1 谢谢大家。校长女士，校董事会的成员们，老师们和行管人员们，学生的父母和朋友们，各位嘉宾和毕业生们，感谢你们邀请我在今天这个盛大的毕业典礼上发表演讲。

2 有一个故事，讲的是关于一对已经结婚40年的夫妻的。一天晚上吃饭的时候，妻子扭头对她的丈夫说："你还记得吗？40年前你在我们的婚礼上对我说了你爱我，从那以后你就再也没有说过那句话了。"他们默默地坐了很久，丈夫终于开口说道："如果我变了心，我会告诉你的。"

3 呵呵，我坐在你们现在坐的地方参加毕业典礼的那个时候距离现在已经有很长一段时间了，我还记得我以无限敬佩、无限喜爱和无限感激的目光仰视着我的老师们。当年坐在台上的一些老师今天依然坐在这里，我想

让他们知道，我的心仍没有变。

4　There's another story. Two newborn babies are lying side by side in the hospital nursery and they glance at each other. Ninety years later, through a remarkable coincidence, the two are back in the same hospital lying side by side in the same hospital room. They look at each other and one of them says, "So what'd you think?"

4　还有一个故事。两个新生儿紧挨着躺在医院的婴儿室里，他们互相瞅了对方一眼。九十年后，一件惊人巧合的事情发生了：两人又回到了同一家医院，并排躺在医院的同一间病房里。他们相互看了彼此一眼，其中一人说道："老兄，你怎么看待这件事？"

5　It's going to be a very long time before you have to answer that question, but time shifts gears right now and starts to gain speed. Just ask your parents whose heads, I promise you, are exploding right now. They think they took you home from the maternity ward last month. They think you learned how to walk last week. They don't understand how you could possibly be getting a degree in something today. They listened to *Cats in the Cradle*① the whole car ride here.

5　在你们必须回答这个问题之前，你们还有一段非常漫长的道路要走，但时间之轮现在就换档并开始加速行驶了。只要问问你们的父母就知道了，我向你们保证，他们现在必定是思绪万千。在他们的记忆里，他们好像是上个月才把你们从产房里抱回了家。他们还以为你们是上个星期才学会了走路。他们想不明白你们怎么可能今天就拿到了某个专业的学位证书。他们是听着《摇篮里的猫》一路来到了这里的。

6　I'd like to say to the parents that I realized something while I was writing this speech, the last teacher your kids will have in college will be me and that thought scared the hell out of me. Frankly, you should feel exactly the same way. But I am the father

6　我想对学生父母们说，当我写这篇演讲稿时，我意识到了一件事，你们的孩子在大学里的最后一位老师将是我，这个想法把我吓得半死。坦率地说，你们

---

① Cats in the Cradle 这是一首从上个世纪七十年代红到九十年代的歌，许多乐队都翻唱过。歌中叙述了一个很简单却很耐人寻味的故事：一个小男孩在接受父亲的礼物——一个球以后，要求父亲和他一起玩，可父亲总是说："改天吧！"虽然总被拒绝，小男孩还是很崇敬父亲，希望长大后可以做父亲那样的人。后来男孩长大了，上了大学、毕业、工作……偶尔去探望父亲的时候，父亲总说："有空多来陪我，可以和我聊聊。"男孩说他很愿意，但是很忙，所以："改天吧！"望着男孩离去时的高大背影，父亲感叹"他真象我……"

of an 11 year old daughter, so I do know how proud you are today, how proud your daughters and your sons make you every day, that they did just learn how to walk last week, that you'll never not be there for them, that you love them more than they'll ever know and that it doesn't matter how many degrees get put in their hand, they will always be dumber than you are.

7   And **make no mistake about it**[②], you are dumb. You're a group of incredibly well educated dumb people. I was there. We all were there. You're barely functional. There are some screw-ups headed your way. I wish I could tell you that there was a trick to avoiding the screw ups, but the screw ups, they're a-coming for you. It's a combination of life being unpredictable, and you being super dumb.

8   Today is May 13th and today you graduate. Growing up, I looked at my future as a timeline of graduations in which every few years, I'd be given more freedom and reward as I passed each milestone of childhood. When I get my driver's license, my life will be like this; when I'm a senior, my life will be like that; when I go off to college, my life will be like this; when I move out of the dorms, my life will be like that; and then finally, graduation. And on graduation day, I had only one goal left, and that was to be part of professional theater. We have this in common, you and I — we want to be able to earn a living doing what we love. Whether you're a writer,

应该和我有同感。但我有个 11 岁的女儿，所以我知道你们今天是多么得自豪，我知道你们的女儿和儿子让你们每一天都感到无比得自豪，他们好像上星期才学会走路，你们会永远在他们身边，而他们永远不知道你们爱他们有多深，所以不管他们拿到多少学位，他们永远都比你们笨。

7   毫无疑问，你们就是笨蛋。你们是一群受过良好教育的笨蛋。我曾经也笨过。我们都曾笨过。你们几乎没有什么用。有一些错误的东西在引导着你们前进。我真希望我可以告诉你们一个避免犯错误的诀窍，但错误总是来找你们的麻烦。不可预测的生活与超级大笨蛋的你们组合在了一起。

8   今天是五月十三日，是你们毕业的日子。我在成长的过程中，我将我的未来视为各类毕业串在一起的时间轴，在这个时间轴上，每隔几年我就会因为跨过人生早期的一个里程碑而得到更多的自由和奖励。当我拿到驾照时，我的生活会是这个样子；当我读高三的时候，我的生活会是那个样子；当我离家去上大学的时候，我的生活会是这个样子；当我搬出宿舍的时候，我的生活会是那个样子；然后一路到了毕

② make no mistake about it 不用有任何疑问

mathematician, engineer, architect, butcher, baker or candlestick maker, you want an invitation to the show. Today is May 13th, and today you graduate, and today you already know what I know, to get where you're going, you have to be good and to be good where you're going, you have to be damned good. **Every once in a while**[3] you'll succeed. Most of the time you'll fail, and most of the time the circumstances will be well beyond your control.

9　When we were casting my first movie, *A Few Good Men*, we saw an actor just 10 months removed from the theater training program at UCLA. We liked him very much and we cast him in a small, but featured role as an endearingly **dimwitted**[4] Marine corporal. The actor had been working as a Domino's Pizza delivery boy for 10 months, so the news that he'd just landed his first professional job and that it was in a new movie that Rob Reiner was directing, starring Tom Cruise and Jack Nicholson, was met with happiness. But as is often the case in show business, success **begets**[5] success before you've even done anything and a week later the actor's agent called. The actor had been offered the lead role in a new,

业的时候。在毕业的那一天，我只剩下了一个目标，那就是成为专业剧团的一员。我们，你和我，有一个共同点，那就是我们都希望能够做我们喜欢做的事情，并以此谋生。无论你是当作家、数学家、工程师、建筑师，还是当屠户、面包师、烛台制造商，你希望的无非就是得到表现的机会。今天是五月十三日，是你们毕业的日子，今天你们已经懂得了我所懂得的道理，知道要想达到目标，你必须优秀，你要想很好地达到目标，你就必须非常非常优秀。有时你会成功，但大多时候你会失败，并且大多时候周围的环境是你无法掌握的。

9　当我们拍摄我们的第一部电影《义海雄风》时，我们看中了一个10个月前才在加州大学洛杉矶分校学完戏剧表演课程的演员。我们非常喜欢他，然后我们给他分配了一个小配角，但是这个角色很有特点，是一个傻得可爱的海军下士。此前那位演员在达美乐披萨店当了10个月的送货员，所以当他知道接到了第一份专业工作，还是在一部由罗布·赖纳执导、汤姆·克鲁斯和杰克·尼克尔森主演的新电影中扮演角色时，他欣喜若狂。但在

③ every once in a while 偶尔；时常

④ dimwitted [dɪmˌwɪtɪd] *adj.* 愚蠢的；笨的

⑤ beget [bɪˈget] *vt.* 产生；招致；引起；当……的父亲

as-yet-untitled Milos Forman film. He **was beside himself**⑥. He felt loyalty to the first offer, but Forman was after all was offering him the lead. We said we understood, no problem, good luck, we'll go with our second choice. Which, we did and two weeks later, the Milos Forman film was scrapped. Our second choice, who was also making his professional debut, was an actor named Noah Wyle. Noah would go on to become one of the stars of the television series *ER* and hasn't stopped working since. I don't know what the first actor is doing, and I can't remember his name. Sometimes, just when you think you have the ball safely in the **end zone**⑦, you're back to delivering pizzas for Domino's. **Welcome to the NFL**⑧.

10   In the summer of 1983, after I graduated, I moved to New York to begin my life as a struggling writer. I got a series of survival jobs that included bartending, ticket-taking, telemarketing, limo driving,

演艺界，往往是你还没干什么，就喜事连连。一个星期后，这位演员的经纪人打电话过来。他说那位演员将在一部由米洛斯·福尔曼执导但尚未命名的新电影中担任主角。那位演员激动得不知道怎么办才好。虽然他珍视第一个工作机会，但毕竟福尔曼让他担任主角。我们对经纪人说，我们理解，没问题，祝他好运，我们会启用我们的第二候选人。我们确实那么做了，两周后，由米洛斯·福尔曼执导的那部影片流产了。我们的第二候选人是一位名叫诺亚·怀尔的演员，他也是在他的职业生涯中初次亮相。后来诺亚继续他的演艺事业，成了电视连续剧《急诊室》里的重要演员，从此后他的星途一往无前。至于我们的第一候选演员，我不知道他现在在做什么，我甚至都不记得他的名字。有时候，就在你认为已经把球带回到了球门安全区的时候，实际上你是回去为达美乐披萨店送货。欢迎加入全国橄榄球联盟。

10   1983年夏天，我毕业后搬到了纽约，开始了我作为一个作家的艰辛生活。为了生存，我打了不少份工，包括当酒保、给人

⑥ be beside oneself 忘乎所以，得意忘形

⑦ end zone（球门线到底线的）球门区；结束区

⑧ Welcome to the NFL 索尔金的名剧 *the West Wing*《白宫风云》里的一句台词

阿伦·索尔金 *Aaron Sorkin*

and dressing up as a moose to pass out leaflets in a mall. I ran into a woman who'd been a senior here when I was a freshman. I asked her how it was going and how she felt Syracuse had prepared her for the early stages of her career. She said, "Well, the thing is, after three years you start to forget everything they taught you in college. But once you've done that, you'll be fine." I laughed because I thought it was funny and also because I wanted to ask her out but I also think she was wrong.

11   As a freshman drama student, and this story is now becoming famous, I had a play analysis class; it was part of my requirement. The professor was Gerardine Clark. If anybody was wondering, the drama students are sitting over there. The play analysis class met for 90 minutes twice a week. We read two plays a week and we took a 20 question true or false quiz at the beginning of the session that tested little more than whether or not we'd read the play. The problem was that the class was at 8:30 in the morning, it met all the way down on East Genesee; I lived all the way up at Brewster/Boland, and I don't know if you've noticed but from time to time the city of Syracuse experiences inclement weather. All this going to class and reading and walking through snow in wind chill that's apparently powered by jet engines was having a negative effect on my social life in general and my sleeping in particular. At one point being quizzed on *Death of a Salesman*, a play I had not read, I gave an answer that indicated that I wasn't aware that at the end of the play the salesman dies and I failed the class. I had to repeat

取票、电话推销、豪华轿车司机以及打扮成驼鹿的样子在商场里发传单。我遇到了一个女人，我在这里读大一的时候她在这里读大四。我问她过得如何，问她雪城大学对她职业生涯的早期阶段有何影响。她说："哦，是这样子的，过个三年你就会开始忘记他们在大学里教你的所有东西。但是一旦你开始这样了，你就会变好了。"我笑了起来，因为我认为这很有趣，也因为我想约她出去，但我也认为她是错的。

11   下面这个故事现在已经成为一个很有名的故事了。我在戏剧学院读大一的时候，我修了一门戏剧分析课；这是我的一门必修课。我们的老师是杰拉丁·克拉克教授。如果有人怀疑的话，戏剧学院的学生们就坐在那边。戏剧分析课一周上两次，每次90分钟。我们一周阅读两部戏剧，课程开始的时候我们要参加一个小测试，试题是20个是非判断题，目的只是想知道我们是否读了剧本。问题是，课程是在早上八点半开始，上课地点在东杰纳西街最南头；而我住在布鲁斯特博兰大街最北端，我不知道你们是否已经注意到了雪城会时不时地遭受恶劣天气的袭击。我一路上读着剧本、顶风冒雪地去上课，刺骨的狂风就像是从喷气式飞机的发动引擎中喷出来的一样，这对我的一般社交生活尤其对我的

it my sophomore year; it was depressing, frustrating and deeply embarrassing and it was without a doubt the single most significant event that occurred in my evolution as a writer. I showed up my sophomore year and I went to class, and I paid attention, and we read plays and I paid attention, and we discussed structure and tempo and intention and obstacle, possible improbabilities, improbable impossibilities, and I paid attention and by God when I got my grades at the end of the year I'd turned that F into a D. I'm joking: it was pass/fail.

12   But I've stood at the back of the Eisenhower Theater at the Kennedy Center in Washington watching a pre-Broadway tryout of my plays, knowing that when the curtain came down, I could go back to my hotel room and fix the problem in the second act with the tools that Gerry Clark gave me. Eight years ago, I was introduced to Arthur Miller at a Dramatists Guild function and we spent a good part of the evening talking. A few weeks later when he came down with the flu he called and asked if I could **fill in for**[9] him as a guest lecturer at NYU. The subject was *Death of a Salesman*. You made a good decision coming to school here.

睡眠产生了负面影响。有一次我们考《推销员之死》，我还没有读这个剧本，我给出的答案表明我不知道在剧本的结尾推销员死了，于是那门课我没及格。我不得不在大二时重修那门课；这是一个令人沮丧、令人灰心、令人难堪的经历，而且毫无疑问这是在我向作家转变过程中发生的最最重要的一件事。大二的时候我出现在了课堂上，我注意听讲；我们读剧本，我集中精力；我们讨论剧本结构、节奏、用意和难点，探讨不可能中的可能性以及不可能中的不可能性，我用心学习。谢天谢地，当我在年底拿到我的成绩单时，我发现我的成绩已由下变成了D。开个玩笑：那门课的成绩只有及格和不及格之分。

12   但当我站在位于华盛顿肯尼迪中心的艾森豪威尔剧院的后面观看我的戏剧在进行走上百老汇舞台之前的试演时，我心想，当帷幕落下之后我就可以回到我下榻的酒店，利用杰瑞·克拉克教授传授给我的方法去修改出现在第二幕中的问题。八年前，在一次由剧作家协会举办的盛大集会上，我经人介绍认识了亚瑟·米勒，我们几乎是彻夜长谈。几周后，他得了流感，他打电话问我是否可以代替他担任纽约大学的客座讲师去上课。上课的主题

---

⑨ fill in for 代替，占据别人的位置

是《推销员之死》。听到这儿你们就庆幸来这里上学是你们的明智决定吧。

13 I've made some bad decisions. I lost a decade of my life to cocaine addiction. You know how I got addicted to cocaine? I tried it. The problem with drugs is that they work, right up until the moment that they **decimate**[⑩] your life. Try cocaine, and you'll become addicted to it. Become addicted to cocaine, and you will either be dead, or you will wish you were dead but it will only be one or the other. My big fear was that I wasn't going to be able to write without it. There was no way I was going to be able to write without it. Last month I celebrated my 11 year anniversary of not using coke. Thank you. In that 11 years, I've written three television series, three movies, a Broadway play, won the Academy Award and taught my daughter all the lyrics to *Pirates of Penzance*. I have good friends.

13 我做了一些错误的决定。我因药物成瘾而浪费了十年的光阴。你们知道我是如何成了一名瘾君子的吗？我试吸了一下。毒品的问题是它确实有效，直到它毁了你的生活。试一下可卡因，你会上瘾的。一旦你沉溺于此，你要么死掉，要么就希望自己死掉，二者必居其一。我很担心离开它我再也无法写作。我担心没有那玩意我根本写不出什么东西来。上个月我庆祝了戒掉药物11周年。谢谢你们的掌声。在这11年里，我已经写了三部电视剧，三部电影，一部百老汇戏剧，获得奥斯卡金像奖，教我的女儿学音乐剧《彭赞斯的海盗》里面的所有歌词。我交了一些好朋友。

14 You'll meet a lot of people who, to put it simply, don't know what they're talking about. In 1970 a CBS executive famously said that there were four things that we would never, ever see on television: a divorced person, a Jewish person, a person living in New York City and a man with a moustache. By 1980, every show on television was about a divorced Jew who lives in New York City and goes on a blind date with **Tom Selleck**[⑪].

14 你们将会遇到很多人，简单地说，他们不知道自己在干什么。1970年，哥伦比亚广播公司的一名高管说过一句名言：有四种人我们永远不会在电视上看到——离婚的人、犹太人、生活在纽约市的人和留着胡子的男人。到了1980年，每个电视节目都是关于一个住在纽约市、离了婚且继续与（留着小胡子的）

---

⑩ decimate [ˈdesəˌmeɪt] *vt.* 十中抽一，取十分之一；大批杀害

⑪ Tom Selleck 美国影星

15   Develop your own compass and trust it. Take risks, dare to fail, remember the first person through the wall always gets hurt. My junior and senior years at Syracuse, I shared a five-bedroom apartment at the top of East Adams with four roommates, one of whom was a fellow theater major named Chris. Chris was a sweet guy with a sly sense of humor and a sunny stage presence. He was born out of his time, and would have felt most at home playing Mickey Rooney's sidekick in *Babes on Broadway*. I had subscriptions back then to *Time* and *Newsweek* and Chris used to enjoy making fun of what he felt was an odd interest in world events that had nothing to do with the arts. I lost touch with Chris after we graduated and so I'm not quite certain when he died. But I remember about a year and a half after the last time I saw him I read an article in *Newsweek* about a virus that was burning its way across the country. The Centers for Disease Control was calling it "Acquired Immune Deficiency Syndrome" or AIDS for short. And they were asking the White House for $35 million for research, care and cure. The White House felt that $35 million was way too much money to spend on a disease that was only affecting homosexuals and they passed. Which I'm sure they wouldn't have done if they'd known that $35 million **was a steal**[12] compared to the $2 billion it would cost only 10 years later. Am I saying that Chris would be alive today if only he'd read *Newsweek*? Of course not. But it seems to me that more and more we've come to expect less and less of each other, and that's got to change. Your friends, your family, this

汤姆·塞莱克相亲的犹太人故事。

15   把握好你自己的人生指南针并相信它。要敢冒风险，敢于失败，要记住第一个穿墙而过的人总是会受伤的。我在雪城大学读大三和大四时，我和四名室友住在东亚当斯街街头的一个五人间公寓里，其中一名室友也是戏剧专业的学生，名叫克里斯。克里斯是一个可爱的家伙，有着狡猾的幽默感和阳光的舞台形象。他生不逢时，如果让他在《百老汇的小鬼》里扮演米奇·鲁尼的小伙伴的话，他会感到最惬意。当时我订阅了《时代》杂志和《新闻周刊》，而克里斯经常取笑我并乐此不疲，因为他觉得关心与艺术无关的世界大事是一种奇怪的兴趣。我们毕业后就失去了联系，所以我不十分肯定他是什么时候去世的。但我记得大约在距离我们最后一次见面的一年半后，我在《新闻周刊》上看到一篇关于一种病毒正在全国蔓延的报道。美国疾病控制中心称之为"获得性免疫缺陷综合征"，或简称为艾滋病。他们请求白宫投入3500万美元用于研究、护理和治疗。白宫认为把3500万美元花在只影响同性恋者的疾病上面太浪费，于是他们不予理睬。我敢肯定，如果他们知道和10年后20

---

⑫ be a steal 便宜货

school expect more of you than vocational success.

16 Today is May 13th and today you graduate and the rules are about to change and one of them is this, decisions are made by those who show up. Don't ever forget that you're a citizen of this world.

17 Don't ever forget that you're a citizen of this world and there are things you can do to lift the human spirit, things that are easy, things that are free, things that you can do every day, civility, respect, kindness, character. You're too good for **schadenfreude**[13]; you're too good for gossip and snark; you're too good for intolerance and since you're walking into the middle of a presidential election, it's worth mentioning that you're too good to think people who disagree with you are your enemy. Unless they went to Georgetown, in which case, they can go to hell. Don't ever forget that a small group of thoughtful people can change the world. It's the only thing that ever has.

亿美元的花费相比，3500 万美元只不过是九牛一毛的话，他们当时是不会拒绝的。我是想说要是克里斯看《新闻周刊》的话多好，那样他就会到现在还活着吗？当然不是。但在我看来，渐渐地，人们对彼此的期望越来越少，这种情况必须改变。你们的朋友、你们的家人、这所学校对你们的期待不只是在职业上取得成功。

16 今天是五月十三日，是你们毕业的日子，即将改变的规则之一就是，决策是由那些挺身而出的人制订的。永远不要忘了你们是世界公民。

17 永远不要忘记你们是世界公民，你们可以做很多事情来鼓舞人们，这些事情很容易做到，又不用花钱，是你们每天都可以做的事情：讲文明礼貌，尊重他人，善待别人，修身养性。你们不屑于幸灾乐祸；你们不屑于飞短流长、危言耸听；你们不屑于打击报复；既然你们正置身于一场总统选举之中，值得一提的是，你们不屑于认为那些与你们意见不同的人都是你们的敌人。除非他们去了你们的死对头乔治敦大学，在那种情况下，就叫他们见鬼去吧。永远不要忘记，少数有思想的人可以改变世界。这是唯一颠扑不破的真理。

---

[13] schadenfreude [ˈʃɑːdənˌfrɔɪdə] *n.* [德语] 幸灾乐祸

18 Rehearsal's over. You're going out there now; you're going to do this thing. How you live matters. You're going to fall down but the world doesn't care how many times you fall down, as long as it's one fewer than the number of times you get back up.

19 For the class of 2012, I wish you joy. I wish you health and happiness and success, I wish you a roof, four walls, a floor and someone in your life that you care about more than you care about yourself. Someone who makes you start saying "we" where before you used to say "I" and "us" where you used to say "me." I wish you the quality of friends I have and the quality of colleagues I work with. Baseball players say they don't have to look to see if they hit a home run, they can feel it. So I wish for you a moment, a moment soon, when you really put the bat on the ball, when you really get a hold of one and drive it into the upper deck, when you feel it. When you aim high and hit your target, when just for a moment all else disappears, and you soar with wings as eagles. The moment will end as quickly as it came and so you'll have to have it back, and so you'll get it back no matter what the obstacles. A lofty prediction, to be sure, but I flat out guarantee it.

20 Today is May 13th and today you graduate and my friends, **you ain't seen nothin' yet**⑭. Thank you, and congratulations.

18 预演已经结束。你们现在就要出发；你们就要去改变世界了。你们如何活着是很重要的。你们会跌倒，但世界并不在意你们跌倒多少次，只要跌倒的次数比你们爬起来继续前进的次数少就行。

19 2012届的毕业生们，我希望你们过得快乐。我祝你们身体健康、生活幸福、事业成功，我祝你们安居乐业，我祝你们在生活中遇到一位你关心对方胜过对方关心你自己的人，遇到一位让你开始用"我们"来代替以前你常常说的"我"的人。我希望你们拥有和我的朋友及同事一样的品质。棒球球员说他们不需要抬头观看他们是否打了一个全垒打，他们全凭感觉即可。所以我希望你们在不久后，当你们真正挥棒击球时，当你们真正击中棒球并将其挥向空中时，你们感受一下。当你们的目标高远并击中它时，当在那一瞬间其他一切都消失时，你就会像雄鹰一样展翅翱翔。那一刻来去匆匆，所以你得让它回来，不惜一切代价也得让它回来。这的确是个崇高的预言，但我向你们保证，它会成为现实。

20 今天是五月十三日，是你们毕业的日子，我的朋友们，好戏还在后头。谢谢各位，祝贺你们。

⑭ you ain't seen nothin' ye *最精彩的还没到来*

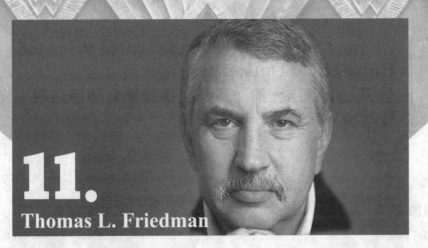

11.
Thomas L. Friedman

托马斯·弗里德曼

在杜兰大学的演讲（2011年）

扫一扫

 人物档案

　　托马斯·弗里德曼（Thomas L. Friedman, 1953 年 7 月 20 日—），美国新闻工作者、专栏作家、作家。弗里德曼出生于美国明尼苏达州，父亲是一家公司副总裁，母亲是家庭主妇。他是三本畅销书的作者：1980 年的著作《从贝鲁特到黎巴嫩》被授予非小说类国家图书奖，至今仍被认为是研究中东问题的必读图书之一；1999 年写就了《凌志车与橄榄树：理解全球化》一书；2002 年，他出版了《经济与态度：探究 9·11 后的世界》。当然弗里德曼最畅销最有影响的著作还是 2005年出版的《世界是平的》。

 场景介绍

　　成立于 1834 年的杜兰大学（Tulane University），位于美国南部路易斯安那州新奥尔良市，是一所著名的综合性大学，同时也是北美大学联盟（AAU：北美 62 所顶尖研究型大学联盟）的成员。2009 年被《美国新闻和世界报道》评为一级国家级大学，历年排名在全美前 50 名左右。

All the Great Change in the World Was Made By Hope-Filled Optimists

世界上所有伟大的改革都是由满怀希望的乐观主义者带来的

经典原文
Original Text

1　Thank you very much President Cowen, thank you the class of 2011. There could be a lot of people with pictures saying who is that guy next to **Stevie Wonder**①. It's a treat to be here today. Thank you for honoring me with this degree. I suspect by now that you have heard every Katrina **metaphor**② in the English language, so, don't worry, I am not going to treat you to any additional ones this afternoon. But I am, though, going to talk about a **hurricane**③.

2　It's one that I experienced firsthand. It was a political hurricane — a real category five — and it still has not **subsided**④. The eye of this storm originally **made landfall**⑤ over Tunisia last December, then it **plowed**⑥　through Egypt and now

中文译文
Suggested Translation

1　非常感谢你，考恩校长。谢谢你们，2011届的毕业生们。可能会有很多人拿着照片说：史提夫·汪达旁边的那个家伙是谁？今天来这里是对我的款待。谢谢你们授予我这个荣誉学位。我猜想你们现在都已经听说了"卡特里娜"在英语里的所有比喻意，所以别担心，今天下午我不打算再给你们增加一个。不过我打算和你们谈谈另外一场风暴。

2　这是一场我亲身经历过的风暴。它是一场政治风暴——真正的5级风暴——到现在仍然没有平息。这场政治风暴的"风眼"最初在去年十二月登陆突尼

---

① Stevie Wonder 史提夫·汪达，1950年5月13日出生，汽车城唱片旗下艺人，美国黑人歌手，作曲家，音乐制作人，社会活动家，盲人。他和弗里德曼一起受邀参加了2011年杜兰大学毕业典礼。

② metaphor ['metəfə] *n.* 暗喻，隐喻；比喻说法

③ hurricane ['hʌrəkən] *n.* 飓风，暴风

④ subside [səb'saɪd] *vi.* 平息；减弱；沉淀；坐下

⑤ make landfall 登陆

⑥ plow [plaʊ] *vi.* [农机] 犁；耕地；破浪前进；开路

托马斯・弗里德曼　Thomas L. Friedman

has **spawned**⑦ a series of tornados that are sweeping across Libya, Syria, Yemen and Bahrain as we speak. Of course, you know what I am talking about — the democracy uprisings across the Arab world, which I had the privilege — and it was a real privilege — to witness firsthand in Cairo's Tahrir Square.

3   Now I know what you're thinking: "Oh my God, he's not going to give us some Middle East politics lecture, is he? He's supposed to give us career advice — 'Do what you love and all that stuff.'" Well, I've given that commencement speech before. As they say, you can Google it.

4   If you'll **bear with**⑧ me today, though, I actually learned a lot of lessons watching that Egyptian revolution unfold in Tahrir Square — lessons that may **have relevance to**⑨ your lives.

5   The first **has to do with**⑩ role of hope and sheer optimism in politics. There is saying that you will often hear from political realists and other **hard-bitten**⑪ types and it goes like this: "Hope is not a strategy."

6   Well, yes, hope alone is not a strategy. But

斯，然后一路穿过埃及，由此引发的一系列"龙卷风"在我们说话的这个时候正席卷利比亚、叙利亚、也门和巴林。当然，你们知道我在说什么——民主崛起于整个阿拉伯世界，我有幸——我真的有幸——在开罗的塔利尔广场亲眼目睹了民主的崛起。

3   我现在知道你们在想什么："噢，我的上帝，他不会要给我们上一堂有关中东的政治课吧？他应该给我们提出职业建议——'做你喜欢做的事情，诸如此类。'"好吧，我以前发表过毕业典礼演讲。正如他们所说，你们可以用谷歌搜到。

4   不过我希望你们今天能忍忍我，看到埃及革命在塔利尔广场爆发，我真的学到了很多经验教训——这些经验教训或许和你们的生活有所关联。

5   第一个经验教训和希望及纯粹的乐观在政治中所起的作用有关。有句话你们会经常从政治现实主义者以及其他强硬派那里听到，这句话是这样说的："希望不是一种策略。"

6   嗯，是的，单有希望并不

---

⑦ spawn [spɒn] *vt.* 产卵；酿成，造成；大量生产

⑧ bear with 忍受；宽容

⑨ have relevance to 和……有关

⑩ have to do with 和……有关

⑪ hard-bitten ['hɑːd'bɪtən] *adj.* 顽强的；不屈服的

hope is the necessary beginning of every strategy for change. People who are inspired by hope, by optimism, "see the world and the people in it as a huge source of possibilities. Hope is what inspires people to get up out of their chairs and lean into the world **against all odds**[12]. If you lose hope you detach from the world and simply **hunker**[13] **down**."[14]

7 Those Egyptian kids who first dared to go into Tahrir Square and call for their president's ouster, their only strategy was hope. They had no idea who would follow, how they would resist the police, how long they might have to stay in the Square and whether they wouldn't all end up in jail, or worse. But they were propelled by a powerful hope and optimism that trumped every other concern.

8 One day walking to Tahrir Square I ran into an Egyptian couple and their two young boys, probably around nine and ten years old. The father stopped me on the Nile Bridge and said: "I just want you to know something. I work in Saudi Arabia but I flew here today for just one reason — to take my two sons to Tahrir Square. I want it **seared**[15] into their minds what freedom feels like, so that they will never **let it go**[16]." That is what hope looks like **in the flesh**[17].

是一种策略。但希望是每一个能产生改变的策略的必要开始。受到希望和乐观精神鼓舞的人们"把世界和人民视为各种可能事件发生的重大来源。希望是能鼓励人们离开座位，投身世界战胜重重困难的东西。如果你失去了希望，你就脱离了世界，就成了缩头乌龟。"

7 那些最先敢于进入塔利尔广场并要求总统下台的埃及孩子们，他们的唯一策略就是希望。他们也不知道谁会跟随，他们要如何抵抗警察，他们会在广场守多久，他们最终会不会去坐牢，或者更糟。但他们被强大的希望和乐观主义精神所驱使着，所有其他担忧都被他们抛在了脑后。

8 有一天我走到塔利尔广场，碰到一对埃及夫妇和他们的两个小儿子，两个孩子大概在九岁和十岁左右。孩子们的爸爸在尼罗河桥上拦住了我，说："我只是想让你知道一件事情。我在沙特阿拉伯工作，但我今天飞来这里只有一个原因——把我的两个儿子带到塔利尔广场。我想让自由的感受铭刻在他们的脑海里，好让他们终生不忘。"这就是我亲身体验到的希望的感觉。

[12] against all odds 困难重重
[13] hunker ['hʌŋkə] vi. 蹲下，盘坐
[14] 这是引自商业哲学家 Dov Seidman 的话
[15] sear [sɪə] vi. 干枯；烧焦；凋谢
[16] let it go 任它去，放下
[17] in the flesh 本人；亲自；以肉体形式

托马斯·弗里德曼 *Thomas L. Friedman*

9　My daughter Natalie graduated college last year and the day before I arrived for commencement, she called me and — knowing that it is my habit to interview people wherever I go — said, "Dad, whatever you do, do not ask my roommates what they are doing next year. Some of them don't have jobs."

10　Sound familiar? Some of you I am sure don't have jobs either. But don't let that stop you from leaning into the world. It is true what they say: Pessimists are usually right. Optimists are usually wrong, but all the great change in the world was made by hope-filled optimists. There were no pessimists in Tahrir Square. Seven years ago, I was in Israel at a dinner with the editor of the *Haaretz* newspaper, which publishes my column in Hebrew. I asked the editor why his newspaper ran my column, and he joked, "Tom, you're the only optimist we have." An Israeli general, Uzi Dayan, was seated next to me and as we walked to the table, he said, "Tom, I know why you're an optimist. It's because you're short." I said, "'Short?' What do you mean?" He said, "You can only see that part of the glass that's half full."

11　Well, I am not that short, but for me all glasses are indeed half full. I hope that is the perspective you are taking from your time at Tulane. Don't let anyone

9　我的女儿娜塔利去年大学毕业，在我参加她的毕业典礼的前一天，她打电话给我——她知道我的习惯就是无论走到哪里都会去采访一些人——说："爸爸，不管你做什么，不要问我的室友他们明年打算做什么。他们中的一些人还没有找到工作。"

10　听起来耳熟吧？我相信你们中的一些人也还没有找到工作。但是不要让这阻止你投身于世界之中。他们说：悲观主义者通常是正确的。这句话是真的。乐观主义者通常是错误的，但在世界上所有伟大的变化都是由满怀希望的乐观主义者带来的。在塔利尔广场上没有悲观主义者。7年前，我在以色列和《国土报》的一位编辑吃晚餐，这家报社用希伯来语发表我的专栏文章。我问那位编辑，为什么他的报纸会刊登我的专栏文章，他开玩笑地说："汤姆，你是我们这里唯一的乐观主义作家。"以色列将军伍兹·达杨就坐在我旁边，当我们走到餐桌边时，他说："汤姆，我知道为什么你是一个乐观主义者。这是因为你短视。"我说："'短视？'你是什么意思。"他说："你只能看到装了半杯水的玻璃杯的下半部分。"

11　嗯，我不短视，但在我看来，所有玻璃杯确实都是半满的。我希望你们在杜兰大学时也

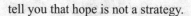

tell you that hope is not a strategy.

12　And whatever you do when you leave here promise me one other thing. It's lesson two from Tahrir Square. Promise me that you won't **get the word**[18]. You see those Egyptians who showed up in Tahrir Square and defended it against the regime's **thugs**[19], well, they just didn't get the word. They just didn't get the word that they were supposed to shut up, remain afraid, mind their own business, and not challenge the **Pharoah**[20] — who kept telling them they were not ready for freedom — and so they just went out and took his political **pyramid**[21] down.

13　Now the reason I raise this is because one of the things I love most about America, and the reason I remain an optimist about this country, is that there is always someone here who just doesn't get the word. They didn't get the word that new immigrants are supposed to wait their turn, that college dropouts are never supposed to start something called Microsoft or Facebook and that people of color are supposed to go to the back of the bus. Instead, they just do it — whatever "it" is — without fear. For all our **ailments**[22] as a country today, our society and economy are still the most open in the world, where individuals with the spark of an idea, the **gumption**[23] to protest or the

是以这样的视角看问题。不要让任何人告诉你希望不是一种策略。

12　不管你们离开这里后做什么，请答应我去做另外一件事。这是从塔利尔广场得到的第二个经验教训。请答应我你们不会接受权威的解释。你们看那些出现在塔利尔广场上的埃及人，他们为了保卫广场而和政府的鹰犬作斗争，是的，他们就是没有接受权威的解释。他们就是没有接受权威的那些要求他们闭嘴、继续害怕、只管自己的事情而不是挑战法老的要求——法老们一直告诉他们，他们尚不具备拥有民主自由的条件——所以他们只管走上街头，将政治金字塔打垮。

13　我之所以提出这一点，是因为我对美国最为热爱的其中一点，也是我仍然对这个国家抱有乐观态度的理由，就是总有人就不理会权威的命令。他们就不理会权威的命令，不理会新移民应该等待轮到自己的时候，不理会大学肄业生永远不可能创立像微软或脸谱网这类的企业，不理会有色人种就应该坐在公共汽车的后面。相反，他们只管做了——不管做了什么——没有恐惧地做了。尽管我们国家今天患有各

---

⑱ get the word 得到权威解释

⑲ thug [θʌɡ] *n.* 暴徒；恶棍；刺客

⑳ Pharoah 法老王；法老

㉑ pyramid ['pɪrəmɪd] *n.* 金字塔；角锥体

㉒ ailment ['eɪlmənt] *n.* 小病；不安

㉓ gumption ['ɡʌmpʃən] *n.* 进取心；气概；精力

passion to succeed can still get up, walk out the door and chase a **rainbow**㉔, lead a **crusade**㉕, start a school or open a business. So Rosa Parks just got on that bus and took her seat, so new immigrants just went out and started 25 percent of the new companies in Silicon Valley in the last decade, so college dropouts named Steve Jobs, Michael Dell, Bill Gates and Marc Zuckerberg just got up and created four of the biggest companies in the world, so Stevie Wonder learned how to play the piano. It was never in the plan, but none of these people got the word. So they just did it.

14　One my favorite interviews in my life was with a Marine Colonel who, when all seemed lost in the Iraq war, and the U.S. military decided to surge instead of retreat, was explaining to me why they did that — why the surge. Here is what he said: "We were just too dumb to quit."

15　So promise me that once you leave here you just won't get the word about what you are not supposed to try, where you are not supposed to travel,

种各样的 "毛病"，但我们的社会和经济在世界上仍然是最开放的，有思想火花的个人、有勇气抗议的个人或者有热情创造成功的个人仍然可以迈出脚步、走出家门，去追逐梦想、去领导改革运动、去开办学校或创办企业。所以罗莎·帕克斯只管上了那辆公交车并坐在了自己的座位上，所以新移民在过去的十年中只管走出家门，在硅谷创办占比 25% 的新公司，所以名叫史蒂夫·乔布斯、迈克尔·戴尔、比尔·盖茨和马克·扎克伯格大学肄业生们只管挺身而出创办了世界上规模最大的四家公司，所以史提夫·汪达学会了如何弹钢琴。这些从来都不是计划之中的事，但这些人一个都没有靠权威的命令行事。所以他们就只管做了。

14　我一生中最喜欢的采访之一是对一位海军上校的采访，当所有人似乎都在伊拉克战争中迷失了方向而美军决定增兵而不是退兵时，他跟我解释他们为什么那么做——为什么他们要增兵。这是他对我说的话："我们只是麻木到不知道退出。"

15　因此，你们要答应我，当你们离开这里的时候，你们不要理会权威命令你们不该尝试做什

㉔ rainbow [ˈreɪnbəu] *n.* 彩虹；五彩缤纷的排列；幻想

㉕ crusade [kruːˈseɪd] *n.* 改革运动；十字军东侵

what chance you're not supposed to take, what crazy dream you are not supposed to chase. Be like that Marine. Be like those young people in Tahrir Square — whatever you decide is your passion or purpose just make sure you're too dumb to quit.

16　The third lesson is more of an observation. And that is what it is like to see a whole people lose their fear and take ownership of their future all at once. Ownership is so important. It is the key to life. When people own things they behave in totally different ways, almost always for the better.

17　It was amazing to watch this happen close up in Egypt. As a journalist who has worked in the Arab world for 30 years I **am conditioned to**[26] asking people whom I have just interviewed only for their first names, because most people are too afraid to give you their last name. Being quoted by a Western reporter can be dangerous. I knew something **was up**[27] in Cairo when I would take out my notebook in Tahrir Square, interview someone and then say, "Excuse, can I just have your first name?" And that person would answer: "My name is Mohammed Akbar Rashid – that's Mohammed with three Ms and two As. I live on Talat Harb Street in Cairo, apartment 46 B. And here is my email and my Twitter handle — and make sure Mubarak reads this." They had lost their fear.

么、不该到哪里旅行、不该抓住什么样的机会、不该追逐什么样的疯狂梦想。你们要像那名海军将领一样。你们要像塔利尔广场上的那些年轻人一样——无论你决定你的热情或目标是什么，只管确保自己麻木到不知道退出。

16　第三个经验教训就是要更多地去观察。这就好像看到整个民族丢掉了恐惧、立刻掌握了自己未来的所有权一样。所有权是非常重要的。它是命脉。当人们拥有自己的东西时，他们的行为方式会完全不同，会几乎总是向更好的方向发展。

17　仔细观察发生在埃及的这件事会让人感到很惊讶。作为一名曾在阿拉伯世界工作了30年的记者，我习惯只询问我刚刚采访的人叫什么名字，因为大多数人都不敢告诉你他们姓什么。被西方记者指名道姓地援引可能是很危险的。当我在塔利尔广场拿出我的笔记本采访某个人，然后说："对不起，我可以知道你的名字吗？"而那人回答道："我的名字是穆罕默德·阿克巴·拉希德——就是含有三个M和两个A的穆罕默德。我住在开罗的塔拉特港街46号B公寓。这是我的电子邮件和推特账户——你要确保穆巴拉克读到这条新闻。"这

㉖ be conditioned to 习惯于；以……为条件　　　㉗ be up 到了，结束了；起床

时候，我就知道某件事情在开罗已经结束了。他们已经丢掉了恐惧感。

18　他们在把家庭住址给我的时候，他们同时就收回了对自己家园和自己国家的所有权。他们说："我不必害怕将我的名字或地址告诉你。现在这是我的国家。"

19　我坚决相信一个众所周知的真理，即有史以来从来没有一个人会去洗一辆租来的汽车。这是真的。真的是这样。在全球历史上，从来没有人洗过一辆租来的汽车。也从来没有人"清洗"过一个租来的国家。去年一月在开罗发生的事情是埃及人从"租房者"变成了"业主"的。

20　这对那些老房东们——那些替穆巴拉克接管了国家的埃及将军们——来说是一件可怕的事。他们看着塔利尔广场上那些年轻人像被关在笼子里长达30年的老虎突然跑了出来一样。关于那只"老虎"，现在有一件事我可以告诉你们：它不会再返回笼子了。那些埃及的将军们知道这一点，所以到最后，他们差不多是对示威者们这样说："你们是听话的老虎，你们是好老虎。老虎想要宪法，老虎就得到了宪法。老虎不会用吃掉穆巴拉克总统的方式吃掉将军们的。"目前我们尚不清楚

18　And in giving me their home addresses they were reclaiming ownership over their homes and their country at the same time. They were saying I don't have to be afraid to give my name or address. This is my country now.

19　I am a huge believer in the **truism**[28] that in the history of the world, no one has ever washed a rented car. Really. It's true. In the history of the world no one has ever washed a rented car. And no one has ever washed a rented country either. And what happened in Cairo last January was Egyptians moved from renters to owners.

20　It was scary for the old landlords — the Egyptian Generals who took over for Mubarak. They looked at those Egyptian young people in Tahrir Square like a caged tiger that had just been released after 30 years behind bars. Now there is one thing I can tell you about that Tiger. It is not going back in its cage. And those Egyptian Generals knew that, which is why, in the end, they basically said to the demonstrators: "Nice tiger, Good, tiger. Tiger want constitution, Tiger get constitution. Tiger just don't eat generals the way tiger just ate President Mubarak." It is still not clear what kind of owners the Egyptian people will turn out to be, but watching them lose their fear and demand the keys was beautiful thing and it leaves me more hopeful than not.

㉘ truism ['truːɪz(ə)m] *n.* 自明之理；老生常谈；老套；众所周知；真实性

21　Lesson four has to do with Facebook. Much has been made of the role of social networking technologies in spurring the uprisings in Tahrir Square. And they certainly did play a role in **facilitating**^㉙ the communication that brought people out and sustained the uprising. But there is one thing you must know: What brought Hosni Mubarak down was not Facebook and it was not Twitter. It was a million people in the streets, ready to die, for what they believed in. We must not forget that. All the buzz around Facebook and Twitter can lull you into a false sense of activism that will be deadly for our own democracy. I see this all the time in the environmental arena.

22　Let me be very **blunt**^㉚. There are a whole bunch of Big Oil companies **standing in the way of**^㉛ the legislation we need today to really create a green, clean-power economy. Sometimes young people will say to me, "Hey, I blogged about that." To which I say, "Really? You blogged about it? That's like firing a mortar into **the Milky Way Galaxy**^㉜."

埃及人民最终将会变成什么样的业主，但看到他们丢掉恐惧、要求得到房屋钥匙就是一件很美妙的事情，它让我更为感到乐观。

21　第四个经验教训和脸谱网有关。社交网络技术在推动塔利尔广场起义方面已经发挥了巨大的作用。它们在帮助人们相互联络以便让人们走上街头、维持起义方面确实发挥了重要作用。但有一件事你们必须要知道：让穆巴拉克垮台的不是脸谱网和推特网，而是走上街头准备为信仰而牺牲的百万民众。我们必须记住这一点。所有在脸谱网和推特网上发表的言论都能让你对行动主义产生错觉，这将对我们自己的民主造成致命的打击。我在环保领域里自始至终看到的就是这种情况。

22　让我非常坦率地说吧。我们今天真的需要制订法律，以便能打造一个使用清洁能源的绿色经济，但是有一大批石油巨头公司在阻碍这项法律的制订。年轻人有时候会对我说："嘿，关于这件事我发表了微博。"对此我会说："真的吗？你发表了微博？这就像把炮弹发射到银河系里一样。"

㉙ facilitate [fə'sɪləˌteɪt] *vt.* 促进；帮助；使容易

㉚ blunt [blʌnt] *adj.* 钝的，不锋利的；生硬的；直率的

㉛ stand in the way of 妨碍，阻碍；阻住……的路

㉜ the milky way galaxy 银河系

23   Please remember: The BPs of the world, they're not on Facebook. They're just in your face. The big fossil fuel companies? They don't have a chat room. They're in the **cloakroom**[33] of the U.S. Congress with bags of political donations. Your life may be digital, but trust me on this one. Politics is still **analogue**[34]. It's still about who can get a million people into Tahrir Square — a million people who will not leave until their demands are met. And if Facebook helps you do that — well then God Bless Facebook. But at the end of the day there is no **substitute for**[35] human beings out in the streets ready to stand and fight for what they believe in. There is no substitute for real people, not mouse clicks or **avatars**[36], going out **in large numbers**[37] and making politicians see that they are insisting on change and are ready to risk something for it. That is how we got civil rights in this country, that is how we got labor rights and that is how we got women's rights. It is how we ended the Vietnam war. It is how the Egyptians ended their tyranny. And it is the only way we will get a green economy. So if you want to get something done in the world, never forget — ultimately — you have to get out of Facebook and into somebody's face.

23   请记住：全世界的英国石油公司都不是在脸谱网上。他们就在你面前。大型化石燃料公司呢？它们没有聊天室。它们拎着政治捐款袋出现在美国国会衣帽间里。你们的生活或许是数字化的，但在这一点上请相信我。政治仍然是模拟信号阶段。其关乎的仍然是谁可以动员一百万人到塔利尔广场上去——让一百万人不离开，直到他们的要求得到满足。如果脸谱网能够帮助你们做到这一点——那么就请上帝保佑脸谱网吧。但归根结底，没有什么可以替代人们走上街头，准备为他们的信仰奋起一战。没有什么可以替代真实的人成群结队地走上街头，让政客们看到他们对改革的坚持并准备为此而冒风险，这不是通过点击鼠标或让阿凡达们显身所能做到的。我们就是这样做才在这个国家得到民权的，我们就是这样做才得到劳动权利和妇女权利的。我们就是这样做才结束了越南战争的。埃及人就是这样做才结束了他们国家的暴政的。这是我们得到绿色经

㉝ cloakroom ['kləʊkruːm] *n.* 衣帽间；寄物处；（英）盥洗室

㉞ analogue ['ænəlɔːg] *adj.* 类似的；相似物的；模拟计算机的

㉟ substitute for 代替，取代

㊱ avatar ['ævətɑː] 天神（以人类、超人类或动物身的形式）显灵；化身，具体化；天神下凡化作人形；《阿凡达》

㊲ in large numbers 大量地

24　And that leads to the fifth lesson: Where innovation comes from today and why it matters more than ever. It is odd to think that you could learn that in Egypt, but it actually offered a very compelling example of this. I have a friend, Curt Carlson, who runs the innovation factory, Stanford Research Institute, now known as SRI, and Curt has a saying, which I have dubbed Carlson's Law. Curt says that when the world gets this flat and connected everything that happens from the top down tends to be dumb and slow. Everything that happens from the bottom up tends to be smart, but chaotic. The **sweet spot**[38] for innovation, though, is moving down — that makes sense, because all of us are smarter than one of us and all of us now have so many more tools to create, connect, communicate and collaborate.

25　That is exactly what happened in Tahrir Square. Every day Mubarak addressed the crowds there he was dumber and slower than the day before. And every day the people stayed there they got more creative, in a slightly chaotic way.

济的唯一方法。所以如果你想让世界上的某件事情得已落实，请永远不要忘记——最终——你必须离开脸谱网，和某人面对面。

24　这就引出了第五个经验教训：今天的创新来自何处，以及为什么它比以往任何时候都更重要。你们可以从埃及那里学到这一经验教训，这想法有些不可思议但它确实为我们提供了一个非常令人信服的例子。我有一个朋友名叫科特·卡尔森，他运营一家创新工厂——斯坦福研究所，现在以其简称 SRI 而闻名。科特有个说法，我称之为"卡尔森定律"。科特说，当世界变平，将从上而下发生的事情联系在一起往往是迟钝的、缓慢的。将自下而上发生的一切联系起来则往往是敏捷的、但却是混乱的。虽然创新的最佳点正在下移——但那是有道理的，因为我们所有人加在一起比我们单独的一个人更聪明，现在我们所有人拥有更多的工具去创造、连接、沟通和协作。

25　那正是在塔利尔广场发生的事情。每一天，穆巴拉克都向那里的人群发表演讲，但他一天比一天变得更为迟钝和缓慢。每一天，人们都待在那里，但他们变得一天比一天更有创意，方式只是稍微混乱了一些。

---

38 sweet spot 甜蜜点；最有效点；最佳击球位置

26   For instance, I was particularly impressed by how the demonstrators held the square when the regime's thugs came on camels and horses and tried to drive them out. They were cornered and unarmed, and someone thought to pull up a steel fence from its **moorings**[39] use it to break up the side walk and create stones — **ammunition**[40] as it were — and it was with those stones, those broken pieces of sidewalk, that they were able to hold their ground.

27   It was equally amazing though to watch, how a people, once free immediately unlocked their imaginations. Every day you came to Tahrir square they had invented something new from the day before. In one corner people were writing poetry, in another they organized a mosque and clinic. In another, people were giving lectures or doing art.

28   What does this have to do with you? A lot. I believe you are **graduating into**[41] a world in which, more and more, you will be required to invent your next job rather than find your next job. You're going to have to dig up your own sidewalk and make your own ammo. Now that may sound **daunting**[42] and, in a way it is, compared to the kind of workplace which my generation found after college. But here is what is exciting: While it is true that this may be the hardest time to find a job, it is equally true that this is the

26   例如，给我留下最深刻印象的是，当政府的爪牙骑着骆驼和马试图把示威者们赶出广场时，示威者们是如何保卫广场的。他们被团团围住，手无寸铁，有人想把停泊处的钢栅栏拔下来，用它打碎人行道，弄出石块——将其当作弹药——而正是那些石块以及那些破碎的人行道使得他们能够固守阵地。

27   但同样使人震惊的是，观察到一个民族一旦获得自由是如何立即释放他们的想象力的。每天你来到塔利尔广场，你会发现他们在前一天发明了一种新东西。在某个角落里，人们正在写诗；在另一个角落里，他们组建了一座清真寺和诊所。还有一个角落里，人们在演讲或进行艺术表演。

28   这些和你们有什么关系吗？有很大关系。我相信你们正逐渐进入一个要求你们越来越多地去创造下一份工作而不是寻找下一份工作的世界。你们将要挖自己的人行道，并制造自己的弹药。现在这听起来好像很吓人，和我们那代人大学毕业后面临的劳动力市场相比，今天的劳动力市场在某种程度上确实很吓人。

㊴ mooring ['muɾɪŋ] *n.* 下锚；停泊处；系船具

㊵ ammunition [ˌæmjuˈunɪʃən] *n.* 弹药；军火

㊶ graduate into 渐渐变为；逐渐进入

㊷ daunting ['dɔːntɪŋ] *adj.* 使人畏缩的；使人气馁的；令人怯步的

easiest time in the history of the world to invent a job.

29　If you have just the spark of a new idea today, you can get a company in Taiwan Province of China to design it; you can get Alibaba in China to find you a low-cost Chinese manufacturer to make it; you can get Amazon.com to do your delivery and fulfillment; you can find a bookkeeper on Craigslist to do your accounting and an artist on freelancer.com to do your logo. All you need is that first spark of extra imagination or creativity.

30　So whatever that spark is that you carry from your time here in Tulane, never **lose sight of**[43] how easily and cheaply you can now turn it into a flame. I am sure many of you saw the movie *The Social Network*. My favorite scene in that movie is the one in the office of then Harvard University President Lawrence Summers. Do you remember what happens? These two Harvard students, Cameron and Tyler Winklevoss, come to complain to Summers that their fellow student, Mark Zuckerberg, has stolen their idea for something called **"Facebook."**[44] Summers hears the twins' **tale of woe**[45] without

但令人兴奋的是：虽然现在的确可能是最难找工作的时期，但说现在是世界历史上最容易创造工作岗位的时期也是事实。

29　如果你今天正好有一个新想法在脑海闪现，你就可以在中国台湾找一家公司将它设计出来；你可以登录中国的阿里巴巴网站去找一个低成本的中国制造商生产它；你可以登录亚马逊网站完成你的交货和订单状态；你可以到克雷格列表网站上找一个会计员做你的会计，在自由职业网站上找一位艺术家设计你的商标。你需要的只是点燃额外的想象力或者创造力火花。

30　所以，无论你们在杜兰大学求学期间携带的火花是什么，请永远不要忽视你们现在可以何等容易又何等低成本地将其变成一团火焰。我相信你们中许多人都看过电影《社交网络》。那部电影里我最喜欢的场景是发生在时任哈佛大学校长劳伦斯·萨默斯的办公室里的一幕。你们还记得发生了什么事吗？那两个哈佛大学的学生卡梅伦和泰勒·温科吾斯来到萨默斯的办公室向他抱

㊸ lose sight of 忽略；不再看见

㊹后来卡梅伦兄弟将扎克伯格告上法庭，这是一场持久的官司。开始双方互相对抗，没有一方肯松口。后来或许实在是不胜其烦，2008 年，扎克伯格终于下定决心，给文克莱沃斯兄弟价值 6500 万美元的股票加现金，以了结此事

㊺ woe [wəu] *n.* 悲哀，悲痛；灾难　ale of woe 悲哀的故事

a **shred**[46] of sympathy, then tosses them out with this piece of advice: "Yes, everyone at Harvard is inventing something. Harvard undergraduates believe that inventing a job is better than finding one, so I'll suggest again that the two of you come up with a new project."

31 That line is supposed to make Summers look arrogant and **clueless**[47]. In fact, his point describes perfectly the challenge for every college grad today: How we dig inside ourselves for that something extra that will distinguish us in this increasingly flat, competitive world. It has never been harder for college grads to find a job. And it has never been easier to invent one. It may take a few tries. Don't let that worry you. Everybody's got something extra to offer, you just have to discover yours.

32 Well, class of 2011, those are the headlines from Tahrir Square — now just one last piece of advice from back home. It is a piece of advice I insist on offering at the close of every commencement speech: "Call your mother." Wherever you go, whatever you do, be sure to call mom.

怨说，他们的同学马克·扎克伯格剽窃了他们创办"脸谱网"的想法。萨默斯听到双胞胎的悲哀故事后，没有表示一点点同情，然后用以下这条建议把他们打发出去了："是的，哈佛里的每个人都在发明着什么东西。哈佛的大学生相信创造工作岗位比找到一份工作更好，所以我再次建议你们两人想出一个新项目来。"

31 这句话被认为是让萨默斯看起来傲慢和愚蠢的一句话。事实上，他的观点完美地描述了每个大学生目前都要面临的挑战：我们如何在内心深处挖掘出额外的东西以我们在这个越来越平坦、竞争越激烈的世界里脱颖而出。大学毕业生找工作从来没有像今天这么难过。大学毕业生创造一个工作岗位又从来没有像今天这么容易过。这可能需要几次尝试。别让这事折磨你。每个人都有额外的东西可提供，你只需发现自己的那一份就行。

32 2011届毕业班的同学们，以上那些提要都是从埃及塔利尔广场运动中得出来的——现在只剩下最后一条来自国内的忠告了。这则忠告是我坚持在每一次毕业典礼演讲结束时讲给大家听的："给妈妈打电话。"无论你去

---

⑯ shred [ʃred] *n.* 碎片；少量剩余；最少量；破布

⑰ clueless ['kluːləs] *adj.* 无线索的；愚蠢的

33　I learned from the legendary University of Alabama football coach, Bear Bryant. Late in his career, shortly after his mother had died, South Central Bell Telephone Company asked Bear Bryant to do a TV **commercial**[48]. As best I can piece together, the commercial was supposed to be very simple — just a little music and Coach Bryant saying in his tough coach's voice: "Have you called your mama today?"

34　On the day of the filming, though, Coach Bryant decided to **ad-lib**[49] something. He reportedly looked into the camera and said: "Have you called your mama today? I sure wish I could call mine." That was how the commercial ran, and it got a huge response from audiences.

35　My mom died three years ago and until her dying day she was my biggest fan. She used to print out my columns in the nursing home — just in case anyone on the staff might have missed one.

36　If you take only one thing away from this talk today, take this: Your parents love you more than you'll ever know and are more proud of you than you will ever know. So when you're off out there conquering the world: Call your mother — and you

哪里，无论你做什么，一定要给妈妈打电话。

33　我是从阿拉巴马大学的传奇橄榄球教练拜耳·布莱恩特那里学到的这则忠告。在拜耳·布莱恩特职业生涯的后期，在他母亲去世后不久，中南贝尔电话公司邀请他拍摄电视广告。就我记忆所及，那个商业广告应该很简单——只是一段短暂的音乐配上布莱恩特教练用他强硬的教练口吻说的一句话："你今天给妈妈打电话了吗？"

34　可是在拍摄广告的那天，布莱恩特教练决定即兴说点什么。据说他对着摄像机说："你今天给妈妈打电话了吗？我真希望我可以给我妈妈打个电话。"那个商业广告就是这样播出的，而且那个广告在观众中引起了极大的反响。

35　我母亲三年前去世了，直到她死的那一天，她都是我最狂热的粉丝。她常常在养老院把我的专栏文章打印出来——只是以防有养老院的员工错过哪一篇文章。

36　如果今天你们只从我的演讲中记住一条忠告的话，记住这点：你们的父母爱你们比你们所知道的要多，他们以你们为傲的程度比你们知道的要更深厚。所

---

⑱ commercial [kəˈmɜːʃəl] *n.* 商业广告　　　　⑲ ad-lib [ædˈlɪb] *vt.* 即兴演唱；即兴讲演

father. You will be glad you did. I wish I could call mine.

以当你们走出校园去征服世界的时候，记住：打电话给你的妈妈——和你的爸爸。你们会为你们的所作所为感到高兴的。我希望我可以给我的妈妈打个电话。

37　Tulane class of 2011, Godspeed and good luck.

37　杜兰大学 2011 届毕业生们，祝你们成功！祝你们好运！

12.

Ariana Huffington

阿里安娜·赫芬顿

在莎拉劳伦斯学院的演讲（2011年）

扫一扫

 人物档案

阿里安娜·赫芬顿（Arianna Huffington），1950年7月15日出生于希腊雅典，毕业于剑桥大学格顿学院，先后获得经济学学士和硕士学位。她是美国政治博客网站赫芬顿邮报（Huffington Post）的共同创始人，开始拥有一个新的身份——网络媒体女王。她为赫芬顿邮报写博客，2010年出版了第13本著作《第三世界美国》。她每周做两档脱口秀节目，包括由公共电台播出的《左、右、中》栏目。她在电视台频频亮相，经常与保守派辩论政务。

 场景介绍

莎拉劳伦斯学院（Sarah Lawrence College）是美国一所私立文理学院，位于纽约州。莎拉劳伦斯学院创办于1926年，创办之初是作为女子学院而存在，1969年开始实行男女同校教育。莎拉劳伦斯学院拥有本科学院和研究生院，可以颁发、授予硕士学位与学士学位。

What We Need from You More than Anything Is Your Wisdom
我们真正最需要的是你们的智慧

1　Thank you so much, President Lawrence, and thank you so much for inviting me to share this glorious moment in your life, graduating class of 2011. I know it's not the most important thing. I know it doesn't matter as much as everything else, but you look amazing.

2　This is a really magical place. I was here for dinner last night, and I met an alum who had been here in college and graduated together with her mother. I love that. She's now a trustee. I met another trustee who is a second man in his family to graduate from Sarah Lawrence. His father was part of the **GI Bill**[1]. And then I met a graduate who told me she was going to Paris and had already written her memoir — How was very Sarah Lawrence.

1　非常感谢你，劳伦斯校长。2011届毕业班的同学们，非常感谢你们邀请我前来分享你们生命中的这一辉煌时刻。我知道大学毕业并非人生中最重要的事。我甚至知道和别的事情相比，它一点都不重要，但你们看上去棒极了。

2　这真是一个神奇的地方。昨晚我在就餐的时候遇到了一位校友，她曾在此学习并和妈妈一起毕了业。我喜欢这个故事。她现在是学校董事。我遇到了另外一位董事，他是他们家族中第二个从莎拉劳伦斯学院毕业的人。他的父亲得益于《退伍军人权利法案》而上了大学。然后我遇到了一位毕业生，她告诉我她要去巴黎并且已经写完了她的回忆录——多么符合莎拉·劳伦斯学

① *GI Bill*《退伍军人权利法案》，美国国会于1944年颁布了的该法案，旨在帮助退伍军人在二战后更好地适应平民生活。法案的基本内容有：美国国会授权联邦政府，对在二战中服兵役超过90天的美国公民提供医疗、卫生、住房等方面的优惠政策；对因战争中断深造机会的美国公民提供资助，让他们有机会接受适当的教育或训练。

3   You are very lucky to have President Lawrence as your President. I love the fact that you have a James Joyce scholar as your President. Because, it's a little known fact but when I was considering launching the Huffington Post in 2005, I first thought I was going to call it Huffington's Wake. It was going to be full of **puns**② and **allusions**③ to Greek mythology. And there is going to be a blog by Leopold Bloom and another by Stephen Daedalus. Nobody was actually going to read it, but everybody was going to pretend to have read it and declare it fabulous.

4   So… you made it! Congratulations! If you look at the world that you are about to inherit, it's a split screen world. On one side of the screen, we see kind of explosion of irrationality, of darkness. We see a world in which the president of the IMF is accused of rape; (a world in which) the former governor of California has fathered a child with his housekeeper incidentally. (**As an aside**④, why is it that women leaders are never accused of rape?)

5   It's also a world in which 70% of people in this country think we're on the wrong track, in which 25 million people are unemployed or underemployed, and in which for the first time, total **outstanding**⑤ student loan debt will be higher than total credit card

院的风格。

3   你们拥有劳伦斯这样的校长是非常幸运的。一个让我高兴的事实是，你们的校长是一名研究詹姆斯·乔伊斯的学者。因为，一个鲜为人知的事实是，当我在2005年考虑推出"赫芬顿邮报"的时候，我首先想到的是我要将其命名为"赫芬顿醒来报"。这将充满双关语和希腊神话故事的意味。网站的博客专栏将由利奥波德·布鲁姆和史蒂芬·代达罗斯主笔。没有人真的会去读它，但每个人都会假装读过它，并宣称它很棒。

4   所以……你们成功了！祝贺你们！如果你们仔细观察你们将要继承的这个世界，你们就会发现，这是一个双面分屏的世界。在世界的一面，我们看到的满是不合理和黑暗。我们看到一个国际货币基金组织的总裁被指控强奸的世界；我们看到一个前加利福尼亚州长和他的女管家不小心有了私生子的世界。（顺便说一句，为什么女性领导人从来没有被指控强奸呢？）

5   在这样的一个世界里，我们国家里有70%的人认为我们走在了错误的道路上，就因为如此，有2500万人失业或没有充分就业，而未偿还的学生贷款债

---

② pun [pʌn] *n.* 双关语；俏皮话

③ allusion [əˈluːʒən] *n.* 暗示；提及

④ as an aside 顺便说一句

⑤ outstanding [aʊtˈstændɪŋ] *adj.* 杰出的；显著的；未解决的；未偿付的

debt, over a trillion dollars. And the percentage of young adults moving back with mom and dad is 34 percent.

6　so clearly if you combine all of that with the fact that we have senators and presidential candidates who don't believe in evolution, who think global warming is a myth and in which they basically think that they don't just have their own set of ideas but their own set of facts, this is really a strange world you're walking out on.

7　But on the other side of the split screen is the world you are creating. While the media are obsessing over **Donald Trump**'s[6] presidential run or Kim Kardashian's latest boyfriend, your generation is busy creating another world. On this part of the split screen there's an explosion of creativity, innovation, empathy, and compassion. You are the most connected and engaged generation in history and to cross the great stage where I am. We used to consume the news and information sitting on the couch, and now we are consuming it **galloping**[7] on a horse. We don't just consume it, we share it, to pass it on, to edit it. We are part of this connected world that we are **at the very moment**[8] absorbing and transforming. And you are asking the big questions and contemplating the cosmic riddles about why we're here and what life is really about, and please don't stop contemplating these cosmic riddles when you get busy earning a living.

务总额将首次高于信用卡债务总额——超过了一兆美元。回家和父母一起住的年轻人的比例是百分之三十四。

6　显然如果你们再联想到以下事实，即我们的参议员和总统候选人不相信进化论，他们认为全球变暖是一个神话，他们基本上认为他们不只是有自己的一套想法他们，还拥有自己的事实，那么你们会觉得即将踏入的这个世界就真是一个光怪陆离的世界。

7　但另一屏面的世界是你们正在创造的世界。尽管媒体沉迷于唐纳德・特朗普参选总统或金・卡戴珊交了新男朋友这样的新闻，但你们这一代人正忙着创造另外一个世界。在双面分屏的这一部分世界里，人们的创造力、创新能力、同理心和怜悯之情呈现大爆发之态势。你们是史上联系最紧密也最忙碌的一代人，你们必将超越我们这代人。过去我们是坐在沙发上吸收着新闻和信息，而现在我们是骑在飞奔的马上吸收着新闻和信息。我们不只是吸收它们，我们还分享它们，我们传递它们，我们编辑它们。我们是这个互通互联的世界的一部分，实际上我们此时此刻就在吸收与转化着它。你们问的是宏观的问

⑥ Donald Trump 唐纳德・特朗普，美国地产大亨，曾参加过美国总统竞选
⑦ gallop ['ɡæləp] *vi.* 飞驰；急速进行；急急忙忙地说
⑧ at the very moment 恰恰在那个时刻

8   I wrote a book about that in the 1990s. Since the book didn't do very well, you haven't heard about it. It was called *The Fourth Instinct*. In that book I explored instinct that takes us beyond our first three — survival, sex, and power — the instinct that drives us to want to find meaning in life, the instinct that drives us to **transcendence**[9], the instinct that drives us to community.

9   Dean Lawrence mentioned Jon Stewart's and Stephen Colbert's Rally. In a moment of irrational **exuberance**[10] on the Jon Stewart' Show, I offered to provide bus rides for anybody who wanted to go to Washington. I didn't realize there would be 10,000 people and 200 buses that left from Citi Field in New York. And when I was there at 5 in the morning, welcoming everyone to the buses, I discovered there were people that were flown from around the country to get on the bus to go to Washington. And one of them said to me, "I just came from Washington to get on the bus to the Washington." And I thought to myself this is obviously a kind of moment of **insanity**[11] in the pursuit of sanity. But at the same time it was a moment illustrating our longing for

题，你们思考的是宇宙之谜，即我们为什么会在这里，以及人生的真正意义是什么，我恳求你们，当你们忙着挣钱的时候，也不要停止思考这些宇宙之谜。

8   我在 20 世纪 90 年代就写了一本关于那个问题的书。因为那本书卖得不好，所以你们没听说过。书的名字是《第四本能》。在这本书中，我探索了让我们超越前三个本能——生存本能、性本能以及权力本能——的本能，即驱使我们要找到生命意义的本能，驱使我们超越自我的本能，驱使我们融入社会的本能。

9   劳伦斯校长提到了由乔恩·斯图尔特和史蒂芬·科尔伯特倡导的集会。在乔恩·斯图尔特主持的节目上，出于一时的冲动，我表示愿意向任何想去华盛顿参加集会的人提供公共汽车。当时我没有意识到会有 1 万人和 200 辆巴士离开纽约市的花旗球场前往华盛顿。当我凌晨 5 点到达那里欢迎大家去坐公共汽车时，我发现有些人从全国各地飞过来乘车去华盛顿。其中一个人对我说："我刚从华盛顿过来想乘车去华盛顿。"我心想：这一刻的人们显然陷入了追求疯狂的非理性

---

⑨ transcendence [træn'sendəns] *n.* 超越；卓越；超然存在

⑩ exuberance [ɪg'zjuːbərəns] *n.* 丰富，茂盛；健康；感情洋溢（或慷慨激昂）的言行；（感情等的）过度（或极度）表现

⑪ insanity [ɪn'sænəti] *n.* 疯狂；精神错乱；精神病；愚顽

community, because getting on the bus together was a **pilgrimage**[12].

10   And in a sense your generation is on this pilgrimage to transform a world that desperately needs transforming. And the key to this is empathy. There is nothing that our world needs more than empathy if we're going to survive and flourish in the 21st century.

11   Just before he died, Jonas Salk said to me we're in a time of the transition. Of course every generation thinks they're in a time of transition. I'm sure Adam turned to Eve in the Garden of Eden and said, "Darling, we're in a time of transition."

12   But some generations actually are in a time of transition. And you are moving from what Jonas Salk called Epoch A (based on survival and competition) to Epoch B (based on meaning and collaboration). And it's a huge huge **seismic**[13] shift that's happening right under our eyes. And the key to it is actually part of your school motto — Wisdom With Understanding. I love that motto, because wherever you look in the world, what we're missing more than anything is not intelligence but wisdom. We have incredibly brilliant leaders with very high IQ's running business, media, politics, making terrible decisions every day. I have a feeling sometimes for example that if Lehman Brothers was Lehman Brothers and Sisters, it might still be around today. What they're lacking is not intelligence but wisdom. Because after all, leadership

状态。但也就是那一刻说明我们渴望融入社会，因为一起乘车就是开启了朝圣之行。

10   从某种意义上说，你们这一代人开启了改造世界的朝圣之旅，而这个世界迫切需要改变。这其中最关键的是要有同理心。如果我们要在二十一世纪生存发展下去，我们的世界最需要的就是同理心。

11   乔纳斯·索尔克在去世之前对我说，我们处于一个转型时期。当然，每一代的人都认为他们处在一个转型时期。我确信伊甸园中的亚当也会对夏娃说："亲爱的，我们正处于转型期。"

12   但某几代人确实是处于一个转型时期。你们正在从一个乔纳斯·索尔克称之为的 A 时代（基于生存和竞争的时代）过渡到 B 时代（基于人生意义和相互合作的时代）。这是一个就发生在我们眼前的巨大转变。这里的关键实际上部分地体现在了你们的校训上——理解与智慧。我喜欢这个校训，因为无论你在什么地方观察这个世界，你会发现，我们缺失的是智慧，而不是智商。我们的领导人非常聪明，他们拥有很高的智商，他们掌管着企业、媒体和政治，他们每天都在做着可怕的决定。例如，有时

⑫ pilgrimage ['pɪlgrɪmɪdʒ] *n.* 漫游；朝圣之行

⑬ seismic ['saɪzmɪk] *adj.* 地震的；因地震而引起的

is about seeing the icebergs before they hit Titanic.

候我有一种感觉，如果雷曼兄弟银行是雷曼兄弟姐妹银行的话，它今天可能仍然存在。他们缺乏的不是智力，而是智慧。因为毕竟领导力就是在泰坦尼克号撞到冰山之前看到冰山的能力。

13　Dean Lawrence talked about transformational knowledge. Well, there was a philosopher I am sure you've all heard of him here at Sarah Lawrence who before even Twitter existed in the third century. A philosopher named Plotinus described three different sources of knowledge: opinion, science, and illumination. In the Internet age we are drowning in opinion; we are drowning in data which is another form of science. But we **are desperate for**⑭ wisdom. And that's really what we need from you more than anything.

13　劳伦斯院长谈到了转换知识。嗯，有一位哲学家我相信你们在莎拉劳伦斯学院都听说过，他生活在连推特网都还没出现的第三世纪。这位叫普罗提诺的哲学家描述了三种不同的知识来源：意见、科学和启迪。在网络时代，我们淹没在意见里；我们淹没在数据里，而数据刚是另一种形式的科学。但我们迫切需要的是智慧。我们真正最需要的是你们的智慧。

14　And for me, one of the most important things about wisdom is to recognize that often the purpose of our life is not obvious as our life is unfolding. Things, especially the biggest heartbreaks... and I have two daughters, one of whom will be a senior next year. So I'm trying to protect them from the biggest heartbreaks, but let me tell you that as you're experiencing in a new way because we all do, the most important thing to remember is that there is a purpose to do that. It may not be obvious at the time you're experiencing it, but there is a purpose to do it.

14　对我来说，关于智慧的最重要的观点之一就是要认识到，当我们的生活画卷展开之时，我们生活的目的往往并不明显。生活中会发生很多事情，尤其是让人伤心欲绝的事……我有两个女儿，其中一个明年就要上大四了。所以我想保护她们不会遭受最让人伤心的事，但让我告诉你们吧，你们会以新的方式经历最伤心的事，因为我们都要经历它，在此过程中，最重要的一点是要记住要有目的地去经历它。在你经历它的时候，你的目的可能不是很明显，但要有目的地去经历它。

⑭ be desperate for 极度渴望

15　let me tell you about one of my heartbreaks. I fell in love with a man when I was 22. He was twice my age and half my size. The love is blind. I actually fell in love with him before I met him. Has that ever happened to you? He was a brilliant writer writing for the *London Times*. His name was Bernard Levin. I used to cut out his columns, and actually put them between pressed flowers in books. And then I met him one night, and completely **tongue-tied**[15]. Nevertheless, he invited me to dinner a week later, and of course I spent the entire week prepping for the dinner not by going to the hair dresser but by reading everything he had written — about Northern Ireland, the Soviet Union. I wanted to be really really smart at the dinner. Of course, he never asked me about Northern Ireland, the Soviet Union. And I ended up spending seven years of my life with him.

16　Then I was 30 and I desperately wanted to have kids. He wanted to have cats. So I did something that I was at that time terrified to do: I left him. I left this man I was very much in love with. And because I didn't trust myself to leave him and stay in London, I left him and moved to New York. So, the rest of my life — my children, my books, The Huffington Post, the fact that I'm standing here speaking to you on your commencements day would not have happened if this man had married me. So, my whole life happened because a man refused to marry me.

15　让我告诉你们我的一件伤心事吧。我在 22 岁的时候爱上了一个男人。他的年龄是我年龄的两倍，身形只有我的一半。爱情总是盲目的。实际上我在遇见他之前就已经爱上了他。这种情况曾经发生在你们身上过吗？他是位聪明的作家，为《伦敦时报》撰稿。他的名字是伯纳德·莱文。我常常把他的专栏剪下来，然后夹在书里面的压花之间。后来在一个晚上我遇到了他，我整个人都呆住了，一句话都说不出来。不过一周之后他邀请我共进晚餐，当然，我花了整整一周的时间准备赴那次晚宴，我不是去美发，而是阅读他写的一切东西——关于北爱尔兰以及苏联的东西。我想在晚餐上表现得很聪明。当然，他从来没有问过我关于北爱尔兰和苏联的事情。最终我和他一起度过了七年的时光。

16　转眼我 30 岁了，我非常想要孩子。而他只想养猫。所以我做了一件当时对我来说不太敢做的事：我离开了他。我离开了这个我深爱着的男人。因为我不相信自己能待在伦敦而不去见他，因此我离开他搬到了纽约。所以，如果这个男人娶了我的话，我后面的生活——我的孩子、我的书、赫芬顿邮报以及在你们的毕业典礼当天我站在这里

---

⑮ tongue-tied [ˈtʌŋtaɪd] *adj.* 结结巴巴的；发音不清的；缄默的

17   So, remember that, okay? In life, the things that go wrong are often the very things that lead to other things going right. Or as Max Teicher, who is graduating today, and who met me last night and told me last night. You know, he said: sometimes you are **bumped from**[16] a class you really want to go to, like he said: I was bumped from an art class but ended up in a class that taught me so much about the Enlightenment and it turned out that and I quote Max "by getting unlucky, I actually got lucky." So that seemed right perfect after my and Bernard Levin stories. So, thank you Max.

18   A key component of Wisdom is also Fearlessness, which is not the absence of fear, but not letting our fears get in the way. I remember one of the low points in my life was when my second book was rejected by 37 publishers. By about rejection 25, you might have thought I might have said, "you know what, there's something wrong here. Maybe I should be looking at a different career. "

19   Instead, I remember walking down St. James Street in London really depressed, and seeing a Barclays Bank there. So I walked in and, with a lot

向你们发表演讲的事实都不会发生。所以，我的整个人生发生了变化是因为一个男人拒绝娶我。

17   所以，请记住这一点，好吗？在生活中，做错了的事情往往会导致做对其他事情。或者正如我昨晚遇见将于今天毕业的学生马克斯·泰彻时他说的那样。他说：有时你真想去一个课堂上课，可是课堂上已经没有了你的位置；就像他说的：我想上艺术课，可是课堂上坐满了人，我最后进了一个课堂，学到了很多很多关于启蒙运动的知识，事实证明（我引用马克斯的原话）"一开始的不走运让我真的很走运"。这句话似乎可以很完美地诠释我和伯纳德·莱文的故事。所以，谢谢你，马克斯。

18   "智慧"的一个关键组成部分就是"无所畏惧"，也就是说，不是没有恐惧，而是不让恐惧妨碍我们。我记得我生命中的一个低潮出现在我的第二本书被37家出版社拒绝出版之时。到大概是第25家出版社拒绝我的时候，你可能认为我会对自己说："你知道吗？这不对啊。也许我应该寻找一份不同的职业了。"

19   我没有那么想，我记得我走在伦敦的圣杰姆斯大街上，心里真的感到很郁闷，然后无意间

16 bump from（没事先通知）挤掉……的座位；取代……的职位

of **chutzpah**[17] just about nothing else, I asked the manager for a loan. And for some reason he gave it to me. And that's what made it possible for me to keep things together for another 13 rejections until my book was finally published. I still send the manager Ian Bell a Christmas card and I think of him as a helpful animal in a fairytale.

20   So remember throughout your life, there will be helpful animals disguised as human beings going to be there to help the hero or heroine of the story to get out of the dark forest. Remember to send them Christmas card, because very often the difference between success and failure is just perseverance. It's getting up one more time. It's getting up one more time than you fall down. And the thing that my mother taught me more than anything is that failure is not the opposite of success. It's just a stepping stone to success.

21   And that means not letting the fears in our heads, the doubts in our heads that I call the **obnoxious**[18] roommates living in my heads get in the way of our dreams. I was recently on Stephen Colbert Show, and I told him, "Stephen, my obnoxious roommate sounds exactly like you." And he said he had to find a place to crash.

看到了巴克莱银行。于是我走了进去，除了厚颜无耻外几乎别无所有，就这样向银行经理申请了一笔贷款。出于某种原因，他批准了我的申请。这让我可以继续遭受另外 13 次拒绝一直撑到我的书最终出版。直到现在我依然会给伊恩·贝尔经理寄圣诞贺卡，我认为他就是童话故事里那个会给予帮助的动物。

20   所以请记住，在你这一生中，总有能帮上忙的动物伪装成人类的模样出现在人们身边，帮助故事中的男主人公或女主人公走出幽暗的森林。记得给他们寄圣诞贺卡，因为成功和失败之间的差异往往仅在于坚持。坚持就是再爬起来一次。坚持就是爬起来的次数比跌倒的次数多一次。我的母亲教导我说，最重要的是要记住，失败不是成功的对立面。失败只是成功的垫脚石。

21   我将恐惧和怀疑称为住在我们的脑海中、阻碍我们梦想之路的可恶室友。所以，不要让恐惧缠绕在我们心头，不要让怀疑在我们脑海中盘旋。称为讨厌的室友住在我们的脑海里，阻碍我们的梦想之路。最近我参加了史蒂芬·科尔伯特真人秀节目，我告诉他："史蒂芬，我那可恶的室友听起来很像你哎。"他说他不得

---

⑰ chutzpah ['hʊtspə] *n.* 肆无忌惮

⑱ obnoxious [əb'nɒkʃəs] *adj.* 讨厌的；可憎的；不愉快的

22 There one of the things I love about Sarah Lawrence is your tradition in its early women-only college days of "productive leisure." Because I feel that as we're living in a more **hyper-connected**[19] world, we need desperately to learn how to unplug and recharge.

23 I work with many great engineers producing great **killer apps**[20] every day. I think what we need and maybe wanna be here to create is a GPS for the soul. We need a killer app that will help us to be very clear in real time when we need to course-correct, when we need to unplug and recharge, connect again with ourselves, which is of course the augment connection.

24 And you know what? I'm going to say something which may seem kind of trivial for a commencement speech. But the most important thing here, the most important the simplest key to daily wisdom, daily unplugging and recharging is sleep. Sleep and Sarah Lawrence's productive leisure are keys to tapping into our wisdom ways. And for some reason, men, I'm sure not Sarah Lawrence men, who are much wiser somehow have **acquitted**[21] sleep deprivation with humility. So you guys here men and women need to change that, because I was recently having dinner with a man who bragged that he had only gotten four hours of sleep the night before.

不找个地方休息一下。

22 我喜欢莎拉劳伦斯学院的一个地方就是，你们的早期女子学院有一个"高效休闲"的传统。因为我觉得，既然我们生活在一个更加超连接的世界里，我们就迫切需要学习如何"拔下插头"以及"再次充电"。

23 我每天都和许多优秀的工程师一起工作去编制优秀的杀手级应用程序。我认为我们所需要的，以及也许想在这里创建的是一个心灵导航系统。我们需要一个杀手级应用程序帮助我们及时弄明白何时需要纠正路线，什么时候需要"拔掉插头"以及"再次充电"，什么时候再次将自己连接起来，当然，是加强式连接。

24 你们知道吗？我打算说一件对于毕业典礼演讲来说似乎是鸡毛蒜皮的小事。但对于日常智慧、日常"断电"和"再充电"而言，最重要的、最关键的也是最简单的事情就是睡眠。睡眠和莎拉劳伦斯学院的高效休闲是开启我们智慧的两把钥匙。因为某种原因，有些男人（我肯定不是莎拉劳伦斯学院的男人）聪明绝顶，但多多少少睡眠不足。所以你们大家，无论男女，都需要改变，因为最近我和一位男士共进

⑲ hyper-connected [ˈhaɪpəkənˈektɪd] *adj.* 超连通
⑳ killer app 杀手级应用软体；极度成功与受欢迎的电脑应用软件
㉑ acquit [əˈkwɪt] *vt.* 无罪释放；表现；脱卸义务和责任；清偿

And I didn't say, but I thought: you know what? If you'd gotten five, this dinner would be a lot more interesting.

25　The final key to wisdom that I want to mention today is that wisdom comes when we're doing something for others. I know that that all of you here at Sarah Lawrence seem to have already discovered it, because I know that you are working in so many different ways to help others: whether it's the Early Childhood Center here, which is called ECC, I'm **hip**[22] to that, the "Right to Write" prison program, I love that, the art exhibition in the Yonkers public library, doing theater outreach in public schools, working on affordable housing and with the homeless, etc., etc. Please don't stop doing these things. And I would love to invite all of you to write on The Huffington Post about what you're doing, because it inspires others and puts the spotlight on the good that's being done.

26　It's really what gives our life meaning, what strengthens our community, what has tapped into our wisdom and I'd love to invite you write about your experiences to inspire others. Just write, just send them to me Arianna@HuffingtonPost.com and we'll post them on the Huffington Post. And you know what? Marketers have realized that something in

晚餐的时候，那位男士吹嘘说他前一天晚上只睡了四个小时。我没说话，但我想：你知道吗？如果你能睡五个小时的觉，这顿晚餐会有趣得多。

25　今天我想说的关于智慧的最后一个关键因素就是，当我们为别人做事的时候，智慧就不期而至。我知道你们莎拉劳伦斯的人似乎已经发现了这一点，因为我知道你们正在以多种不同的方式去帮助别人：无论是在这里的幼儿教育中心（该中心被称为ECC，我非常熟悉）帮助别人，还是参与"有权写作"的监狱项目（我喜欢这一项目），无论是在纽约郊区杨克斯公共图书馆举办艺术展览，还是在公立学校里做剧场外表演，无论是参与经适房的建设，还是帮助无家可归人，等等等等。请不要停止做这些事。我想邀请你们所有人给赫芬顿邮报写文，发布你们正在做的事情，因为这可以激励别人，并让正在进行的好事成为人们关注的焦点。

26　行善真的给了我们生活的意义，巩固了我们的社区，启发了我们的智慧，我想邀请你们写下自己的经历好去激励别人。尽管写，尽管把写好的东西发到我邮箱：Arianna@HuffingtonPost.com。我们会发布在赫芬顿邮报上。你们

---

⑫ hip [hɪp] *adj.* 熟悉内情的；非常时尚的

desire guides around doing good. And they're tapping into that collective wisdom. Have you seen the explosion of cause marketing? Even Chivas whiskey now is advertising on cellphone or TV by pointing out "Millions of people," the ad says, "are out only for themselves... Can this really be the only way?" That is the ad for Chivas whiskey. You know there is something happening, when they're using our appeal to collective goodness to sell scotch.

27　So let's reject this by saying that this moment in history quite simply demands that we stop waiting on others — especially others living in Washington — to solve the problems and right the wrongs of our times. So as you are leaving this magical place, please don't wait for leaders on a white horse to save us. Look in the mirror and discover the leader in the mirror. Tap into your own leadership potential because the world desperately needs you. And that means daring to take risks and daring to fail, as many times as it takes, along the way to success — and, more important, to re-making the world. And to do it all with more boldness, with more joy, with more sleep, and with more gratitude. Congratulations and thank you so much.

知道吗？营销人员已经意识到人们有做好事的欲望了。他们深入挖掘集体的智慧。你们看到了公益营销广告呈现爆增了吗？甚至芝华士威士忌现在都在手机或电视上做广告。它的广告是这么说的："成千上万的人都只为自己而出门忙碌……这真的是唯一的生活方式吗？"这是芝华士威士忌的广告。你们清楚，当他们利用我们对集体善良的诉求而出售苏格兰威士忌时，就有猫腻发生。

27　让我们拒绝这一做法，人类历史上的这一刻非常明确地要求我们不要再继续等待别人——尤其是居住在华盛顿的那些人——去解决问题并纠正我们时代的错误。所以，当你离开这个神奇的地方时，请不要等待骑着白马的领导人来拯救我们。照照镜子，你会发现镜子里的那个人就是领袖。挖掘你们自己的领导潜力，因为世界迫切需要你们。这意味着在成功之路上，要无数次地敢于承担风险，勇于面对失败——更重要的是重塑这个世界。更大胆、更快乐地去做吧，当然还要有更多的睡眠和更多的感激之情。祝贺你们，非常感谢各位。

13.
Elie Wiesel

埃利·威塞尔

在华盛顿大学的演讲（2011年）

扫 一 扫

 人物档案

　　埃利·威塞尔（Elie Wiesel）是1986年度的诺贝尔和平奖得主，美籍犹太人作家和政治活动家。1928年出生在罗马尼亚。二战期间，他和三个姐妹以及父母被送进奥斯维辛集中营，最后只有他一人生还。他的写作主题是关于大屠杀的记忆。他至今已经出版了57本书，其中1958年出版的自传《夜》与《安妮日记》并列为犹太人大屠杀的经典作品。1986年威塞尔因为通过写作"把个人的关注化为对一切暴力、仇恨和压迫的普遍谴责"而荣获和平奖。

 场景介绍

　　华盛顿大学（University of Washington）创建于1861年，位于美国西雅图，是一所世界顶尖的著名大学，世界大学学术排名第8位，上海交通大学世界大学排名第15位。华盛顿大学医学领域全球排名第三位，生命科学领域全球排名第五位，计算机领域全美排名第六位。教授队伍中拥有252位美国院士，167位美国科学委员会学部委员和12位诺贝奖得主。华盛顿大学是美国太平洋沿岸历史最悠久的大学，同宾夕法尼亚大学和密歇根大学齐名。

13 Memory and Ethics
记忆和道德

经典原文
Original Text

1　Chancellor, Chairman of the Board of Trustees, members of the distinguished faculty, families, parents, grandparents and friends, and especially, of course, the graduating class:

2　I congratulate you together with my other fellow recipients of the honorary degree. What you have learned here should not stay only in memory, but you must open the gates of your own memory and try to do something with what you have learned.

3　I speak to you, of course, not only as a teacher, but also as a witness. And therefore I must maybe define myself. You should know that I am Jewish. Maybe you don't know it. But to me, to be Jewish is what? It's not exclusive — it's an opening. It is really as when the conductor here conducts his orchestra; he offers the person to sing or to play a certain part, a certain tune. And I offer my memory to you. You should know something about what is there, inside.

中文译文
Suggested Translation

1　校长、校董事会主席、尊敬的老师们、毕业生的家人父母祖父母和朋友们、当然特别是毕业班的同学们：

2　我向你们以及和我一起接受荣誉学位的朋友们表示祝贺。你们在这里学到的东西不应该只停留在记忆里，你们必须还要打开自己的记忆大门，尝试用你们学到的东西去做一些事情。

3　当然，我不仅是作为一名教师，而且还作为一名证人对你们进行演讲。因此，我必须对自己进行一下说明。你们应该知道我是个犹太人。也或许你们并不知道。但对我来说，身为犹太人意味着什么呢？它意味着不是独家享有——它意味着公开。这就像乐队指挥在这里指挥乐队一样；他让人演唱某一段歌曲或演奏某一段特定的乐曲。我为你们提供的是我的记忆。你们应该了解我的脑袋里面装的是什么。

4　But what I say, that a Jew, the more Jewish he or she is, and the more universal is the message, I say that anyone else could say the same thing, whether as Protestant, Unitarian, Catholic, Buddhist or even **agnostic**①. We must be before we give. We must shield and protect the identity, the inner identity that we have and that makes us who we are.

5　Now, the topic is memory. In the Bible, the expression is "Remember, don't forget." And when you study the text, you realize there is something wrong there. It's enough to say, "remember." Or it's enough to say, "don't forget." Why the repetition? It could mean, "Remember not to forget." It could also mean, "Don't forget to remember." I say that knowing one thing: that this is a very great university. I have been here before you were born, most of you. I have been here some 35 years ago or so. And so humbly I realize that it took the leaders of this university 35 years to invite me again.

6　Now, a story. A man is lost in the forest. And he tries to find the exit and fails. It takes him hours in night and day, and he's still lost in the forest. On the third day, he notices that someone else is in the forest. He runs to him and he says, "Ah! I'm so glad to meet you. Show me the way out." And he said, "I am like

4　可是我要说的是，一个犹太人，他或她身上的犹太味越浓，他或她传递出的消息就越具普遍性，其他任何人也都会说同样的话，不管他是新教徒、天主教徒、佛教徒甚至是个不可知论者。在我们给予之前，我们必须先拥有。我们必须保护和捍卫我们的身份，保护我们所拥有的内在身份，让我们保持本色的身份。

5　现在把演讲主题转回到记忆上来。在《圣经》中，关于记忆的描述是"记住，别忘了。"当你们学习课文时，你们知道这种表达是错的。说"记住"就足够了。或者说"别忘了"也就足够了。为什么要重复呢？它可能是想表示"记得别忘了"。也可能是想表示"别忘了要记住"。我这么说是因为我知道一件事：这是一所非常了不起的大学。在你们大多数人出生之前，我就一直在这里。35年前左右我就在这里了。所以我谦卑地意识到，这所大学的领导人用了35年的时间再次邀请我。

6　现在我来讲个故事。一个人在森林里迷路了。他试图找到出口，但失败了。他夜以继日，花了大量的时间，但他仍然迷失在森林里。到第三天的时候，他在森林里看到了另外一个人。他

---

① agnostic [æg'nɒstɪk] *n.* 不可知论者

you — I am lost in the forest. One thing I can tell you: You see that road there? Don't go there. I have just come from there."

7   I belong to a generation that tells you that. Where you now can start your life, and you've of course entered a lot of roads, cities, maybe new universities, and remember, there is something that you must remember: Don't go where I come from.

8   The 20th century was one of the worst centuries in the history of humankind. Why? Because it was dominated by two fanaticisms. Political fanaticism: capital, Moscow. Racist fanaticism: capital, Berlin. And therefore, that century has caused more deaths than any time before.

9   What do we know now? A new trend is hanging upon us, and the name is **fanaticism**②. We must do whatever we can to, first of all, unmask. Second, to denounce. And, of course, to oppose fanaticism wherever it is. What is fanaticism? Perversion. You can take a beautiful idea — like religion in the Middle Ages — but fanaticism can turn it into something which is anti-human because a group of human beings decide that they know who is worthy of life, who is

跑到他面前，对那人说："啊！我真高兴见到你。请指给我出去的路吧。"那人说："我和你一样，我也在森林里迷了路。不过我可以告诉你一件事：你看到那条路了吗？不要朝那儿走。我刚从那里过来。"

7   我属于可以告诉你们那句话的一代人。你们现在可以开始你们的新生活了，你们当然有很多条路可以选择，你们可以踏入很多城市，你们也许要进入新的大学继续学习，但要记住，有一点你们必须要记住：不要走我来时的路。

8   20 世纪是人类历史上最糟糕的世纪之一。为什么？因为它由两个狂热主义所主导。一个是政治狂热主义，其首都在莫斯科。另一个是种族狂热主义，其首都在柏林。因此，20 世纪造成的死亡人数比此前任何时候都多。

9   我们现在知道什么？一种新趋势正弥漫在我们身边，它的名字就是狂热主义。我们必须尽我们所能，首先要撕下它的假面具，其次要谴责它，第三当然就是要反对狂热主义，无论它出现在哪里。狂热主义是什么？它就是变态。你可以拥有一个美丽的思想——像在中世纪的宗教那

---

② fanaticism [fəˈnætɪsɪzəm] *n.* 狂热，著迷；盲信
③ redemption [rɪˈdempʃən] *n.* 赎回；拯救；偿还；实践

worthy of **redemption**[3].

10　And today, fanaticism has reached an even lower point in its development: the fanatic who becomes a suicide murderer. That is a kind of atomic bomb. A suicide murderer who becomes himself, and, in some cases, herself, a weapon! They do not want simply to die. For that, they could simply jump into the ocean. They want to kill innocent people mainly, including children, and therefore that is an option that you must resist in your own life.

11　What else have we learned? That we are not alone in this world. God alone is alone. Human beings are not. We are here to be together with others, and I insist on the others — which means, in some places, in some groups, they are suspicious of the other. Don't. I see the otherness of the other, which appeals to me. In fact it is the otherness of the other that makes me who I am. I am always to learn from the other. And the other is, to me, not an enemy, but a companion, an ally, and of course, in some cases of grace, a friend. So the other is never to be rejected, and surely not humiliated.

12　What else? I quote from the Bible, I continue, because after all that is my study — that's my upbringing. The greatest commandment, to me, in the Bible is not the Ten Commandments. First of all,

样——但狂热主义可以将其变成反人类的东西，因为一群人认为他们知道谁值得活着，而谁应该得到救赎。

10　今天，狂热主义已经发展到了的一个更为低级的阶段：狂热分子变成了自杀凶手。这是一种原子弹。一个自杀凶手将他自己（在某些情况下是她自己）变成了武器！他们不想一死了之。因为如果是那样的话，他们完全可以直接跳进海里。他们主要想杀死包括儿童在内的无辜之人，因此，这是一个你必须在你自己的人生中予以抵制的选项。

11　我们还学到了什么？我们在这个世界上并不孤单。上帝是孤独的。人类不是。我们来到这里是为了跟别人在一起，而我则强调别人的重要性——这意味着，在一些地方，在一些群体中，人们怀疑对方。不要这样。我看到了别人的差异性，而差异性吸引了我。事实上，正是别人的差异性才使我有了自己的身份。我总是向别人学习。对我来说，他人不是敌人，而是伙伴，是盟友，当然，在某些情况下，是朋友。所以永远不要拒绝别人，当然更不要羞辱别人。

12　还学到了什么？我继续援引《圣经》，因为毕竟我从《圣经》里得到学问——我从《圣经》里获得教养。对我来说，《圣

it's too difficult to observe. Second, we all pretend to observe them. My commandment is, "Thou shall not stand idly by." Which means when you witness an injustice, don't stand idly by. When you hear of a person or a group being persecuted, do not stand idly by. When there is something wrong in the community around you — or far way — do not stand idly by. You must intervene. You must interfere. And that is actually the motto of human rights. Human rights has become a kind of secular religion today. And I applaud it — I am part of it. And therefore wherever something happens, I try to be there as a witness.

13　One of my last dramatic visits was to Bosnia. I was sent by President Clinton as a Presidential Envoy. And I would go there, really, to those places in Bosnia, to speak with the victims. My interest is in the victims. And I would go literally from person to person, from family to family, from **barrack**④ to barrack, from tent to tent, asking them to tell me their stories. And they always began, but they stopped in the middle. Not one of the people I interviewed or interrogated ended the story. The story was usually about rape in the family, and murder, they were tortured, there was humiliation — no one finished the story! Because they all burst into tears.

经》里最大的戒律不是"十大戒律"。首先，遵守"十大戒律"太难了。其次，我们都是在假装遵守它们。我的戒律是"你不能袖手旁观"。这意味着当你目睹不公正之事时，不要袖手旁观。当你听到一个人或一群人受迫害时，不要袖手旁观。当你周围的社会——或在远方的社会——里有错误的事情发生时，不要袖手旁观。你必须干预。你必须进行干预。这实际上是人权口号。今天人权已成为一种世俗化的宗教。我为它喝彩——我是其中的一部分。因此，无论发生什么事，我试着去作证。

13　我上一次戏剧性访问是在波斯尼亚。我是被克林顿总统作为总统特使派去的。我真的愿意到那里去，愿意到波斯尼亚的那些地方去，愿意和受害者说话。我对那里的受害者感兴趣。毫不夸张地说，我是从一个人到另一个人、从一个家庭到另一个家庭、从一个军营到另一个军营、从一座帐篷到另一座帐篷地去走访，请人们告诉我他们的故事。他们总是有开始没结尾，因为他们停在了故事中间。我采访或询问过的人之中，没有一个人将故事讲完。故事通常涉及到家人遭强奸和谋杀，他们遭受折磨和羞

④ barrack ['bærək] n. 营房；兵舍

辱——没有人讲完故事！因为他们讲着讲着就突然放声大哭起来。

14　And then I realized. Maybe that is my mission, as a teacher, as a witness: to finish the story for them. Because they were crying and crying and crying. And I felt like the prophet Elijah, when I sat down in private to do what I had to do. I said I'm going to collect their tears, and turn them into stories.

14　然后我明白了。也许作为一名教师，作为一名证人，我的使命就是完成他们的故事。因为他们在不停地哭、哭、哭。当我独自一人坐下来做我必须做的事情时，我觉得自己像先知以利亚一样。我说我要收集他们的泪水并把这些泪水变成故事。

15　Now, you have already known something which I did not before I came here. This university is great not only because of its great faculty and its marvelous students, but also because it has a tradition. The commencement speaker should speak only for 15 minutes. I am sure they **meant well**⑤ because they felt sorry for you, graduates. You are waiting here patiently for the moment when the Chancellor will come and offer you the degree. So why should I expose you to torture, the torture of waiting?

15　现在，你们已经知道了一件我在来这里之前并不知道的事情。这所大学之所以伟大，不仅是因为它有出色的教师团队和出色的学生，还因为它有一个传统。毕业典礼演讲嘉宾应该只讲15分钟。我相信他们本意是好的，因为他们觉得对不起你们这些毕业生。你们在这里耐心等待着校长给你们颁发学位证书的那一刻。所以我何必要折磨你们、让你们久等呢？

16　I want you to know, with all that I have gone through in life: I still have faith in humanity. I still have faith in humanity. I have faith in language, although language was **perverted**⑥ by the enemy. I have faith in God, although I quarrel with Him a lot of time. I don't know whether he feels upset or not, but I do. Why? Because I don't want to break the chain that links me to my parents and grandparents and theirs, and theirs, and theirs.

16　我想用我全部的生活经历让你们知道：我仍然相信人性。我仍然相信人性。我相信语言，尽管语言曾被敌人滥用。我相信上帝，虽然我用很多时间跟他争论。我不知道他是否感到沮丧，但我确实感到沮丧。为什么？因为我不想打破联系我和父母、祖父母以及他们的父母祖父母的那个链条。

---

⑤ mean well 对……怀有善意　　　　⑥ pervert [pə'vɜːt] vt. 使堕落；滥用；使反常

17 And furthermore, I believe that the human being — any human being of any community, any origin, any color — a human being is eternal. Any human being is a challenge. Any human being is worthy of my attention, of my love occasionally. And therefore I say it to you: When you are now going into a world which is hounded, obsessed with so much violence, often so much despair — when you enter this world and you say the world is not good today, good! Correct it! That's what you have learned here for four years from your great teachers. Go there, and tell them what you remember. Tell them that the nobility of the human being cannot be denied.

18 I'm sure you have learned French literature. I'm sure you have learned about Albert Camus, the great philosopher and novelist. In his famous novel, *The Plague*, at the end Dr. Rieux, who was the main character of the novel, sees a devastated city, thousands and thousands of victims from the plague. And this doctor at the end says, it's true, all that is true.

19 But nevertheless, I believe, he said, there is more in any human being to celebrate than to **denigrate**[7]. I repeat: There is more in any human being to celebrate than to denigrate.

20 Let's celebrate. Thank you.

17 而且，我相信人——任何社会、任何出身、任何肤色的任何人——都是永恒的。任何人都是一个挑战。任何人都值得我注意，都值得我偶尔去热爱。因此，我要对你们说：当你进入一个被这么多暴力所纠缠、常常让人无比绝望的世界的时候——当你进入这样一个世界的时候，你会说，今天的世界不怎么样，好啊！那就去纠正它！你们在这里用了四年时间从你们了不起的老师那里学到的东西正好有了用武之地。出发吧，告诉他们你们都记住了什么。告诉他们，高尚的人性是不能被否认的。

18 我相信你们已经学习了法国文学。我相信你们已经了解了伟大的哲学家、小说家艾伯特·加缪。在他著名的小说《瘟疫》的末尾部分，小说的主人公李欧医生看到了满目疮痍的城市以及成千上万的瘟疫患者。这位医生最后说：这是真的，这一切都是真的。

19 但是，我相信他说的话：在人类身上值得庆祝的地方多于值得诋毁的地方。我再重复一遍：在人类身上值得庆祝的地方多于值得诋毁的地方。

20 让我们一起庆祝吧。谢谢你们。

---

⑦ denigrate ['denɪgreɪt] *vt.* 诋毁；使变黑；玷污

14.
John Grisham

约翰·格里沙姆

在北卡罗来纳大学教堂山分校毕业典礼上的演讲（2010年）

扫一扫

 人物档案

约翰·格里沙姆（John Grisham，1955年—），美国畅销书作家，他的小说在全球销售已逾2.5亿册，被翻译成29种语言，是全球第二位首印卖200万册的作家（另一位是J.K.罗琳）。格里沙姆以法律惊悚小说见长。值得一提的是，格里沙姆的多部小说被翻拍成电影后也取得佳绩，特别是《公司》、《塘鹅暗杀令》和《造雨人》等影片，上映后受到观众的广泛欢迎。

 场景介绍

北卡罗来纳大学教堂山分校（University of North Carolina at Chapel Hill，简写UNC），是一所男女同校的公立研究型大学，位于北卡罗来纳州教堂山。该校和我们熟悉的加州伯克利、洛杉矶加利福尼亚大学、弗吉尼亚大学和密西根大学并称为"公立常青藤"。北卡罗来纳大学教堂山分校有一个最为显著的特征就是性价比非常高，在公立大学中是无可争议的第一，在全国也是性价比最高的十所高校之一。

14 Find the Voice in Which to Tell the Story
寻找能够用来讲故事的心声

经典原文
Original Text

1　Thank you, **Holden Thorp**[①]. Thanks to you, the University, and the Board of Trustees, the administration, the faculty, and the graduates for the invitation to be here. I am honored to address the Class of 2010.

2　To the graduates, congratulations upon this day. Your hard work and perseverance have brought you to this milestone, and you are to be commended. Your families and friends are here and they are very proud. Make this day last as long as possible. Take lots of pictures. Give lots of smiles and hugs. Savor it. It is truly unique.

3　I have been here before. Two years ago, I was sitting out there as a proud parent watching my daughter graduated from **UNC**[②]. That day was not quite as pretty as today. The weather looked bad. The forecast was dreadful. The skies were dark and

中文译文
Suggested Translation

1　谢谢你，侯登·绍普。北卡罗来纳大学，校董会，行政管理人员，教职员以及毕业生们，谢谢你们邀请我来到这里。我很荣幸能向2010届毕业生发表演讲。

2　值此你们毕业之际，我谨向毕业生们表示祝贺。你们的努力与坚持换来的是今天里程碑式的成就，你们值得表扬。你们的家人和朋友共聚此地，他们感到非常自豪。让今天的时光慢些流逝吧。多拍些照片，留下美好回忆吧。脸上露出微笑，尽情地拥抱吧。尽情品味成功的喜悦吧。今天这样的日子不会再有。

3　我曾经来过这里。两年前，我就坐在那里自豪地看着女儿毕业于北卡罗来纳大学。那天的情况比今天可惨多了。天气看上去非常糟糕。天气预报不容乐观。

---

① Holden Thorp 侯登·绍普，是该校校长。
② UNC 是 University of North Carolina 的缩拼。

threatening. It looked bad. **At the last moment**③, the decision was made to keep the **festivities**④ here and not move them indoors. Just as the graduates were preparing to march in, a **tropical depression**⑤ settled on Chapel Hill and **the bottom fell out**⑥. The rain began, driving, howling, cold wind with no end in sight. James Moeser was the chancellor then. Most of the crowd scattered. We were soaked. It was awful. It was wonderful. James Moeser, who was also soaking wet, finally decided to just **dispense with**⑦ all **formalities**⑧. With one wave of the hand, sort of like **Moses**⑨, he **conferred**⑩ 5,000 degrees, and we got out of here. It was a very short commencement. There were no speeches. Maybe it wasn't all bad, I don't know.

4   With that day in mind, I am very grateful to see sunshine and a sky that is **Carolina blue**⑪. I've been

天空黑压压的，吓人得很。天气看起来不怎么样。校方最终决定，毕业典礼不移到室内，仍然在这里举行。就在毕业生们准备列队进入的时候，热带低气压在教堂山上方登陆，顿时天像要塌下来一样。雨哗哗地下了起来，冷风怒号着漫无边际地刮着。詹姆斯·姆泽是当时的校长。参加典礼的大多数人四散逃离。我们浑身都湿透了。既狼狈，又好玩。詹姆斯·姆泽也像落汤鸡一样浑身湿透，终于他决定省去典礼的繁文缛节。只见他一只手不停地挥舞，一气儿颁发了5000个学位证书，动作有点像摩西，之后我们便离开了这里。那是一次非常简短的毕业典礼，没有任何演讲。也许下雨不全是坏事，我不知道是不是这样。

4   由于老是惦记着那天的天气，因此看到今天阳光灿烂，天

③ at the last moment 最后一刻，刚刚赶上

④ festivity [fe'stɪvɪtɪ] *n.* 庆祝活动，庆典

⑤ tropical depression 热带低气压，气象图简写为 TD，是热带气旋的一种，中心持续风力达每小时 41-62 公里，即强风级的级别，属于强度最弱的级别，对下一级为低压区或热带扰动，对上一级为热带风暴。

⑥ the bottom fell out 出现……的暴跌；出现……的垮台，暴跌

⑦ dispense with 摒弃，省掉

⑧ formality [fɔː'mælɪtɪ] *n.* 拘泥形式，拘谨；遵守礼节

⑨ Moses ['məʊzɪz] *n.* 摩西，《圣经》故事中犹太人古代领袖。《圣经》记载摩西带领以色列人逃离埃及来到红海的时候，他挥舞着手中的神杖将红海一分为二，以色列人得以逃脱埃及人的追赶。这里演讲者用隐喻手法让人联想詹姆斯·姆泽校长雨中颁发学位证书的滑稽情形。摩西的这一故事成为了西方文化里的一个经典符号，一个经典的例子就是《冒牌天神》里金·凯瑞用意念将碗里的咖啡一分为二的镜头。

⑩ confer [kən'fɜː] *vt.* 授予，赋予

watching the weather for two months.

5   I am just as proud today because my wife, Renee, is a member of the Class of 2010. She is finishing her work for a degree in English, work I interrupted almost 30 years ago when I convinced her to marry me. I'm not sure she wanted to back then, but we did anyway. It's a big day for our family.

6   Some of you are sad to be leaving, probably in shock that your time here has **gone by**⑫ so quickly. Others are, no doubt, thrilled to be getting out of here. Regardless of how you feel now, your emotional attachment to this place will only deepen as the years go by, and you will find yourself drawn back time and time again.

7   I have never met a **Tar Heel**⑬ who did not let it be known, usually within the first 30 seconds of a conversation, that he was in fact a Tar Heel, or that she loved her days in Chapel Hill. Let's face it. It's a great school. We all know it. There is so much to be proud of.

空蓝蓝的，我感到非常高兴。两个月来我一直在注意着天气。

5   今天让我同样感到自豪的是我妻子蕾妮也是2010届毕业班中的一员。她完成了她的工作拿到了英语专业学位，这是一项差不多30年前被我中断了的工作，当时我说服她嫁给了我。我不确定她那时有没有想打退堂鼓，但不管怎么说，我们结了婚。今天对我们一家人来说是个大喜日子。

6   你们中的一些人为即将离开而感到伤心，也许对大学时光如此匆匆流逝惊叹不已。另外一些人则无疑因马上离开这里而莫名兴奋。不管你们现在的感觉如何，你们对这个地方的情感牵挂随着岁月的流逝只会加深，你们将会发现自己会一次又一次地回来看看。

7   我还没有碰到过一个不会泄露自己"焦油脚后跟"身份的人。通常谈话不超过30秒，你就会发现他实际上就是个"焦油脚后跟"，或者她喜爱在教堂山度过的日子。让我们面对现实。这是一所伟大的学校。我们大家都清楚这一点。这里有很多令人骄傲的东西。

⑪ Carolina blue 北卡蓝。指的是淡蓝色，类似的表达方式有light blue、sky blue、powder blue和baby blue。因北卡大学的校色为淡蓝色而得名

⑫ go by 时光流逝。

⑬ Tar Heel 焦油脚后跟。北卡罗来纳州的别名为 Tar heel State，因此 Tar heel 就成了北卡罗来纳州和北卡罗来纳州人民的昵称，它也是北卡罗来纳大学教堂山分校运动队统一的称呼。

8   You are leaving today, but you will not be forgotten. Whether you are graduating with honors, or without; regardless of what you studied, or didn't study, you will not be forgotten. There are people on this campus who work in what's called development, that's another word for fundraising, and they are watching you even as we speak. They will follow you. They are very friendly. They will send you letters, birthday cards, Christmas cards, and at first you may be flattered, but you will soon learn that these cards are very expensive. They will expect cards **in return**[14] — pledge cards, commitment cards, they even take credit cards. They will follow you well into your old age. And when you die, they will expect a sizeable chunk of your estate. You will not be forgotten.

9   But don't be irritated. They are good folks and they really, really want you to succeed.

10   The generosity of others has played a major role in building this great institution. Those who have walked here before you have enriched your learning experience. It's important for you to give, as a way of saying thanks, but also to invest in future generations. Give, because others have given for you.

11   Now I have never written a long book, and

8   你们今天就要离开，但是你们将不会被遗忘。无论你是否以优等生的成绩毕业，无论你学没学到什么，你们都不会被忘记。在这个学校里有些人从事所谓"学校发展"的工作，其实就是筹款工作，他们在我们说话的时候甚至就在盯着你。他们会跟踪你。他们非常友善。他们会给你寄信，寄生日贺卡，圣诞卡。一开始你受宠若惊，可是不久后你就会知道这些卡是很昂贵的。他们期待着从你那里得到回报——捐款承诺卡、保证卡，他们甚至收取你的信用卡。他们将一直跟踪你到你风烛残年的时候。而当你辞世的时候，他们将期待得到你房产的一大部分。所以你们将不会被忘记。

9   不过不要生气。他们都是好人，他们真的真的希望你取得成功。

10   另外一些人的慷慨大方在这所伟大学校的建设中起到了重要作用。那些从你们前面走过这里的人丰富了你们的学习经历。重要的是你要捐赠，把捐赠作为向他们表示感谢的方式，不过你也是在未来的子孙身上投资。之所以要捐赠，是因为别人先行为你进行了捐赠。

11   我从来没有写过长篇小

⑭ in return 作为报答

I have never given a long speech. This one will last for 17 minutes, from top to bottom, so hang on, I'm almost finished.

12　Before I close, though, I'm expected to at least attempt to say something significant, something you might remember for more than 24 hours. Certain things are expected in commencement speeches, and I would **hate for**[15] you to leave here feeling as though you didn't get your money's worth. Not that I'm getting paid, but that's no big deal.

13　On campuses this spring across the country, commencement speakers are saying such things as: "The future is yours." "Take control of your destiny." "Set your goals high." **And so on**[16] **and so forth**[17]. These **platitudes**[18] are not worth much, so I don't use them. You don't really want to hear them. Of course, the future is yours. Who else would want it? Take it. You can have it. We've had our chance and **made a royal mess of**[19] things. I'm sure you can do better. I expect you will.

14　Advice is common theme during these speeches. Someone who has been out there comes back here and shares a few **nuggets**[20] of wisdom, a few tips on how to succeed. Advice is very easy to give and even easier not to follow, so I don't **fool with**[21]

说，也从来没有发表过长篇演讲。本次演讲从头到尾将要持续 17 分钟，因此耐心点，我就要讲完了。

12　但是在结束之前，我至少应该说点有意义的话，说点你们 24 小时后也许还能记住的话。某些话应该出现在毕业演讲里，而如果你们带着自己的钱花得不值的感觉离开这里的话，我会感到遗憾的。不是因为我得到了报酬，那没有什么大不了的。

13　今春在全国校园里，毕业典礼演讲者们说着这样的话："未来是你们的"、"把命运牢牢抓在自己的手里"、"要志存高远"，如此等等，如此这般。这些陈词滥调没有多少价值，因此我不说它们也罢。你们的确不想听到这些。未来理所当然是你们的。还有谁想要它？拿去吧。你们可以拥有它。我们已经拥有了自己的机会，还把事情搞得一团糟。我相信你们能够做得更好。我期待你们做得更好。

14　在这类演讲里，忠告是家常便饭。某某人在外面混出了名堂，然后回来和大家分享他的一些智慧心得，分享他的一些成功经验。忠告很容易给出，但是忠

⑮ hate for 为……感到抱歉

⑯ and so on 等等

⑰ and so forth 等等

⑱ platitude [plætɪtjuːd] *n.* 陈词滥调

⑲ make a royal mess of 扰乱，弄乱

⑳ nugget ['nʌgɪt] *n.* 天然金块；珍闻，珍品

㉑ fool with [非正] 摆弄；玩弄；浪费

约翰·格里沙姆 *John Grisham*

it. You don't' want to hear it. You don't need the advice. You've got the brains, the talent and now the education to live your life the way you want. You'll figure it out.

15　On a couple of occasions, I have given a speech entitled: "The Top Ten Reasons You Should Stay in College until you're Thirty Years Old." It got a few laughs, had a little wisdom to it, but I realized it really wasn't being heard. You wouldn't hear it now. Let's face it — you're done, you're finished, you're ready to get out of here, it's time to move on. I stopped giving that speech because the **hate mail**[22] from the parents was so **vicious**[23].

16　Actually, I do have one piece of advice. I guess sometimes we can't just help ourselves. Call home at least once a week. It's a proven fact that we call home less frequently the older we get. And that's wrong. It should be **the other way around**[24]. As we get older, our parents get older. E-mail, Facebook, text, that's all good. Call home once a week so your parents can hear your voice, and you can hear theirs.

告更容易不被遵循，因此我不会在这上面浪费口舌。你们不需要听这些。你们不需要忠告。你们有头脑，有才华，现在又接受了教育，你们会过上自己想过的生活。你们将会自己悟出人生良言。

15　曾有那么几次，我发表了题为"你30岁前应该待在大学里的10大理由"的演讲。它给人们带来了一些笑声，也有点智慧格言，但是我意识到人们真的不想听那样的演讲。你们现在不想听那样的演讲。让我们正视这样的事实吧——你们的学生生涯结束了，你们的学业结束了，你们准备离开这里，继续前行的时刻到来了。我不再发表那样的演讲，因为来自父母们的抱怨信太尖刻。

16　实际上，我的确有一则忠告。我猜想我们有时候就是控制不住自己。那就是：至少每周给家里打一次电话。事实证明，我们越是少打电话回家，我们老得就越快。错了。我们应该从相反的角度看这个问题。当我们变老时，我们的父母亲变得更老。发电子邮件、上脸谱网站、发短信，这些形式都很好。每周给家里打一次电话，这样你的父母会听到你的声音，而你也可以听到

---

22 hate mail 抱怨信

23 vicious ['vɪʃəs] *adj.* 恶的，邪恶的；恶意的；

怀恨的

24 the other way around *adv.* 从相反方向

17   Okay, one more piece of advice. Read at least one book a month. That may not sound like much, but the big publishing companies in New York have spent a lot of money studying you and your reading habits. You have terrified them. They cannot figure you out. They don't know how many of you, in five years, will be reading books on Kindles, iPads, Nooks, Kobos, and Sony E-Readers. About half the research suggests that you will read more because of these incredible devices. About half the research says you will read even less. They can't figure you out. As far as I'm concerned, I don't care if it's a hardback, paperback, e-book or library book. Read. Reading stimulates the brain and the imagination. A video takes away your imagination.

18   Now, this is **self-serving**[25], obviously. It's a proven fact that people who read buy more books than people who don't read, so I'm always thinking about book sales. I can't help it. Truthfully, I wish you'd read 10 books a month, or at least buy that many.

19   The most difficult part of writing a book is not devising a plot which will captivate the reader; it is not developing characters the reader will have strong feelings for or against; it is not finding a setting which will take the reader to a place he or she has never been; it is not the research, whether in fiction or non-fiction. The most difficult task facing a writer is to find a voice in which to tell the story.

20   A voice is pronunciation, diction, syntax,

他们的声音。

17   好的，还有另外一条忠告。一个月至少读一本书。这听起来并不算多，但是纽约市的大出版商花费了大笔银子来研究你们和你们的阅读习惯。你们让他们惶恐不安。他们揣摩不透你们。他们不知道5年之后你们会有多少人使用Kindle、iPad、Nook、Kobo以及索尼的E-Reader读书。他们算不出来。就我个人而言，我不在乎你们读的书是精装书、平装书、电子书还是图书馆藏书。读书吧。读书可以刺激大脑，激发想象力。视频会剥夺你们的想象力。

18   显然我这么说是有私心的。事实证明，读书的人比不读书的人买的书要多，因此我常常考虑书的销量问题。我无法克制自己。老实讲，我真希望你们一个月读10本书或者至少买10本书。

19   写书最困难的部分不是设计一个能够迷住读者的故事情节，不是设计一些读者强烈喜欢或讨厌的人物，不是设计一个读者从来没有见过的场景，不是调查研究，对于小说创作是如此，对非小说创作也是如此。作家面临的最大困难是找到一个声音，一个可以带来故事的声音。

20   声音是发音，是措辞，是

㉕ self-serving ['self's3ːvɪŋ] *adj.* 自私的，自私自利的

dialogue, plot, character, the ABC's of writing. But a writer's voice is much more. A writer's voice is the tone, the mood, the point of view, the consciousness, the sense of credibility. I have never thought of writing as hard work, but I have worked hard to find a voice. All writers do. Sometimes we are successful, often we are not. But long before the first chapter is finished, and often before the first chapter is started, we search and search to find a voice.

21 Students of creative writing are constantly urged, find the voice, find the voice in which to tell the story, and to do so they are taught to try different techniques, different narrations, different points of view — all in an effort to find the voice.

22 When a writer finds the voice, the words flow freely, the sentences become paragraphs and pages and chapters and the story is told, the writer is heard and the reader is rewarded.

23 In this respect, writing is a lot like life itself. In life, a voice is much more than the sound we make when we talk. Infants and preschoolers have voices and can make a lot of noise, but a voice is more than sound.

24 The voice of change, the voice of compassion, the voice of the future, the voice of his generation, the voice of her people. We hear this all the time. Voices, not words.

语法，是对话，是情节，是人物，是写作基础知识。但是一个作家的声音远不止这些。一个作家的声音是音调，是情绪，是观点，是良知，是诚信。我从来不认为写作是一种劳作，但是我却辛辛苦苦地去寻找一种声音。所有作家莫不如此。有时候我们成功了，但我们面对的常常又是失败。远在第一章结束之前，甚至常常在动笔写第一章之前，我们找啊找啊，去寻找一个声音。

21 人们常常敦促那些具有创造性写作能力的学生们说，去寻找那个声音吧，寻找那个能够带来故事的声音吧，为此人们教导他们，要尝试不同的技巧，不同的叙述，不同的观点——所有这些努力都是为了寻找那个声音。

22 一旦作家找到了那个声音，则下笔如有神，句子成为段落，段落成为章节，最后故事被讲述了出来，作家的声音被听到，而读者也得到了享受。

23 在这方面，写作就像生活本身。在生活中，声音的内涵远比我们谈话时制造的声响要丰富得多。婴儿和学龄前儿童有嗓门，他们能够制造很大的噪音，但是声音不只是声响。

24 变革之声，同情之声，未来之声，时代之声，人民之声。我们每时每刻都能听到这些声音。是声音，不是单词。

25　There are over 5,600 of you in the Class of 2010, and I doubt seriously right now if anyone of you believes that you will leave here today, go out into the world, start your career, and not be heard. Isn't that one of our greatest fears? We will not be heard? No one will listen to us when we are ready to lead, there's no one to follow?

26　To be heard, you must find a voice. For your ideas to be accepted, for your arguments to be believed, for your work to be admired, you must find a voice.

27　A voice has three **essential elements**[26].

28　The first is clarity. When I was in high school, I discovered the novels of **John Steinbeck**[27]. He was and is my favorite writer. *The Grapes of Wrath* is a book I've read more than all others. I admire his talent for telling a story, his compassion for the **underdog**[28], but what I really admire is his ability to write so clearly. His sentences are often rich in detail and complex, but they flow with a clarity that I still envy. His characters are flawed and tragic, often complicated, but you understand them because they have been so clearly presented.

25　你们 2010 届毕业班的人数超过了 5600 人，此刻我真怀疑你们有谁会相信，你们今天就要离开这里走向世界，开创在即的事业，而居然没有人听到你们的声音。那难道不是我们最大的恐惧吗？没人会听到我们的声音？当我们做好领导者的准备时，居然没人听到我们的声音？没有一个人追随我们？

26　如果想被听到，那就必须找到一个声音。如果希望人们接纳自己的思想，相信自己的观点，尊重自己的工作，你必须先找到属于自己的声音。

27　声音包含三个主要因素。

28　第一个是清晰性。当我还在上中学的时候，我发现了约翰·斯坦贝克的小说。他过去是我最喜欢的作家，现在依然是。《愤怒的葡萄》是一本我百读不厌的书。我羡慕他讲故事的才华以及他对失败者的同情心，但是真正让我羡慕的是他能够如此清晰地写故事的能力。他用的句子内涵丰富而又结构复杂，但是它们清晰流畅，让我至今都羡慕不已。他笔下的人物有缺陷且都是悲剧人物，内心常常充满矛盾，但是你能够理解他们，因为他们被如

㉖ essential element（生命）必需元素；主要元素
㉗ John Steinbeck 约翰·斯坦贝克（*John Steinbeck*, 1902—1968）美国作家，是 20 世纪 30 年代大萧条期间美国文坛上涌现出的一批反映社会和经济主题的杰出小说家之一，1962 年获得诺贝尔文学。代表作就是《愤怒的葡萄》。

29 In life, we tend to ignore those who **talk in circles**⁽²⁹⁾, saying much but saying nothing. We listen to and follow those whose words, and ideas and thoughts and intentions are clear.

30 The second element is **authenticity**⁽³⁰⁾. Few things I like better in life than getting lost in a good book written by an author who is **in full command of**⁽³¹⁾ his **subject matter**⁽³²⁾, either because he has lived the story, or so thoroughly researched it. I read a lot of books written by other lawyers — legal thrillers, as they are called — I read them because I enjoy them, also I have to **keep an eye on**⁽³³⁾ the competition. I can usually tell by page 3 if the author has actually been in a fight in a courtroom, or whether he's simply watched too much television.

31 In life, we tend to discredit those who claim to be what they are not. We respect those who know their subject matter. We **long for**⁽³⁴⁾, and respect credibility.

32 The third element is **veracity**⁽³⁵⁾. In the past few years, the publishing industry has been **scandalized**⁽³⁶⁾ by **a handful of**⁽³⁷⁾ writers who wrote very compelling

此清晰地呈现在了你面前。

29 在现实生活中，我们往往忽略那些说话饶来绕去、说了半天不知所云的人。我们聆听并跟随那些说话直截了当、思想和意图都很清晰的人。

30 第二个要素是真实性。一生中很少有什么事情比迷失在一本好书之中更让我欢喜的了，作者把这本书的主题完全置于自己掌控之下，或是因为他亲身经历过书中的故事，或是他进行过仔细的研究。我阅读大量由其他律师写的书，这些书被称为法律惊悚故事书，我读这些书是因为我喜欢它们，另外的一个原因是我必须留意这个行业里的竞争情况。通常我读 3 页就知道作者是否真的在法庭上进行过辩论，还是他只不过是电视看多了。

31 在现实生活中，我们往往不相信那些弄虚作假的人。我们敬重那些了解自己写作主题的人。我们渴望并尊重真实性。

32 第三个要素是诚实性。在过去几年里，出版业因一小撮作家蒙了羞，他们写了一大堆自己

㉘ underdog [ˈʌndədɒg] *n.* 失败者，受压迫者
㉙ talk in circles 说话绕弯子，说话兜圈子，意思是说话不直截了当
㉚ authenticity [ˌɔːθenˈtɪsɪti] *n.* 确实性，真实性
㉛ in command of 指挥，掌控
㉜ subject matter *n.* 主题，主旨

㉝ keep an eye on 照看，照管；留心；注意
㉞ long for 渴望；羡慕
㉟ veracity [vəˈræsəti] *n.* 诚实；真实
㊱ scandalize [ˈskændəlaɪz] *vt.* 使……震惊；使……起反感；使……受耻辱；使……愤慨
㊲ a handful of 少量的

stories of their real-life adventures. These were good stories, they were well written, the voices were clear and seemingly authentic. They sold for big money, they were marketed aggressively, they were reviewed favorably, and then they were exposed for being what they really were — frauds fabrications, lies. The real-life adventures never happened. The books were pulled from the shelves. The publishers were embarrassed. Lawsuits were filed to retrieve the advances. And the writers' voices have been forever silenced.

33 In life, finding a voice is speaking and living the truth.

34 Each of you is an original. Each of you has a distinctive voice. When you find it, your story will be told. You will be heard. The size of your audience doesn't matter. What's important is that your audience is listening.

35 You are lucky to have studied here. Lucky, and deserving. Many, many applied, and only you were chosen. You have been **superbly**[38] educated, but now your time is up. You have to go. You can't stay here until you're 30; and besides, on August 21, the freshmen will be here to replace you.

36 One final thought: right now, you want to **be something**[39]. You have big dreams, big plans, big

真实经历的引人入胜的故事。这些故事本身是好故事，写得也很好，声音是清晰的，而且看起来也是真实的。它们卖得很好，市场反应热烈，它们得到了很好的书评，可是随后它们被曝光称根本不是那么回事——它们是被编造出来的谎言。所谓的真实历险从来没发生过。书被下架。出版商很尴尬。要求收回预付款的诉讼随之发生。这些作家从此销声匿迹。

33 在现实生活中，找到自己的声音就是说真话、办真事。

34 你们每个人都是原创。你们每个人都有自己独特的声音。一旦你找到了自己的声音，你的故事将为众人所知。人们会听到你的声音。属于你的听众规模大小并不重要，重要的是你的听众在倾听。

35 你们能在此学习是幸运的。你们是幸运的，也是应得的。很多很多人申请到这里读书，但只有你们被选中。你们接受了极好的教育，但是现在你们在这里的时间结束了。你们必须离开。你们不能一直在这里赖到30岁；再说，到了8月21号，新生将来到这里取代你们。

36 最后一点想法：从现在起，你们就要有成就一番事业的

㊳ superbly [supˈɜ:blɪ] *adv.* 雄伟地，壮丽地；[口] 极好地；超等地

㊲ be something 了不起，很重要

ideas, big ambitions. You want to be something. Don't ever forget what you want to be right now.

想法。你们要有远大梦想，要有宏伟蓝图，要有开阔的视野，要有雄心壮志。你们想成就一番事业。永远不要忘了你想要成为一个什么样的人。

37 The future has arrived.

38 It commences now.

39 Good luck.

37 未来已经到来。

38 它始于现在。

39 祝你们好运。

15.

Sue Monk Kidd

苏·蒙克·基德

在斯克里普斯学院的演讲（2010年）

扫一扫

 人物档案

　　苏·蒙克·基德（Sue Monk Kidd，1948 年 8 月 12 日—），一位来自美国南部的著名女作家，代表作有《蜜蜂的秘密生活》、《美人鱼椅子》、《翅膀的发明》等。

 场景介绍

　　斯克里普斯学院（Scripps College）是一所女子学院，1926 年成立，位于美国加利福尼亚州克来蒙特。是克来蒙特联校成员，在全美女校排名第三。致力于培养学生成为独立、智慧的女性，校内有比较强烈的女权意识。

You Have Untold Strengths and Resources Inside
在你内心深处有无尽的力量和资源

经典原文
Original Text

1　I am so happy to add my voice to my daughter's and tell you what an honor it is to be at Scripps College and to offer a commencement address, along with her. About all a commencement speaker can really do is to suggest a couple of things that she believes really matters. And Ann has offered this idea, along with your senior speaker, I think. It was a very similar idea, in fact. That it is important, that it matters, to listen to what is inside of yourself and discover your necessary fire, and that, in fact, this may be the way your particular genius is found.

2　What I'd like to add to that is that your necessary fire is not only necessary for you, it is necessary to the world itself. Years ago, I came upon a memorable line by the writer Fredrik Beatner. "You are called to the place where your deep gladness and the world's deep hunger meet." I would even go so far as to say that one of the more powerful outbreaks of happiness and meaning in your life will occur when you pair your passion and the world's need. Even as

中文译文
Suggested Translation

1　我很高兴继我的女儿之后，告诉你们我和她一起来到斯克里普斯学院为大家献上一场毕业典礼演讲是多么光荣的一件事。大概一位毕业典礼演讲嘉宾真正能做的就是提出几件她认为真正重要的事。我想安已经和你们的毕业生代表一起在演讲中提出了这个想法。事实上，她们的思想观点非常类似。那就是倾听自己内心想要什么，并发现你必需的激情之火，这很重要，很要紧，事实上，这可能是发现你特殊天赋的方式。

2　我想补充的一点是，你那必需的激情之火不仅对于你而言是必需的，它对于整个世界而言也是必需的。若干年前，我偶然读到由作家弗雷德里克·比特纳写下的一句令人难忘的话："你被召唤到了一个你的大欢喜和世界的大饥饿交织在一起的地方。"我愿意狗尾续貂地加上一句：当

a child, my passion was writing. I felt back then, that I had found my small true light. Later on, of course, I lost it. Actually it was more like turning my back on it and finding something more practical. When I went to college in the sixties you found something that you could **fall back on**[①]; at 29, however, I began to feel an internal sense of exile, a kind of homesickness, for my own place of belonging in the world. And on the morning of my 30th birthday I announced to my husband and to my two toddlers who were sitting at the table that I was going to become a writer, and they went right on eating their cereal.

3　I spent years studying the craft, practicing the art, developing my own voice. What I was doing during that time was having this conversation with myself about my own reach for excellence. And that is a very important conversation to have with your work.

4　However, I found out that it's about half the conversation.

5　Finally, one day I began to ask the other half of the question. And that is, "What does my work serve?" Not just, "How can I serve my work?" but "What does my work serve in the world?" And then the conversation got really interesting. I was in Chicago at a book signing for *The Secret Life of* Bees

你的热情与世界的需要同路而行时，你的生活会更加快乐，你的生命会更有意义。我还是个小孩子的时候，我的激情就是写作。我觉得那时我就像在黑夜里找到了一点光亮一样。当然，我后来失去了这种激情。实际上更应该说是我背叛了它，因为我找到了更实际的东西。20世纪60年代当我在上大学时，我找到了可以退而求其次的东西；然而当我到了29岁的时候，我开始对我在世界上的归属之处有了一种放逐感，有了一种思乡之情。在我30岁生日那天早上，我对坐在餐桌旁的丈夫和两个小孩说，我打算成为一名作家，而他们头也不抬，照常喝粥。

3　我花了几年的工夫研究写作技巧，练习写作艺术，提升自己的影响力。我当时做的是就与自己展开对话，讨论如何追求自己的卓越。那种对话对你的工作非常重要。

4　然而，我发现那种对话只进行了一半。

5　终于有一天，我开始问问题的另一半。那就是："我的工作有什么用？"而不仅仅是："我怎么能做好我的工作？"而是："我的工作到底有什么用？"后来的对话就很有趣了。有一次我

---

① fall back on 退到；求助于；回头再说

when a man approached me and he said, "I didn't want to read your book, but I read it anyway." It's not exactly the greeting you hope for. I ask him why he was resistant. And he said, "Well, I'm a 48 year old corporate executive from a large city in **New England**②. I grew up in a very privileged family." And he pointed out to me that my novel was about a 14-year-old girl who grew up on a peach farm in the South and endures a lot of hardship. He said, "These worlds couldn't be more different."

6　I said, "Well why did you read it?" And he said, "My wife made me."

7　I teasingly ask him, "Well, was it very painful for you?" At which point he smiled and he confessed that he had actually made a surprising connection with my 14-year-old Lily and with the African-American women in the book. And he said this, and I have not ever forgotten exactly how he said it. "They had an effect on me that I can't explain. I just know that now I **am more disposed to**③ the South, to black women, and to little girls who need their mothers."

8　And I understood then that he had given me a reason to write fiction that was better than anything

在芝加哥为我的书《蜜蜂的秘密生活》进行签售活动，一个男人走到我跟前对我说："我不想看你的书，但我还是看了。"这句打招呼的话不是我希望听到的。于是我就问他为什么不愿意看我的书。他说："是这样的，我今年48岁，是新英格兰地区一个大城市里的企业高管。我在一个非常不一般的家庭里长大。"他指出我的小说描写的是一个出生在南方一个桃园里的14岁小女孩忍受了许多艰难困苦的故事。他说："我们的世界大不相同。"

6　我说："那你为什么要读它？"他说："我老婆逼着我读的。"

7　我开玩笑地问他："那么，这让你很痛苦吗？"此时他笑了笑，承认实际上他吃惊地发现自己已经和小说中14岁的莉莉以及非洲裔美国妇女联系在了一起。他说了下面这句话，而我永远也不会忘记他是怎么说这句话的。"我无法解释她们对我的影响：我只知道现在我更同情南方，更同情黑人妇女和需要妈妈关爱的小女孩。"

8　于是我明白了他给了我一个写小说的理由，那个理由比我

---

② **New England** 新英格兰，当地华人常称之为"纽英仑"，是位于美国大陆东北角、濒临大西洋、毗邻加拿大的区域。新英格兰地区包括美国的六个州，由北至南分别为 缅因州、新罕布什尔州、佛蒙特州、马萨诸塞州（麻省），罗得岛州、康涅狄格州。

③ **be disposed to** 倾向于；太容易相信的；易受骗的

I was really coming up with, beyond just fulfilling my own need and desire to do it: Because it creates empathy. Most people, unfortunately, tend to go through the world maintaining their separation from others, more or less preserving that. But when we read fiction, we participate intimately in other people's lives. In their sufferings and ecstasies, in all the ways their lives fall apart and are shattered and are put back together again. And if their experience is different from ours, **all the better**④.

9　The man in the bookstore helped me to deepen my conversation with myself about the purpose of my work in the world. What did it serve? Did it serve the world somehow? The truth is, it is hazardous to leave this out of the conversation. We no longer live in a **paradigm**⑤ of **rugged**⑥ individualism. We live in a paradigm of global community. And it seems to me that a vast number of our planetary ills can be traced back to one thing: a breakdown of community, from our inability to truly belong to the family of Earth — with all the care that that implies.

10　Now, understanding one's particular genius, one's particular purpose in the community is going to be perhaps the most indispensible ethic in the years ahead. In one of her poems, Edna St. Vincent Millay wrote, "Oh, world, I cannot hold thee close enough." Now we have to be honest and say that the

想到的任何理由都充分，远远超过满足自己写小说的需要和欲望之外：因为小说激发了同理心。遗憾的是，大多数人倾向于和别人保持或多或少的距离。但当我们读小说时，我们很深入地卷入进其他人的生活之中——分享他们的喜怒哀乐，目睹着他们的生活先是分崩离析，后来又破镜重圆。如果他们的经历与我们的不同，我们便读得更加津津有味。

9　书店里的那个男人帮助我加深了我与自己关于工作目的的对话。它有什么用？它对世人有用吗？事实上，省略这一部分的对话是危险的。我们不再生活在一个以顽强的个人主义为范式的世界上。我们生活在一个以地球村为范式的世界上。在我看来，我们星球上的大量问题都可以追溯到一件事上：社会的分裂，这是由于我们无法真正归属于地球大家庭——蕴含其中的所有关心也就消失了。

10　了解一个人在社会里的特殊天赋及其特定目的可能是未来若干年里最不可或缺的一件事。埃德娜·圣文森特·米莱在她的一首诗里写道："哦，世界啊，我不能把你抱得更紧了。"现在我

---

④ all the better 反而更好，更加
⑤ paradigm ['pærə'daɪm] *n.* 范例；词形变化表
⑥ rugged ['rʌgɪd] *adj.* 崎岖的；坚固的；高低不平的；粗糙的

world is not easy to cuddle up to. Neither is it is easy to embrace this big dysfunctional crazy family that populates the world. The world **is rife with**[7] agonizes and with horrors. But it's also rife with beauty and goodness. For all its darkness, it is still ours.

11   And there simply comes a time in the maturation of a human being when you must embrace the world. Mother it a little, sister it, befriend it. It is your place of belonging. There is a provocative new idea afoot — I think it's very alive here at Scripps College — that says women are the emerging architects of change in the world. And it is now largely recognized that, it is now largely recognized that women are the largest untapped resource on the planet.

12   Melanie Vanere, the new American ambassador for global women's issues said that, "The major problems in our world cannot and will not be solved without the massive involvement of women." Well, that would be you! That would be the applied genius, the applied genius of Scripps College women. Genius in Women: such a brilliant thing. The particular genius in you — which you all have — will only truly flourish when it is practiced on behalf of our world.

13   Speaking from personal experience however, it can be daunting to put your true self and your

们必须诚实地说，拥抱世界并不容易。拥抱居住于这个世界的功能失调的疯狂大家庭也不是很容易。这个世界充斥着痛苦和恐怖。但它也充满了美好与善良。尽管这个世界有它的黑暗面，但它仍然是我们的。

11   一个成熟的人必须拥抱这个世界。像母亲般关怀它，像姐姐般爱护它，像朋友般帮助它。它是你的归属之地。现在有一种新的说法——我认为这种说法在斯克里普斯学院非常流行——说女人是改变世界的新兴设计师。而现在得到广泛共识的一点是，妇女是地球上最大的未开发资源。

12   梅兰妮·范尼勒是解决全球妇女问题的新一代美国代表，她曾说过这样一句话："没有大量女性的参与，我们世界中的主要问题不能也不会得以解决。"嗯，她说的就是你们！她说的就是你们的有用天赋，来自斯克里普斯学院女生的有用天赋。女性身上的天赋：这是多么有灵性的一件东西。只有当你们身上的特殊天赋——你们都拥有这种天赋——为我们的世界而展现时，这种特殊天赋才会真正迸发出来。

13   然而从个人经验来说，当你怀揣希望想为世界做贡献时，

⑦ be rife with 充满

particular genius in the world in the hopes of making your contribution. Whenever there is a turning point in life — and you are at such a grand one — it is common for fear and thoughts of inadequacy to rise up in the vacuum of the unknown.

14　The trick is: do not let them keep you from diving in anyway. I assure you, I became a novelist by jumping in over my head, by airing on the side of audacity.

15　In my novel, *The Secret Life of Bees*, 14-year-old Lily, a motherless runaway, finds refuge among a group of African American women. One of these women is August Boatright, who lives with her two sisters in a pink house in which presides the statue of a black Madonna. The women turn to this icon for strength and consolation.

16　One day August says to Lily, "Listen to me now. I'm going to tell you something I want you to always remember. Okay? The black Madonna is not some magical being out there, like a **fairy godmother**[8]. She's not the statue in the parlor. She's something inside of you. When you're unsure of yourself, when you start pulling back into small living and into doubt, she's the one inside of you saying, 'Get up from there and be the glorious girl you are.' That voice sits in your head, all day long saying, 'Lily,

把你真实的自我和你特别的天赋展现于世可能是一件让你感到害怕的事。每当在生命中出现转折点的时候——你们现在就处于这样一个重大的转折点之上——对准备不足的担心和思虑像水银在未知真空领域里一样上升是很常见的现象。

14　诀窍是：不要让它们阻止你行动起来。我向你们保证，我是靠头脑发热以及厚颜无耻才成为小说家的。

15　在我的小说《蜜蜂的秘密生活》里，14岁的莉莉是一个没有母亲、离家出走的女孩，她在一群非洲裔美国妇女那里找到了庇护之所。其中一位叫奥格斯特·博特莱特的妇女与她的两个姐妹住在一间粉红色的房子里，房间里有一座黑色圣母像异常醒目。妇女们从这座圣像中寻求力量和安慰。

16　有一天，奥格斯特对莉莉说："现在听我说。我要告诉你一件事，我希望你永远记住这件事。好吗？那座黑色圣母像不是供在那里的类似仙女教母一样的神灵。她不是放在客厅里的雕像。她是你内心里的某种东西。当你不相信自己的时候，当你开始缩小生活圈子并怀疑自己的时候，她是你心中的一个自我，她

⑧ fairy godmother *n.* 充当临死孩童教母的仙女;（民间传说中）保护婴儿的仙女

苏·蒙克·基德 Sue Monk Kidd

don't be afraid. Don't ever be afraid. I am enough. We are enough.'"

17　I'm not August Boatright, but I want to say something like that to you. Find a purpose grand enough for your life. And whatever your necessary fire is, your genius turns out to be, remember, in some way, it is necessary for the world too. Try to love the world despite what you see out there. Go make your big beautiful dent, and as you do so come down on the side of boldness. If you err, may it be for too much audacity, and not too little. For you really are enough.

18　You have untold strengths and resources inside. You have your glorious self.

对你说：'振奋起来，成为原本的你，那个光荣的女孩吧。'那声音盘旋在你脑海里，整天说：'莉莉，不要害怕。永远不要害怕。我足够强大。我们足够强大。'"

17　我不是奥格斯特·博特莱特，但我想对你们说类似那样的话。找到你生活中足够宏伟的一个目标。不管你心中那团必须燃烧的激情之火是什么，不管你的天赋最终是什么，请记住，在某种程度上，你的激情之火对于世界来说也是必须燃烧的。试着去爱这个世界吧，不管你看到的世界是怎样的面目。请在这个世界上留下你的美丽大脚印吧，当你这么做的时候，请你无所畏惧。如果你犯了错，但愿是因你太胆大而不是太胆小而犯的错。因为你真的足够强大。

18　在你内心深处有无尽的力量和资源。你们拥有辉煌的自我。

16.
Louise Erdrich

路易丝·厄德里克

在达特茅斯学院的演讲（2009年）

扫一扫

  人物档案

　　路易丝·厄德里克（Louise Erdrich，1954年—）是美国当代创作最盛、得奖最多且声望最高的印第安女作家之一。她的创作涉及小说、诗歌、儿童文学等，尤以小说见长，代表作有《爱药》《踪影游戏》《鸽灾》。她出版小说13部，其中《哥伦布的桂冠》（The Crown of Columbus）系厄德里克与已逝前夫迈克尔·道里斯（Michael Dorris）的合璧之作。

  场景介绍

　　达特茅斯学院（Dartmouth College）成立于1769年，是美国历史最悠久的学院之一，也是闻名遐迩的常春藤学院之一。依照利扎维洛克牧师当初成立这个学校的目的，是为了培养当地印第安部落的年轻人和年轻白人。这所学院在最初的两百年中只收男生，直到一九七二年才改为男女合校，是常青藤学院中最晚接纳女生的一个。

Do Your Best for This Beautiful Old World
请为了这个古老而又美丽的世界做出你最大的贡献吧

1　I am tremendously moved, and happy, to stand before you today. Thank you all for welcoming me. Thank you President Wright and Susan DeBovoise Wright. Congratulations on your new President, Jim Yong Kim. I offer my admiration to the other recipients of honorary degrees, and acknowledge my ancestors and relatives, **Nindinawemagonidok**[①], including the first Native people educated on this very ground, Abenaki homeland, Dartmouth College.

2　Class of 2009, I'm delighted to be your speaker. Although I've written many long books, I am also a former Kentucky Fried Chicken waitress and understand brevity. This speech will last 11½ minutes, and there will be chickens in it.

3　I am a member of the class of 1976, the first class that included women, the first class in the newly **recommitted**[②] Native American Program, and to

1　今天站在你们面前，我非常感动，也非常高兴。谢谢大家对我的欢迎。感谢莱特校长和苏珊·狄波沃斯·莱特夫人。祝贺你们有了新校长，他就是金永吉。我向其他荣誉学位获得者致敬，向我的祖先和亲戚致谢，Nindinawemagonidok，包括第一批就在这片土地上、就在阿布纳基人的家园里、就在达特茅斯学院接受教育的原住民。

2　2009 届毕业生们，我很高兴成为你们的演讲嘉宾。虽然我写了很多长篇小说，但我也是前肯塔基炸鸡店服务员，明白简洁的重要性。这篇演讲将持续 11.5 分钟，而且其中有关于小鸡的事情。

3　我是 1976 届毕业班的一员，那一届是第一届开始招收女学生的，也是重新审查"美国原住民

---

① Nindinawemagonidok 印第安语，即"我的亲戚们"

answer a question I was recently asked — yes, in those days we did play an ancient form of (beer) pong.

4　I am a storyteller, so that's where I'm going to begin.

5　Story One: The Courage of Chickens

6　The morning I was to leave for Dartmouth, from my home in Wahpeton, North Dakota, which I'd hardly ever left, I was so afraid that I almost did not go. I applied in the first place because my mother, a strong Turtle Mountain Chippewa woman, had seen a picture of the winter **carnival**③ ice sculpture in a *National Geographic Magazine*, and noted Dartmouth's historic commitment to educating American Indians. We didn't think about co-education, or what it would mean to be so far from home. I'd never been on a plane. I negotiated the change at Boston's Logan Airport. The smaller plane I boarded also at that time carried mail, freight, whatever was needed in the Upper Valley, including livestock. On that day, they were carrying **crates**④ of baby chicks in the back hold of the cabin. Every time the plane went over a bump of warm air, the chicks started **peeping**⑤.

计划"的第一届，最近有人问我一个问题，我的回答是——是的，在那时候，我们的确玩一种古老的（啤酒）乒乓球游戏。

4　我是个讲故事的人，所以，我要开始讲故事了。

5　第一个故事：小鸡的勇气

6　那天早上，我离开位于北达科他州瓦皮顿市的家前往达特茅斯，此前我从未离开过家，我很害怕，差一点就没有去成。我最初之所以申请去达特茅斯，是因为我的母亲是一个坚强的乌龟山齐佩瓦族女人，她曾在《国家地理杂志》上面看到一张关于冬季嘉年华冰雕的图片，她注意到了达特茅斯对教育美国印第安人做出了具有历史性意义的承诺。我们没有想过接受合作教育，也没有想过远离家乡意味着什么。此前我从来没有坐过飞机。我在波士顿洛根机场还商量要改变行程。我那时登上的小飞机还携带着邮件、货物以及康乃狄克河上游河谷所需要的任何东西，包括家畜。那天，他们在机舱后面放了一箱子的小鸡仔。每当飞机遇到暖气流颠簸的时候，小鸡们就开始吱吱地叫。

---

② recommit [ˌriːkə'mɪt] *vt.* 再犯；再委托；重新提交（议案等）讨论
③ carnival ['kɑːnɪvl] *n.* 狂欢节，嘉年华会；饮宴狂欢
④ crate [kreɪt] *n.* 板条箱；篓
⑤ peep [piːp] *vi.* 窥视；慢慢露出，出现；吱吱叫

7　"Ppeeeeeppppeeeeepp…"

8　"PPPeeepppppePpeeeeeep…"

9　They were terrified. But in their fear they did not cower or go silent. They stood up together and made noise. They didn't even know the plane was going to land. The lesson was this: when you're afraid, get your friends around you and don't panic. Picture exactly what you fear. Most of the time, once you analyze your fear it can be managed. Unless you are in a life or death situation, your main fear is probably failure, or possible humiliation.

10　Story Two. The Uses of Humiliation, or The Law of the Onion

11　By the end of the year and on into the next, I was probably cracking the very eggs those chickens laid onto the Thayer Dining Hall breakfast grill. My boss was a former army cook converted to vegetarianism. A man ahead of his time. He also made the **flunky**[6], me, do the prep work. So one morning before class, I peeled and chopped a sixty pound bag of onions. Then I went straight to Introduction to the Problems of Democracy.

12　My problem that day was that I smelled like an onion. You know how it is when you smell like an onion. You can't smell how badly you smell. I walked into class and everybody moved away from me. I was

7　"吱吱吱吱……"

8　"吱吱吱吱……"

9　它们都被吓坏了。但它们在感到恐惧的时候并没有退缩或沉默。它们站起一起鼓噪着。它们甚至不知道飞机就要着陆了。从这里得到的经验教训就是：当你害怕的时候，和你的朋友们围拢在一起，不要惊慌。准确地描绘出你所恐惧的事情。在大部分时间里，一旦你分析出你恐惧的是什么，它就是可控的。除非你在生死关头，否则你主要担心的可能就是失败或者是羞辱。

10　第二个故事：羞辱的用途或者洋葱法则

11　到那一年的年底以及第二年，我的工作可能就是把那些小鸡下的蛋打到塞耶餐厅的早餐烧烤盘子里。我的老板以前在军队里做炊事员，后来成了一个素食主义者。他是一个走在时代前面的人。他也让我这个打工妹做好了成为素食者的准备工作。所以有一天早上在上课前，我把一袋重 60 磅的洋葱去皮切碎了。然后我就直奔课堂上"民主问题导论"课。

12　我那一天的问题是我闻起来就像一棵洋葱。你们知道当你闻起来像棵洋葱的时候会是什么味道。你闻不到自己的气味有多

⑥ flunky ['flʌŋkɪ] n. 仆人，奴才；走狗

frozen with embarrassment. Now, I was sure anyway, coming from North Dakota, that everyone was smarter than me. And at the moment, not only were they smarter, but I was the only one who smelled like an onion.

13　Lesson. If you smell like an onion, hold your nose and take notes. I passed the class, but did not become a philosophy major. Instead, I became a writer. Even if people were smarter, I had the advantage of knowing onions. I had stories. Most important of all, I had humiliation. If there's one this we all have in common, it is absurd humiliation, which can actually become the basis of wisdom.

14　The experience caused me to invent The Law of the Onion. It goes something like this: You have to risk humiliation if you want to move forward. But the Law of the Onion also states: Don't take things personally. If other people's opinions are not personal to you, good or bad, you have a kind of freedom to be who you are. You have the freedom to do the work that is most meaningful to you.

15　My third story is not simple. This is because I decided that for this occasion I would finally solve a problem that bothered me the entire time I was at Dartmouth.

16　This is the problem of Orozco's Skeletons.

17　My last and favorite job was at the old reference library microfilm desk under the **mural**[7]

难闻。我走进课堂，每个人都躲着我。我满脸尴尬。来自北达科他州的我再怎么样都知道他们每个人都比我聪明。那一刻，他们不仅比我聪明，我还是唯一一个闻起来像一棵洋葱的人。

13　经验教训？如果你闻起来像一棵洋葱，捂上你的鼻子做笔记。我通过了那门课程的考试，但我并没有成为一位哲学家。相反，我成为了一名作家。即使人们比我聪明，但我有了解洋葱这一优势。我有故事。最重要的是，我遭受过羞辱。如果有一种经历是我们大家都共同拥有的，那就是遭受可笑的羞辱，而它其实是智慧的基础。

14　这次的经历让我发明了"洋葱法则"。它大致是这样的：如果你想前进，你就必须冒着被羞辱的危险。但洋葱法则也规定：对事不对人。如果其他人的观点不是针对你个人的，无论观点好或坏，你都有一种我行我素的自由。你有自由去做对你来说最有意义的事情。

15　我的第三个故事就不简单了。这是因为我认为在这样一个场合，我应该解决一个困扰我整个在达特茅斯求学生涯的问题。

16　这就是奥罗斯科的骷髅骨架问题。

17　我的上一份工作也是我最喜爱的工作，就是坐在文献图书

painted by Jose Clemente Orozco beginning in 1932. Of course, this is one of Dartmouth's greatest treasures, and perhaps the most powerful and **exquisite**[8] mural in North America.

18 The doorway to my little office was close to the part of the mural called *Gods of the Western World*. And now, as Gods have entered the speech, I must say this:

19 Whatever does not turn away from you in hard times and in your deepest hours — that is God. But remember, however deep your faith, however hard you pray, there is another person in the world with a faith as deep as yours, praying just as hard, only their God has a different name. The Gods have this in common: they are mysterious, ungraspable, and unknowable. The Gods raise questions. Who are we? How did we get here? Can we make a car that runs on carbon dioxide and gives off oxygen, like a tree? You are put here to answer unanswerable questions.

20 To get to my office I passed beneath section of the mural where a huge skeleton, assisted by other skeletons in **academic gowns**[9], violently gives birth to baby skeletons in academic hats. Not only that, but

馆微型胶卷室的一张旧桌子前，桌子上方是一幅由若泽克莱门特奥罗斯科在 1932 年开始绘制的壁画。当然，这幅画乃是达特茅斯大学最大的财富之一，也许是北美最具影响力、最精美的壁画。

18 紧靠我的小办公室门口的那部分壁画被称为《西方诸神》。现在，既然诸神已经进入了演讲之中，我必须说下面这段话：

19 无论是在什么样的困难时刻，即使在你跌入最深的深渊的时刻，对你不离不弃的只有上帝。但要记住，无论你的信仰有多笃定，无论你的祈祷有多虔诚，世界上总有一个人的信仰和你一样笃定，他的祈祷和你一样虔诚，只是他们的神有不同的名字。诸神有一个共同点：他们都是神秘的、难以理解的和不可知的。神提出一些问题：我们是谁？我们怎么会在这儿？我们可否制造用二氧化碳驱动、排放出氧气的汽车，就像树一样？你们来到这里就要回答这些无法回答的问题。

20 我在进入办公室的时候要从一部分壁画的下面通过，这部分的壁画是由一个巨大的骷髅骨架构成，这个骨架由其他几个身

---

⑦ mural ['mjʊərəl] *n.* 壁画；（美）壁饰

⑧ exquisite [ɪk'skwɪzɪt] *adj.* 精致的；细腻的；优美的，高雅的；异常的；剧烈的

⑨ academic gown 学位袍

the skeleton babies are in bell jars. Now again, this mural is a work of the highest genius, however, to an undergraduate that part of the mural is also seriously creepy. And you do know what I'm talking about. I noticed that not very many people liked to study by that part of the mural. As I passed beneath it every day, I tried to **get a handle on**[10] what it meant.

21 Well, obvious, at least at first. It meant that we were all dry skeletons absorbing dry knowledge giving birth to little **vacuum packed**[11] boney skeletons.

22 So is this us? Sitting here today? I don't think so. Look around you, feel the wind, the sun, the energy from the great-branched trees. Something very different is going on. We are so vital, so alive. And we are all here one final time, in order to celebrate the fact that you have acquired knowledge.

23 With this knowledge you have the makings of mino bimaadiziwin, in Ojibwe, the good life. Knowledge with Courage. Knowledge with Fortitude. Knowledge with Generosity and Kindness.

着学位袍的小骷髅骨架扶持着，它在努力地分娩戴着学位帽的婴儿骷髅骨架。不仅如此，所有的婴儿骷髅骨架还都被装在钟形玻璃罩里。我再次声明，这幅壁画是一位超级天才的作品，但对于一个本科生而言，壁画的这一部分也够毛骨悚然的了。你们知道我的意思。我发现很多人不是很喜欢在那部分壁画旁边学习。每天当我走过它的时候，我都试图弄明白那幅壁画的意思是什么。

21 其实，意思很明显，至少最初的意思很明显！它指的是我们所有人都是干巴巴的骷髅，吸收着枯燥的知识，然后生下包装在真空里的瘦骨嶙峋的小骷髅。

22 那么这就是我们吗？今天坐在这里的我们就是这个样子吗？我不这么认为。看看你的周围吧，感受一下微风和阳光吧，感受一下有着巨大枝杈的大树的能量吧。一些截然不同的事正在发生。我们是如此重要，是如此生龙活虎。我们最后一次在这里聚会，为的是庆祝你们获得了知识。

23 有了这些知识，你们就可以编织美好的生活（布瓦族语是mino bimaadiziwin）。知识加上勇气，知识加上毅力，知识加上慷慨与仁慈。

---

⑩ get a handle on [口语] 控制，掌握，驾驭，左右
⑪ vacuum packed 预抽真空密封的

24　This is mino bimaadiziwin.

25　This concept of mino bimaadiziwin resonates with the message of Orozco's **ferocious**[12] skeletons. It says knowledge without compassion is dead knowledge. Beware of knowledge without love.

26　Now I don't mean romantic love – *Harlequin*[13] *Romance Love* — I don't write those books. It is the kind of love you have: devotion to the world.

27　A world that needs you right now, worse than it ever has.

28　Have you ever been in a relationship where you took someone for granted, where you treated that person badly but he or she seemed resilient? A relationship in which you had the feeling that things were going to be all right in spite of how you'd acted and then, boom, all of a sudden you got dumped?

29　That is the relationship we are in right now with the earth. But if the earth dumps us, we actually do die of broken hearts. We get **extirpated**[14], ended, exterminated, finished. The numbers are **crunched**[15]; the science is done. Our planet, which at best estimate might support 2 billion modest lifestyles, will see our population jump to 7 billion in just two years. We're in a nosedive unless we can change as a species.

24　这就是美好的生活。

25　布瓦族语 "mino bimaadi-ziwin" 这一概念和奥罗斯科凶猛的骷髅所传达的信息是一样的。它表示的是没有同情心的知识就是死知识。它让我们谨防没有爱的知识。

26　我这里说的爱不是指浪漫的爱情——《小丑的浪漫爱情》——我不写那类书。我指的是那类你所拥有的爱：对世界的奉献。

27　现在世界需要你们，比以往任何时候都需要你们。

28　你们曾处于这样一种关系中过吗？就是你把某人视为理所当然，你欺负他，但他或她似乎不放在心上？在这样一种关系中，你觉得一切都会好起来的，不管你以前是怎么做的，可是突然有一天，你就被甩了？

29　现在我们与地球就是这样的关系。但如果地球抛弃了我们，我们真的就会伤心死了。我们被灭绝，我们被终结，我们被消灭，我们完蛋了。数字被反复计算；科学也无能为力。按照最乐观的估计，我们的星球或许能支持 20 亿人以适度的生活方式

---

⑫ ferocious [fə'rəʊʃəs] *adj.* 残忍的；惊人的

⑬ harlequin ['hɑːləkwɪn] *n.* 丑角；滑稽角色；花斑眼镜蛇

⑭ extirpate ['ekstɜːpeɪt] *vt.* 使连根拔起；灭绝，破除

⑮ crunch [krʌnʃ] *vt.* 压碎；嘎扎嘎扎的咬嚼；扎扎地踏过

We're like chicks in a crate, peeping, and we don't know if we're going to land. We don't know what's going to happen. There's no pilot. There's just this plane.

30　So while the plane is diving one chick in the crate turns to the other and says, "Which came first, the chicken or the egg?. And the other chick says, "That's not the question. The question is why did the chicken cross the road? And the third chick says, "Shut up, stop arguing and help me steer!"

31　No matter what we believe, no matter what our political convictions, ethnicities or religious faiths, we have to get together and steer this thing. We must stop fighting endless wars and act to heal and love this world. Nindiniwemaganidok. You are my relatives. We are all related through our common humanity and through this college and all who endeavor, here, as one, to make this the best world possible.

32　So take love away with your diploma. Knowledge with love.

33　It is love of peace that makes you a warrior, love of process that binds you to your work, love of family that steadies you in all that you do. Often, the only answer to the questions that will be posed

生存，但在短短两年内，我们将看到我们的人口一下子猛增到70亿。我们现在处于一种俯冲状态，除非我们作为一个物种能够发生变化。我们就像装在箱子里的小鸡，吱吱乱叫，但我们不知道是否就要着陆。我们不知道会发生什么。我们没有飞行员。我们只有这架飞机。

30　所以当飞机正在俯冲的时候，箱子里的一只小鸡扭头对另外一只小鸡说："是先有鸡，还是先有蛋呢？"被问的那只小鸡说："这算是什么问题啊。问题是为什么小鸡过马路？"第三只小鸡说："都给我闭嘴，不要争论这些无聊的问题了，快帮我把舵！"

31　不管我们相信什么，不论我们的政治信仰、种族或宗教信仰是什么，我们必须一起把好舵。我们必须停止无休止的战争，立即行动起来，去愈合创伤，去热爱这个世界。你们是我的亲戚。我们都是通过我们共同的人性、通过这所大学联系在了一起，我们齐心协力，努力让这个世界变成可能是最好的世界。

32　所以，带上你的爱与文凭吧。带上你的知识与爱吧。

33　是对和平的热爱使你成为了一名战士，是对过程的热爱让你和你的工作联系在了一起，是对家庭的热爱让你在做事情时稳

all through your life is a mute and fierce love, an irrational love, a love that simply answers I am here.

34　So don't hold back, don't punt. DO WHAT YOU LOVE BEST. Make your life doing what you love best, but do it as if it meant you were out to save the world. Because you are. And if you are criticized and not every one agrees with you, say to yourself, I must be doing something original; and if your efforts are rejected, say I will persevere; and if your work fails at first, fail again, fail better, until you triumph.

35　The words of **Samuel Beckett**[16] , "Ever tried. Ever failed. No matter. Try again. Fail again. Fail better."

36　My words: until you triumph. And when you do, help young people get where you are.

37　While I was at Dartmouth, my parent wrote letters to me every week. I saved them all. I reread them before I came here and thought I'd leave you with two lines of their wisdom. My father, a North Dakota schoolteacher, often closed his letters with the Latin phrase — Magnum vectigal est parsimonia.

重坚定。通常，能解答你一生所遇到的问题的唯一答案是无声却又猛烈的爱，是一种非理性的爱，是一种简单地回答我为什么在这里的爱。

34　所以不要退缩，不要放弃。做你最爱做的事情。让做你最爱做的事情成为你的生命之歌，但在这么做的时候，就像你是去拯救世界一样。因为你的确是。如果你受到了批评，不是每个人都赞同你，请你对自己说：我一定是在做一些具有创造性的事情。而如果你的努力遭遇了失败，请对自己说：我会坚持下去。如果你的工作一开始就失败了，那就让它再次失败，在失败中进步，直到你取得成功。

35　塞缪尔·贝克特教导我们："努力过，失败过，没关系，屡战屡败，屡败屡战，在失败中进步。"

36　我送给你们的话是：一直到你成功。当你成功时，帮助年轻人取得你今天的成就。

37　当我在达特茅斯上学时，我父母每星期都给我写信。我把所有的信都保留起来。来这里之前我又重读了这些信，我想给你们留下两行他们写的智慧之语。我父亲是北达科他州的一名

---

⑯ **Samuel Beckett** 塞缪尔·贝克特（1906—1989），20 世纪爱尔兰、法国作家，创作的领域包括戏剧、小说和诗歌，尤以戏剧成就最高。他是荒诞派戏剧的重要代表人物。1969 年，他因"以一种新的小说与戏剧的形式，以崇高的艺术表现人类的苦恼"而获得诺贝尔文学奖。

Thrift is a source of revenue. Those with banking careers ahead, take note. My mother always closed her letters with I love you.

38 And now in the remaining 30 second, I'd like to ask you all to rise. This is not about me. Please turn around, Class of 2009, and look at everyone gathered around you. Look at this view you've seen so often, with your loved ones honoring you under the generous trees. I'd like to ask you to recognize all of the people who got you through Dartmouth. Cheer for your professors and Dartmouth faculty. Your President and future President. Your unsung administration. The roommates you chose and the ones you didn't choose, but got anyway, the ones who taught you frustration and tolerance. Cheer the people in the town of Hanover. Cheer the towering trees and sweet old buildings. The people who set the chairs up and are waiting to clean this area. Cheer the Baker librarians. Cheer the cooks. Those who serve the food and cut the lawns. And of course, applaud your dear friends. Cheer for your **fraternity**[⑰] brothers and **sorority**[⑱] sisters. Applaud your family and most of all, last of all, cheer for your grandparents and your parents, who made it all possible.

教师，他常常在信的结尾写上一句拉丁语—Magnum vectigal EST parsimonia。意思是，节俭就是一顶收入之源。那些以后要从事银行职业的同学们，请记下这句话。我母亲总是在信的最后写上一句"我爱你"。

38 现在在剩下的30秒演讲里，我想请你们全体起立。这和我没关系。请你们转身，向四周看看，2009届毕业生们，看看聚集围绕在你身边的每个人。看看你们习以为常的景象，你们所爱的人在繁盛的大树下面向你们致敬。我想请你们向所有让你们顺利从达特茅斯毕业的人致敬。请为你们的教授们和达特茅斯学院的全体教员欢呼吧。请为你们的校长和未来的校长欢呼吧。请为默默无闻的幕后管理人员们欢呼吧。请为你们选择的室友们欢呼吧，也请为那些你们没有选择做室友、但不管怎样教会，挫折和宽容的同学们欢呼吧。请为汉诺威镇的人们欢呼吧。请为高耸入云的树木和可爱的古老建筑欢呼吧。请为那些把椅子摆好并清理这个区域的人们欢呼吧。请为贝克图书馆的馆员们欢呼吧！请为厨师们欢呼吧！请为那些供应食品和修剪草坪的人们欢呼吧！当

⑰ fraternity [frəˈtɜːnəti] n. 友爱；兄弟会；互助会；大学生联谊会
⑱ sorority [səˈrɒrəti] n. 妇女联谊会；女学生联谊会

路易丝 · 厄德里克　*Louise Erdrich*

39　This is your day. Think of everyone who means something to you. Appreciate them all. Class of 2009, cheer hard. You've graduated from Dartmouth. Now you have the freedom and skills to love this world like crazy. We need her. Do your best for this beautiful old world.

然，请为你们亲爱的朋友们鼓掌吧。请为你们兄弟会里的兄弟们和女生联谊会的姐妹们欢呼吧。请为你们的家人鼓掌吧，最重要的也是最后的，请为你们的祖父母和父母欢呼吧，是他们使这一切成为了可能。

39　今天是属于你们的日子。想想每一个对你有意义的人吧。向他们表示感谢吧。2009届毕业生们，大声欢呼吧。你们已经从达特茅斯毕业。现在，你们有了疯狂热爱这个世界的自由和能力。我们需要这个世界。请为了这个古老而又美丽的世界做出你最大的贡献吧。

17.
David Foster Wallace

大卫·福斯特·华莱士

在凯尼恩学院的演讲（2005年）

扫一扫

 ## 人物档案

　　大卫·福斯特·华莱士（英语：David Foster Wallace，1962年2月21日—2008年9月12日）出生于美国纽约州伊萨卡，美国著名作家，擅长写作小说、短篇故事。华莱士的作品具有深邃的知识性和精密的逻辑思辨性，擅长讥讽嘲笑，为现代派小说开辟了新道路。华莱士喜欢用繁琐的长句子，而且脚注和尾注比正文都要长，他擅长打断正常的句子结构，将其弄得支离破碎，吸引读者的注意力。代表作有《系统的笤帚》《头发奇特的女孩》《无尽的玩笑》《与丑陋人物的短暂会谈》《忘却》。2008年，华莱士在加利福尼亚州的家中自杀，年仅46岁，此前他一直长期服用抗抑郁症的药物。

 ## 场景介绍

　　凯尼恩学院（Kenyon College），美国著名私立学校，位于俄亥俄州的甘比亚。由主教费兰德·蔡斯建立于1824年，与欧柏林学院、丹尼森大学等同属于俄亥俄五校联盟。学校在2007、2008年度均名列全美第27位及地区第7位。

17 This Is Water
这就是水

经典原文
Original Text

1　If anybody feels like perspiring [cough], I'd advise you to go ahead, because I'm sure going to. In fact I'm gonna [mumbles while pulling up his gown and taking out a handkerchief from his pocket].

2　Greetings, thanks and congratulations to Kenyon's graduating class of 2005. There are these two young fish swimming along and they happen to meet an older fish swimming the other way, who nods at them and says, "Morning, boys. How's the water?"And the two young fish swim on for a bit, and then eventually one of them looks over at the other and goes，"What the hell is water?"

3　This is a standard requirement of US commencement speeches, the deployment of didactic little parable-ish stories. The story ["thing"] turns out to be one of the better, less bullshitty **conventions**① of the **genre**②, but if you're worried that I plan to present

中文译文
Suggested Translation

1　如果你要出汗 [咳嗽]，我建议你就尽管出汗吧，因为我肯定要出汗了。事实上我要擦汗[喃喃自语地拉起学位服，从口袋里拿出一个手帕]。

2　向凯尼恩学院 2005 届毕业班的同学们表示问候、感谢和祝贺。话说有两条小鱼并排向前游着，他们遇见了一条大鱼正朝相反的方向游去，那条大鱼冲他们点了点头，说："早上好啊，小伙伴们。你们觉得水怎么样？"这两条小鱼继续向前游了一会儿，突然其中一条侧过身来对另外一条小鱼说："水到底是啥玩意？"

3　对美国大学毕业典礼演讲的标准要求就是要讲一些带有说教性质的小寓言故事。事实证明，讲故事会让这类体裁的演讲变得更精彩、更言简意赅而不废

---

① convention [kən'venʃən] *n.* 大会；[法] 惯例；[计] 约定；[法] 协定；习俗
② genre ['ʒɒnrə] *n.* 类型；种类；体裁；样式；流派；风俗画

myself here as the wise, older fish explaining what water is to you younger fish, please don't be. I am not the wise old fish. The point of the fish story is merely that the most obvious, important realities are often the ones that are hardest to see and talk about. Stated as an English sentence, of course, this is just a **banal**③ **platitude**④, but the fact is that in the day to day trenches of adult existence, banal platitudes can have a life or death importance, or so I wish to suggest to you on this dry and lovely morning.

4   Of course the main requirement of speeches like this is that I'm supposed to talk about your liberal arts education's meaning, to try to explain why the degree you are about to receive has actual human value instead of just a material payoff. So let's talk about the single most pervasive cliché in the commencement speech genre, which is that a liberal arts education is not so much about filling you up with knowledge as it is about quote teaching you how to think. If you're like me as a student, you've never liked hearing this, and you tend to feel a bit insulted by the claim that you needed anybody to teach you how to think, since the fact that you even got admitted to a college this good seems like proof that you already know how to think. But I'm going to **posit**④ to you that the liberal

话连篇，但是如果你们担心我打算在这里扮演那条聪明的大鱼向你们这些小鱼解释什么是水，就请你们打消这种疑虑吧。我不是那条聪明的大鱼。我讲这则鱼故事的主要目的仅仅是想说明一个道理，就是最明显、最重要的现实往往最容易被人视而不见、避而不谈。当然，被表述成一个英语句子的大道理只不过是个老生常谈的道理，但事实是，在日复一日的成人现实世界里，老道理的重要性可能关乎生死，至少在这个干燥清爽的早晨，我希望能够引起你们的注意。

4   当然，对这类演讲的主要要求是我应该谈谈你们接受素质教育的意义，试图解释你们就要拿到的学位为什么具有实际的人文价值而不只是物质上的回报。那么就让我们谈一谈在毕业典礼演讲中最为普遍出现的陈词滥调吧，即素质教育与其说是灌输给你们知识，不如说是"教导你们如何思考"。如果你们和学生时代的我一样，你们就永远不会喜欢听这些话，你们会觉得别人说你们需要学会如何思考是对你们的侮辱，因为事实上，你们能被这样的好大学录取似乎已经证

---

③ banal [bəˈnɑl] *adj*. 陈腐的；平庸的；老一套的
④ posit [ˈpɒzɪt] *vt*. 安置；假定

arts cliché turns out not to be insulting at all, because the really significant education in thinking that we're supposed to get in a place like this isn't really about the capacity to think, but rather about the choice of what to think about. If your total freedom of choice regarding what to think about seems too obvious to waste time discussing, I'd ask you to think about fish and water, and to bracket for just a few minutes your skepticism about the value of the totally obvious.

5 Here's another didactic little story. There are these two guys sitting together in a bar in the remote Alaskan wilderness. One of the guys is religious, the other is an atheist, and the two are arguing about the existence of God with that special intensity that comes after about the fourth beer. And the atheist says，"Look, it's not like I don't have actual reasons for not believing in God. It's not like I haven't ever experimented with the whole God and prayer thing. Just last month I got caught away from the camp in that terrible blizzard, and I was totally lost and I couldn't see a thing, and it was fifty below, and so I tried it: I fell to my knees in the snow and cried out，'Oh, God, if there is a God, I'm lost in this blizzard, and I'm gonna die if you don't help me.'" And now, in the bar, the religious guy looks at the atheist all puzzled. "Well then you must believe now，" he says, "After all, here you are, alive." The atheist just rolls his eyes." No, man, all that was was a couple Eskimos happened to come wandering by and showed me the

明了你们知道如何思考。但我断定，关于素质教育的这一老套说法其实不带有任何侮辱性质，因为我们应该在这样的地方得到的重要思考方面的重要教育实际上和思考的能力无关，而是和选择什么样的问题去思考有关。如果你们认为完全自由地选择什么样的问题去思考是一件太过简单的事，不值得浪费时间去讨论，那么我想请你们想想刚才讲的鱼和水的故事，并且暂时不去怀疑那个太过简单之事本身的价值。

5 我再讲一个带有说教性质的小故事。有两个家伙并排坐在一间位于偏远的阿拉斯加荒野的酒吧里。其中一人是教徒，另一人则是个无神论者，这两个家伙在争论上帝是否存在，当他们喝到大概第四瓶啤酒的时候，争论已经到了白热化的程度。那位无神论者说："你听着，我不相信上帝存在不是没有真正的理由。我不是没有试过向全能的上帝祈祷之类的事。就在上个月，我在远离营地的地方遇上了一场可怕的暴风雪，我完全迷了路，什么也看不见，气温在零下五十度，所以我尝试了祈祷：我双膝跪在雪地里，大声喊叫：'啊，上帝呀，如果上帝存在的话，我迷失在这暴风雪里，如果您不帮我，我会死的。'酒吧里的教徒看着无神

way back to camp."

6　It's easy to run this story through kind of a standard liberal arts analysis: the exact same experience can mean two totally different things to two different people, given those people's two different belief templates and two different ways of constructing meaning from experience. Because we prize tolerance and diversity of belief, nowhere in our liberal arts analysis do we want to claim that one guy's interpretation is true and the other guy's is false or bad. Which is fine, except we also never end up talking about just where these individual templates and beliefs come from. Meaning, where they come from inside the two guys. As if a person's most basic orientation toward the world, and the meaning of his experience were somehow just hard-wired, like height or shoe-size; or automatically absorbed from the culture, like language. As if how we construct meaning were not actually a matter of personal, intentional choice. Plus, there's the whole matter of arrogance. The nonreligious guy is so totally certain in his dismissal of the possibility that the passing Eskimos had anything to do with his prayer for help. True, there are plenty of religious people who seem arrogant and certain of their own interpretations, too. They're probably even more repulsive than atheists, at least to most of us. But religious dogmatists's problem is exactly the same as the story's unbeliever:

论者一脸茫然的样子。"那么你现在必须相信了，"他说，"毕竟你现在还活着啊。"无神论者朝他翻了翻白眼。"不是，老兄，这一切都是因为有几个爱斯基摩人刚好从我身边路过，是他们指给我返回营地的路。"

6　通过标准的素质教育分析可以很简单地总结这个故事：考虑到两个不同的人具有不同的信仰模式以及从经历中提炼人生意义的不同方式，两个不同的人从完全相同的经历中可以得到完全不同的人生启迪。因为我们珍视信仰的包容性和多样性，所以我们在素质教育分析中不会声明一个人的解读是对的，而另外一个人的解读是错的或糟糕的。这样是好的，问题是我们永远也不会停止讨论个人的信仰模式从何而来，也就是说，那两个人的信仰模式来自内心世界的什么地方。就好像一个人最基本的世界观和他对人生阅历的解读就如身高或鞋子的尺寸般是固定了的；或者如语言般会自动从文化里吸收养分。就好像我们如何提炼人生意义并不是个人的事、并不是有意的选择一样。另外，还有傲慢态度在作祟。那个无神论者就那么肯定路过的爱斯基摩人和他的祷告一点关系都没有。没错，有不少教徒看上去也对自己的解释趾高气扬、深信不疑。他们甚至可

blind certainty, a close-mindedness that amounts to an imprisonment so total that the prisoner doesn't even know he's locked up.

7　The point here is that I think this is one part of what teaching me how to think is really supposed to mean. To be just a little less arrogant. To have just a little critical awareness about myself and my certainties. Because a huge percentage of the stuff that I tend to be automatically certain of is, it turns out, totally wrong and deluded. I have learned this the hard way, as I predict you graduates will, too.

8　Here is just one example of the total wrongness of something I tend to be automatically sure of: everything in my own immediate experience supports my deep belief that I am the absolute center of the universe; the realest, most vivid and important person in existence. We rarely think about this sort of natural, basic self-centeredness because it's so socially repulsive. But it's pretty much the same for all of us. It is our default setting, hard-wired into our boards at birth. Think about it: there is no experience you have had that you are not the absolute center of. The world as you experience it is there in front of you or behind you, to the left or right of you, on your TV or your monitor. And so on.Other people's thoughts and feelings have to be communicated to you somehow, but your own are so immediate, urgent, real.

能比无神论者更令人讨厌，至少对我们大多数人来说是这样。但宗教里的教条主义者存在的问题完全和故事里的无神论者一样：盲目自信、思想狭隘到了极点，以至于思想的囚犯甚至不相信自己被关在了思想的监牢里。

7　这里的关键就是，我认为这个故事就表现了是什么教会我如何思考才是真正有意义的这一点。少一点傲慢即可。对自我和自信要有一点批判意识。因为我潜意识里肯定的很多事情后来都被证明是完全错误的、自欺欺人的。我是经过一个艰难的历程才学到这个教训的，我预测你们毕业生也将如此。

8　这里有一个例子来说明我自动认为是正确的东西其实是错误的：我亲身经历的一切事情都让我深信我就是宇宙的绝对中心；我是存在于宇宙之中的那个最真实、最生动、最重要的人。我们很少想到这种天生的、基本的个人主义，是因为它会遭到社会的严重排斥。但个人主义对我们所有人来说都是一样的。它是我们与生俱来的固有本性。想想看：你的所有经历无不说明你是绝对的宇宙中心。你所经历的世界要么在你前面，要么在你后面；要么在你的左面，要么在你的右面；要么在你的电视里，要么在你的显示器里。如此等等。

9   Please don't worry that I'm getting ready to lecture you about compassion or other-directedness or all the so-called virtues. This is not a matter of virtue. It's a matter of my choosing to do the work of somehow altering or getting free of my natural, hard-wired default setting which is to be deeply and literally self-centered and to see and interpret everything through this lens of self. People who can adjust their natural default setting this way are often described as being well-adjusted, which I suggest to you is not an accidental term.

10   Given the triumphant academic setting here, an obvious question is how much of this work of adjusting our default setting involves actual knowledge or intellect. This question gets very tricky. Probably the most dangerous thing about an academic education, least in my own case, is that it enables my tendency to over-intellectualize stuff, to get lost in abstract argument inside my head, instead of simply paying attention to what is going on right in front of me, paying attention to what is going on inside me.

11   As I'm sure you guys know by now, it is extremely difficult to stay alert and attentive, instead of getting **hypnotized**[5] by the constant monologue inside your own head (may be happening right now). Twenty years after my own graduation, I have come gradually to understand that the liberal arts cliché about hosed teaching you how to think is actually

尽管你不得不以某种方式和其他人交流思想感情，但你自己的思想感情是如此直接、迫切和真实。

9   请不要担心，我不准备向你们讲同情心或利他导向或所有所谓的美德。这不关美德的事。它关乎的是我如何选择改变或摆脱我那一天性，那一固有本性，即以自我为中心的严重的个人主义，并戴着这副有色眼镜去看待世间万物。透过这种方式调整固有本性的人们通常被描述为调整得不错的人，我告诉你们，这可不是一句随随便便说的话。

10   考虑到这里浓厚的的学术氛围，一个明显的问题是，这种调整我们固有本性的努力和实际的知识或智力有多大关系。这是个很棘手的问题。至少在我看来，学术教育最危险之处大概是它使我倾向于过度理智化，让我的大脑迷失在抽象的论据上，而不是简单地关注在我眼前发生了什么事，关注我内心在想什么。

11   我相信你们现在都知道，保持清醒的头脑和高度的注意力而不被你脑海里的唠唠叨叨（可能你们的大脑现在就在开小差）所迷惑是非常困难的。我毕业二十年后才逐渐明白，关于素质教育教你如何思考的陈词滥调实

---

⑤ hypnotize ['hɪpnətaɪz] vt. 使着迷；对……施催眠术；使恍惚

shorthand for a much deeper, more serious idea: learning how to think really means learning how to exercise some control over how and what you think. It means being conscious and aware enough to choose what you pay attention to and to choose how you construct meaning from experience. Because if you cannot exercise this kind of choice in adult life, you will be totally hosed. Think of the old cliché about quote the mind being an excellent servant but a terrible master.

12　This, like many clichés, so lame and unexciting on the surface, actually expresses a great and terrible truth. It is not the least bit coincidental that adults who commit suicide with firearms almost always shoot themselves in the head. They shoot the terrible master. And the truth is that most of these suicides are actually dead long before they pull the trigger.

13　And I submit that this is what the real, no bullshit value of your liberal arts education is supposed to be about: how to **keep from**[6] going through your comfortable, prosperous, respectable adult life dead, unconscious, a slave to your head and to your natural default setting of being uniquely, completely, imperially alone day in and day out. That may sound like **hyperbole**[7], or abstract nonsense. Let's get concrete. The plain fact is that you graduating seniors do not yet have any clue what day in day out really means. There happen to be whole,

际上表达的是一个更深刻、更严肃的理念：学习如何思考实际上意味着学会控制如何思考和思考什么。这就意味着你要保持足够清醒的头脑以来选择你关注什么以及选择如何从经历中提炼生活的意义。因为如果你在成年生活中不能学会进行这种选择，你将会受到严厉的惩罚。想想这句老话吧："思想是个优秀的仆人，但是个糟糕的主人。"

12　就像许多俗话一样，这句俗话表面上平淡无奇，实际上表达了一个伟大而可怕的真理。用枪支自杀的成年人几乎总是打爆自己的头，这完全不是什么巧合之事。他们是开枪杀死糟糕的主人。事实上，大多数自杀者在他们扣动扳机之前其实就已经死了。

13　我认为这就是你们接受的素质教育所应该具有的没有水分的真正价值：如何避免死气沉沉、浑浑噩噩地度过你那舒适、富有、可敬的成人生活，如何避免成为你大脑的奴隶，如何避免成为那种日复一日唯我独尊的自然本性的奴隶。这听起来可能很夸张，或像是一堆抽象的废话。让我们具体说明一下。一个简单的事实就是，你们毕业生对日复一日的真正含义还没有任何头

---

⑥ keep from 隐瞒；阻止；抑制

⑦ hyperbole [haɪˈpɜːbəlɪ] n. 夸张的语句；夸张法

large parts of adult American life that nobody talks about in commencement speeches. One such part involves boredom, routine, and petty frustration. The parents and older folks here will know all too well what I'm talking about.

14 By way of example, let's say it's an average adult day, and you get up in the morning, go to your challenging, white-collar, college-graduate job, and you work hard for eight or ten hours, and at the end of the day you're tired and somewhat stressed and all you want is to go home and have a good supper and maybe unwind for an hour, and then **hit the sack**[8] early because, of course, you have to get up the next day and do it all again. But then you remember there's no food at home. You haven't had time to shop this week because of your challenging job, and so now after work you have to get in your car and drive to the supermarket. It's the end of the work day and the traffic is apt to be very bad. So getting to the store takes way longer than it should, and when you finally get there, the supermarket is very crowded, because of course it's the time of day when all the other people with jobs also try to squeeze in some grocery shopping. And the store is hideously lit and infused with soul-killing Muzak or corporate pop and it's pretty much the last place you want to be but you can't just get in and quickly out; you have to wander all over the huge, over-lit store's confusing aisles to find the stuff you want and you have to maneuver

绪。它碰巧主宰了成年美国人的绝大部分生活，而没有人在毕业典礼演讲中谈及这一点。成年美国人的这部分生活由无聊、例行公事和小挫折构成。在座的学生家长和年长者们非常清楚我在说什么。

14 举例来说吧，假如今天是你作为一个成年人的普通一天，你早上起床，然后去上班，干一份和大学毕业生相称的具有挑战性的白领工作，你努力工作了八或十个小时，到了下班的时候你累了，感到有点压力，你只想赶回家吃上一顿美味可口的晚餐，也许再放松上一个小时，然后早点上床睡觉，因为第二天你当然必须早早起床重复这一切。但忽然你想起来家里还没有吃的东西。这一周你没有时间去购物，因为你的工作很难搞定，所以下班后你就得跳进车子开车去超市。一天的工作结束了，交通变得非常拥挤。所以去商店的时间比平时要长得多，当你终于到达那里的时候，超市里人山人海，因为这当然是一天当中所有其他职场人士也匆匆赶来购物的时间。商店里灯火通明，四处飘荡着摄人心魄的助兴音乐或公司流行曲，这差不多是你最不想去的

⑧ hit the sack 睡觉，就寝

大卫·福斯特·华莱士 *David Foster Wallace*

your junky cart through all these other tired, hurried people with carts (et cetera, et cetera, cutting stuff out because this is a long ceremony) and eventually you get all your supper supplies, except now it turns out there aren't enough check-out lanes open even though it's the end-of-the-day rush. So the checkout line is incredibly long, which is stupid and infuriating. But you can't take your frustration out on the frantic lady working the register, who is overworked at a job whose daily tedium and meaninglessness surpasses the imagination of any of us here at a prestigious college.

15　But anyway, you finally get to the checkout line's front, and you pay for your food, and you get told to have a nice day in a voice that is the absolute voice of death. Then you have to take your creepy, flimsy, plastic bags of groceries in your cart with the one crazy wheel that pulls **maddeningly**⑨ to the left, all the way out through the crowded, bumpy, littery parking lot, and then you have to drive all the way home through slow, heavy, SUV-intensive, **rush-hour traffic**⑩, et cetera et cetera.

地方，但你又不可以快进快出；你只好在灯火通明的庞大商店里那些混乱的过道上漫步徘徊去寻找要买的东西，你不得不推着你的购物车穿梭于脸上写着疲惫、形色匆匆、也推着购物车的人群（等等等等，这里省去若干字，因为这是个漫长的仪式），最终你找到了所有的晚餐食材，只是现在才发现开放的结账通道不够多，尽管现在是下班后的高峰时间。因此，等着结帐的队伍非常长，这真是愚蠢之至，让人愤怒之极。但你还不能把怨气发泄在手忙脚乱的女收银员身上，她得超负荷工作，而且日常工作的单调和乏味程度超过了我们任何一个著名大学里的人的想象。

15　但不管怎样，你终于来到了收银台前，你为买到的食物付了钱，同时一个死人般冷冰冰的声音对你说：祝你生活愉快。然后你必须把那些令人毛骨悚然的、薄薄的塑料购物袋放进购物车里，令人抓狂的是购物车的一个车轮抽风似的老是向左转，你推着这么一辆车一路穿过拥挤不堪、高低不平、杂乱无章的停车场，然后你驾车回家，一路上行驶缓慢，因为正值下班高峰期，路上还充斥着运动型多用途汽车

⑨ maddeningly ['mædnɪŋlɪ] *adv.* 使人恼火地；令人发狂地
⑩ rush-hour traffic 交通高峰时间

16 Everyone here has done this, of course. But it hasn't yet been part of you graduates' actual life routine, day after week after month after year.

17 But it will be. And many more dreary, annoying, seemingly meaningless routines besides. But that is not the point. The point is that petty, frustrating crap like this is exactly where the work of choosing is gonna come in. Because the traffic jams and crowded aisles and long checkout lines give me time to think, and if I don't make a conscious decision about how to think and what to pay attention to, I'm gonna be pissed and miserable every time I have to shop. Because my natural default setting is the certainty that situations like this are really all about me. About my hungriness and my fatigue and my desire to just get home, and it's going to seem for all the world like everybody else is just in my way. And who are all these people in my way? And look at how repulsive most of them are, and how stupid and cow-like and dead-eyed and nonhuman they seem in the checkout line, or at how annoying and rude it is that people are talking loudly on cell phones in the middle of the line. And look at how deeply and personally unfair this is.

18 Or, of course, if I'm in a more socially

（SUV），所以交通十分堵塞，等等等等。

16 当然，在座的每个人都有过这样的经历。但这还没有成为你们毕业生年复一年月复一月周复一周日复一日的实际日常生活的一部分。

17 但它会的。除此之外还有许多更沉闷、更恼人、看似更毫无意义的日常琐事在等着你。但那不是关键。关键是像在做这样的鸡毛蒜皮令人沮丧的小事时，恰恰就是该做选择工作的时候。因为交通堵塞和拥挤的过道以及长长的结款队伍给了我思考的时间，而如果我不有意识地决定如何思考和关注什么，我在每一次购物的时候就会感到愤怒和痛苦。因为我的固有本质让我坚信像这样的情况其实都是针对我的。它让我感到饥饿和疲劳，它让我只想回家，似乎世界上所有其他人都在和我作对。那些挡我道的人是谁？瞧瞧他们中的大部分人有多么讨厌，看看排在结帐队伍里的人有多么愚蠢，他们看上去像牛一样愚蠢，双眼无神，简直就不是人，或者看看站在队伍里的人们拿着手机大喊大叫的样子是多么让人恼火，显得是多么粗鲁。瞧瞧这对个人来说是多么不公平。

18 当然，也可以换一种想

conscious liberal arts form of my default setting, I can spend time in the end-of-the-day traffic being disgusted about all the huge, stupid, lane-blocking SUV's and Hummers and V-12 pickup trucks, burning their wasteful, selfish, forty-gallon tanks of gas, and I can dwell on the fact that the patriotic or religious bumper-stickers always seem to be on the biggest, most disgustingly selfish vehicles, driven by the ugliest [responding here to loud applause] (this is an example of how not to think, though), most inconsiderate and aggressive drivers. And I can think about how our children's children will despise us for wasting all the future's fuel, and probably screwing up the climate, and how spoiled and stupid and selfish and disgusting we all are, and how modern consumer society just sucks, and so forth and so on.

19　You get the idea.

20　If I choose to think this way in a store and on the freeway, fine. Lots of us do. Except thinking this way tends to be so easy and automatic that it doesn't have to be a choice. It is my natural default setting. It's the automatic way that I experience the boring, frustrating, crowded parts of adult life when I'm operating on the automatic, unconscious belief that I am the center of the world, and that my immediate needs and feelings are what should determine the world's priorities.

法，如果我对我的本性进行更具社会意识的素质教育形式思考的话，我可以在晚上下班回家的路上对所有庞大、笨重、阻塞车道的 SUV 和悍马以及 V-12 皮卡车心生厌恶，它们用的是四十加仑的油箱，既浪费又自私，我还可以思索这样一个事实，即带有爱国主义色彩或宗教色彩的车尾贴似乎总是贴在最大型、最令人讨厌、最自私的车辆上面，由最丑陋 [这里赢得了热烈的掌声]（虽然这是一个如何不去思考的例子）、最轻率和最具攻击性的司机驾驶。我想到我们孩子们的孩子们会看不起我们浪费未来燃料的行为，也许是厌恶我们搞坏了气候，厌恶我们大家是多么任性、愚蠢、自私、恶心，厌恶现代消费者社会是多么得烂，等等等等。

19　你们懂得我的意思。

20　如果我选择在商店和高速公路上也这样想，那很好。我们中很多人都这么做。但这样想往往太过简单和自动化，它不必成为一项选择。这是我的固有本性。当我自动地、无意识地相信我就是世界的中心、我眼前的需要和感情应该决定世界的优先顺序的时候，我经历的就是成人生活里那无聊、令人沮丧、拥挤的部分，这就是自动的方式。

21 The thing is that, of course, there are totally different ways to think about these kinds of situations. In this traffic, all these vehicles stopped and idling in my way, it's not impossible that some of these people in SUVs have been in horrible auto accidents in the past, and now find driving so terrifying that their therapist has all but ordered them to get a huge, heavy SUV so they can feel safe enough to drive. Or that the Hummer that just cut me off is maybe being driven by a father whose little child is hurt or sick in the seat next to him, and he's trying to get this kid to the hospital, and he's in a bigger, more legitimate hurry than I am: it is actually I who am in his way.

22 Or I can choose to force myself to consider the likelihood that everyone else in the supermarket's checkout line is just as bored and frustrated as I am, and that some of these people probably have harder, more tedious and painful lives than I do.

23 Again, please don't think that I'm giving you moral advice, or that I'm saying you are supposed to think this way, or that anyone expects you to just automatically do it. Because it's hard. It takes will and effort, and if you are like me, some days you won't be able to do it, or you just **flat out**[11] won't want to.

24 But most days, if you're aware enough to give

21 当然，最重要的是我们可以用完全不同的方式去思考这类问题。在交通堵塞的路上，所有车辆都停在路上挡住了我，一个可能的解释就是坐在 SUV 上的一些人对过去发生的交通事故还心有余悸，他们现在发现开车是一件多么可怕的事，于是他们的心理治疗师差不多是命令他们驾驶一辆庞大又笨重的 SUV，这样他们驾车就可以有足够的安全感。或者说那个突然变道超我车的悍马或许正由一位父亲驾驶，而坐在他旁边的孩子受了伤或生了病，他正急着送孩子去医院，跟我比起来，他有一个更大、更合理的着急的理由：其实是我挡了他的路。

22 或者我也可以选择强迫自己认为在超市结账的其他人和我自己一样无聊和沮丧，而且他们中的一些人可能比我活得更累、更烦闷、更苦。

23 再说一遍，请不要以为我在给你们进行道德说教，也不要以为我在劝说你们应该这样思考问题，更不要以为有人期望你们自动那么做。因为这很难。它需要毅力和努力，如果你们像我一样，有朝一日你们会没有能力这么做，或者你们根本就不想做。

24 但大多数时候，如果你们

⑪ flat out 竭尽全力；用全速；疲惫

yourself a choice, you can choose to look differently at this fat, dead-eyed, over-made-up lady who just screamed at her kid in the checkout line. Maybe she's not usually like this. Maybe she's been up three straight nights holding the hand of a husband who is dying of bone cancer. Or maybe this very lady is the low-wage clerk at the motor vehicle department, who just yesterday helped your spouse resolve a horrific, infuriating, red-tape problem through some small act of bureaucratic kindness. Of course, none of this is likely, but it's also not impossible. It just depends want you what to consider. If you're automatically sure that you know what reality is, and you are operating on your default setting, then you, like me, probably won't consider possibilities that aren't annoying and miserable. But if you really learn how to pay attention, then you will know there are other options. It will actually be within your power to experience a crowded, hot, slow, consumer-hell type situation as not only meaningful, but sacred, **on fire**[12] with the same force that made the stars: love, fellowship, the mystical oneness of all things deep down.

25　Not that that mystical stuff is necessarily true. The only thing that's capital-T True is that you get to decide how you're gonna try to see it.

足够清醒地给自己一个选择，你们可以选择用不同的眼光来看待这个长着一对死鱼眼睛、化妆化成妖精一样、在排队结帐的时候对孩子大喊大叫的胖女人。也许她平常不是这样的。也许她已经连续三天三夜握着即将死于骨癌的丈夫的手了。也许这位女士是一位任职于汽车部门的低薪职员，她就在昨天通过一件小小的官僚善举帮助你的配偶解决了一个可怕的、令人恼火的、繁琐的问题。当然，没有一件事是可能发生的，但也不是不可能的。这仅仅取决于你想去怎么想。如果你自以为你知道现实是什么，而且你根据自己的本性去行事，那么你就会和我一样，可能不会考虑那些不恼人和不痛苦的事情发生的可能性。但如果你真的学会如何去关注别人，那么你会知道还有其他的选择。拥有一次拥挤的、闷热的、缓慢的、对消费者来说好似炼狱般的经历实际上是你可以承受的事情，这不仅是有意义的，而且还是神圣的，我们崇拜的是和上帝造星一样的力量：爱、友谊、内心深处一切想法的神秘统一性。

25　不是说神秘的东西就一定是真的。唯一的真理就是你开始决定你打算如何努力去认识它。

---

⑫ on fire 着火；起火；在兴头上；非常激动

26   This, I submit, is the freedom of a real education, of learning how to be well-adjusted. You get to consciously decide what has meaning and what doesn't. You get to decide what to worship.

27   Because here's something else that's weird but true: in the day-to-day trenches of adult life, there is actually no such thing as atheism. There is no such thing as not worshipping. Everybody worships. The only choice we get is what to worship. And the compelling reason for maybe choosing some sort of god or spiritual-type thing to worship be it JC or Allah, bet it YHWH or the Wiccan Mother Goddess, or the Four Noble Truths, or some inviolable set of ethical principles is that pretty much anything else you worship will eat you alive. If you worship money and things, if they are where you tap real meaning in life, then you will never have enough, never feel you have enough. It's the truth. Worship your body and beauty and sexual allure and you will always feel ugly. And when time and age start showing, you will die a million deaths before they finally grieve you. On one level, we all know this stuff already. It's been codified as myths, proverbs, clichés, **epigrams**[13], parables; the skeleton of every great story. The whole trick is keeping the truth up front in daily consciousness.

26   我承认这是真正教育的自由，是学习如何调整好的自由。你开始有意识地决定什么有意义而什么没有意义。你开始决定信奉什么。

27   因为还有一件事虽奇怪却是真实的：在日复一日的成年人真实生活中，其实是没有无神论这一词汇的。也没有不敬拜这样的事。每个人都会去敬拜。我们要做的唯一选择是敬拜什么。也许选择某个神或某种精神之类的东西去敬拜（无论是基督耶稣，还是真主，无论是耶和华，还是巫婆，还是四圣谛，还是一套神圣不可侵犯的伦理原则）的充分理由就是你所敬奉的几乎其他任何东西都会活活吞噬了你。如果你敬拜金钱和物质，如果它们是你活着的真正意义，那么你将永远不会满足，你永远不觉得你有足够的金钱和物质。这是真理。敬拜你的身体、你的美和性感，那你就永远觉得自己难看。当时间的痕迹开始出现在脸上时，在你最终为此感到悲伤之前，你宁愿死上一百万回。从某种层面上说，我们早都知道这个道理。它被编成了神话、谚语、俗话、警句、寓言；它成了每一个精彩故事的纲要。关键在于要让真理在

⑬ epigram ['epɪgræm] *n.* 警句；讽刺短诗；隽语
⑭ insidious [ɪn'sɪdɪəs] *adj.* 阴险的；隐伏的；暗中为害的；狡猾的

28　Worship power, you will end up feeling weak and afraid, and you will need ever more power over others to numb you to your own fear. Worship your intellect, being seen as smart, you will end up feeling stupid, a fraud, always on the verge of being found out. But the **insidious**[14] thing about these forms of worship is not that they're evil or sinful, it's that they're unconscious. They are default settings.

29　They're the kind of worship you just gradually slip into, day after day, getting more and more selective about what you see and how you measure value without ever being fully aware that that's what you're doing.

30　And the so-called real world will not discourage you from operating on your default settings, because the so-called real world of men and money and power hums merrily along in a pool of fear and anger and frustration and craving and worship of self. Our own present culture has harnessed these forces in ways that have yielded extraordinary wealth and comfort and personal freedom. The freedom all to be lords of our tiny skull-sized kingdoms, alone at the center of all creation. This kind of freedom has much to recommend it. But of course there are all different kinds of freedom, and the kind that is most precious you will not hear much talk about much in the great outside world of wanting and achieving. The

日常生活意识中保持在最重要的位置上。

28　如果崇拜权力，你就最终会感到虚弱和恐惧，你会永远需要比别人更大的权力来麻痹你自己的恐惧。如果崇拜你的智慧，醉心于被视为智者，那么你最终会感到愚蠢，总觉得自己是一个骗子，马上就会被别人发现。但是这些形式的崇拜其有害之处不在于它们是邪恶或罪恶的，而在于它们是无意识的。它们都是人的固有本性。

29　你们只是逐渐陷进那种崇拜之中，日复一日，你对要看什么以及如何衡量其价值越来越挑剔，但你从来都完全没有意识到你所做的只是陷入其中。

30　而所谓的真实世界不会阻止你运用你的固有本性，因为所谓的现实世界里的人、金钱和权力都围绕着恐惧、愤怒、挫折、渴望和自我崇拜快乐地歌唱着。我们自己现有的文化已经利用了这些力量创造出了非凡的财富、舒适自在和个人自由。那种所有人都想成为自己那一亩三分地的领主、独自一人位于万物中心的自由。这类自由备受推崇。当然，世界上有各种各样的自由，而最珍贵的那种自由是你在外面

⑮ rat race 激烈竞争

really important kind of freedom involves attention and awareness and discipline, and being able truly to care about other people and to sacrifice for them over and over in myriad petty, unsexy ways everyday.

31 That is real freedom. That is being educated, and understanding how to think. The alternative is unconsciousness, the default setting, the **rat race**⑮, the constant gnawing sense of having had, and lost, some infinite thing.

32 I know that this stuff probably doesn't sound fun and breezy or grandly inspirational the way a commencement speech is supposed to sound. What it is, as far as I can see, is the capital-T Truth, with a whole lot of **rhetorical**⑯ **niceties**⑰ stripped away. You are, of course, free to think of it whatever you wish. But please don't just dismiss it as just some finger-wagging Dr. Laura sermon. None of this stuff is really about morality or religion or dogma or big fancy questions of **life after death**⑱.

33 The capital-T Truth is about life BEFORE death.

34 It is about the real value of a real education, which has almost nothing to do with knowledge, and everything to do with simple awareness; awareness of what is so real and essential, so hidden in plain

那个你争我夺的大千世界里不会听到太多、也不会谈论太多的自由。真正重要的那类自由包含的是专注、意识和纪律，能够真正地关心他人，每天以无数琐碎而不露骨的方式为他人不断地作出牺牲。

31 那是真正的自由。这是受过教育且懂得如何思考的人的自由。此外你也可以选择无意识，固有本性，激烈的竞争，对某些无穷尽的东西患得患失带来的痛苦感。

32 我知道这些东西可能听起来并不轻松愉快或鼓舞人心，不像毕业典礼演讲应该讲的话。在我看来，它是真正重要的真理，不需要一大堆华丽辞藻修饰。你当然可以随便地按照你所希望地认为。但请你们不要误认为这是某个劳拉博士指手画脚的说教。这里没有一句话关乎道德、宗教、教义或死后来生的大问题。

33 真正的真理讲的都是今世今生的问题。

34 它讲的是真正教育的真正价值，它几乎和知识无关，而完全和简单的意识有关；它让我们意识到在我们周围总是有一些东

---

⑯ rhetorical [rɪ'tɒrɪkl] *adj.* 修辞的；修辞学的；夸张的

⑰ nicety ['naɪsəti] *n.* 精密；美好；细节；拘泥细节

⑱ life after death 来世，来生

sight all around us, all the time that we have to keep reminding ourselves over and over:

35　This is water.

36　This is water.

37　It is unimaginably hard to do this, to stay conscious and alive in the adult world day in and day out. Which means yet another grand cliché turns out to be true: your education really is the job of a lifetime.

38　And it commences: now.

39　I wish you **way**[19] more than luck.

西，它们是如此真实的存在，是如此得不可或缺，看似显而易见实则隐藏很深，因此我们务必不断提醒自己：

35　这就是水。

36　这就是水。

37　在成人的世界里日复一日地保持头脑清醒活跃是非常难得的一件事。但这也意味着另一个冠冕堂皇的陈词滥调原来是真理：教育真的是一辈子的事。

38　现在就开始吧。

39　我祝福你们的不只是好运气。

---

⑲ way [weɪ] *adv.* 大大地；远远地

18.

Anna Quindlen

安娜·昆德兰

在维拉诺瓦大学的演讲（2000年）

扫一扫

人物档案

安娜·昆德兰（Anna Quindlen，1953年7月8日—）美国著名作家，出生于宾夕法尼亚州的费城。父亲是爱尔兰人，母亲则是意大利人。她是美国历史上第三个为《纽约时报》撰写社论对页专栏的女性。她是普利策评论奖得主。畅销小说有《主题课程》《亲情无价》（曾改编为电影）以及《黑与蓝》。

场景介绍

维拉诺瓦大学是位于美国宾夕法尼亚州费城西北郊拉德诺镇的一所私立大学。维拉诺瓦大学（Villanova University）成立于1842年，是宾夕法尼亚州历史最悠久、规模最大的天主教大学。十年多来，在美国新闻与世界报道的排名中，在美国北部最佳硕士项目大学分类中，维拉诺瓦大学一直排名第一。

安娜·昆德兰 *Anna Quindlen*

Don't Be Perfect, Be Yourself
不追求完美，只追求自我

经典原文
Original Text

1　President Creighton, members of the board, the faculty and adminstration, family and friends, and members of class of 1999.

2　I feel like a bit of a fraud wearing **this thing**[①]. When I came down those steps over there, I was wearing what I really deserve, my basic BA black. It has it would be happy to be here been enough. It was twenty-five years ago that I actually earned the degree, and that's from your sister school — Barnard College.

3　So I look at all of you today and I cannot help but see myself some twenty-five years ago, at that commencement. I sometimes seem, in my mind, to have as much in common with that young woman as I do with any stranger I might pass in the doorway of a Starbucks or in the aisle of an airplane. I cannot remember what she wore that day or how she felt. But I can tell you this about her without question: she was perfect.

中文译文
Suggested Translation

1　克赖顿校长、董事会各位成员、老师们、领导们、毕业生家人和朋友们以及1999届的全体毕业生们：

2　我觉得围着这玩意有点像骗子。当我从那些台阶走下来的时候，我穿戴的是我应该穿戴的服装，就是文学士的黑色学位服。我是在二十五年前获得了该学位，而且是在你们的姊妹学校——巴纳德学院获得的。

3　因此，我今天看着眼前的你们，不由得看到了大约二十五年前在毕业典礼上的我自己。在我的记忆里，我有时觉得我和当年那个小女孩身上的共同点与我和在星巴克门口或在飞机过道通上擦肩而过的任何陌生人身上的共同点一样多。我不记得在毕业典礼的那一天她穿的是什么或她感觉如何。但我可以毫无疑问地

---

① this thing 这里指作者被授予荣誉博士学位时被围在脖子上的白色绶带

4 Let me be very clear what I mean by that. I mean that I got up every morning and tried to be perfect in every possible way. If there was a test to be had, I had studied for it; if there was a paper to be written, it was done and redone. I smiled at everyone on campus, because it was important to be friendly, and I made fun of them behind their backs because it was important to be witty. And I worked as a residence counselor and I sat on housing council. If anyone had ever stopped and asked me why I did those things — well, I'm not sure what I would have said. But I can tell you, today, that I did them to be perfect, in every possible way.

5 Being perfect was hard work, and the hell of it was, the rules of it changed. So that while I arrived at college in 1970 with a trunk full of perfect **pleated**[2] **kilts**[3] and perfect **monogrammed**[4] sweaters, by Christmas vacation I had another perfect uniform: overalls, turtlenecks, **Doc Martens**[5], and the perfect New York City Barnard College affect — part hyperintellectual, part **ennui**[6]. This was very hard work indeed. I had read neither **Sartre**[7] nor **Sappho**[8], and the closest I ever came to being

告诉你们：她是那么得完美无暇。

4 请让我很清楚地告诉你们我指的是什么。我的意思是说，那个时候我每天早上醒来后就努力以任何可能的方式让自己表现完美。如果要参加一门课程的考试，我提前复习它；如果要写一篇论文，我提前写完它并不断修改。我向校园里的每个人投以微笑，因为表示友好很重要，我在背后才取笑他们，因为保持机智很重要。我担任居委会顾问，我成为住房委员会成员。如果有人问我为什么要做这些事情——嗯，我不知道那时候的我会如何回答。但我今天可以告诉你们答案，那就是我所做的一切都是为了完美，以一切可能的方式追求完美。

5 追求完美是一项艰苦的工作，而它最可恶的地方就是完美的规则发生了改变。所以，我在1970年秋天拖着装满堪称完美的褶裥短裙和印字毛衣的箱子到达达特茅斯学院，但到了圣诞假期时，我穿上了另外一套完美的校服：吊带裤、高领毛衣、马丁大夫靴，受到到了纽约市巴纳德学院的完美影响——部分是具有超

---

② pleated ['pli:tɪd] *adj.* 起褶的

③ kilt [kɪlt] *n.* 苏格兰式短裙

④ monogrammed ['mɒnəgræmd] *adj.* 有交织字母的；有花押字的

⑤ Doc Martens [复数][商标] 马丁大夫靴 [亦

作 Doctor Martens]

⑥ ennui [ɒn'wɪ:] *n.* （法）厌倦，无聊；倦怠

⑦ Sartre ['sɑ:trə] *n.* 萨特（法国哲学家、小说家、剧作家）

⑧ Sappho ['sæfəu] *n.* 莎孚（古代希腊的女诗人）

安娜·昆德兰 *Anna Quindlen*

bored and above it all was falling asleep. Finally, it was harder to become perfect at Barnard, because I realized that I was not the smartest girl in the world. Eventually being perfect day after day, year after year, became like always carrying a backpack filled with bricks on my back. And oh, how I secretly yearned to lay my burden down.

6   So what I want to say to you today whether you are 21 or 51 is this: if this sounds, in any way, familiar to you, if you have been trying, in one way or another, to be perfect too, then make today, when for a moment there are no more grades to be gotten, classmates to be met, terrain to be scouted, positioning to be arranged — make today the day that you put down that backpack. Trying to be perfect may be sort of inevitable for people like us, who are smart and ambitious and interested in the world and in its good opinion. But at one level it's too hard, and at another, it's too cheap and easy. Because it really requires you mainly to read the **zeitgeist**⑨ of wherever and whenever you happen to be, and to assume the masks necessary to be the best of whatever the zeitgeist dictates or requires. Those requirements shapeshift, sure, but when you're clever like us and female like us you can read them and do the imitation required.

人智慧的，部分则很无聊。追求完美确实很辛苦。此前我既没有读过萨特的书，也没有读过萨福的诗，而当我读它们的时候，是我感到最无聊的时候，然后我居然睡着了。终于，我感到在巴纳德学院达到完美更加困难，因为我意识到我不是世界上最聪明的女孩。最终日复一日年复一年地追求完美就好像总是背着一个装满砖块的背包。噢，我背地里多么希望能扔掉这个沉重的负担啊。

6   所以在座的名位，无论是21岁的年轻人还是51岁的中年人，我今天要对你们说的是：如果你无论从哪个角度想，都觉得我的故事听起来很熟悉，如果你也一直试图以这样或那样的方式寻求完美，那么就让今天成为你放下那个包袱的日子吧，暂时忘了要拿到的成绩，忘了要见面的同学，忘了要侦察的地形，忘了要设置的定位。追求完美可能就是像我们这样聪明、雄心勃勃并对世界及世人对我们的评价感感兴趣的人的宿命。但一方面这太难，而另一方面它又太廉价、太容易。因为它真的需要你主要做好两件事：一是无论何时何地，你都要读懂你所处时代的潮流；二是戴上必要的面具以便最好地满足时代潮流的使命和要求。当

⑨ Zeitgeist ['zaɪtgaɪst] *n.* 时代思潮，时代精神

然，这些要求会随时发生变化，但是当你像我们一样聪明并和我们一样是女性的话，你就可以读懂时代潮流并进行必要的模仿。

7　But nothing important, or meaningful, or beautiful, or interesting, or great ever came out of imitations. The thing that is really hard, and really amazing, and really like jumping out of the plane day after day is giving up on being perfect and beginning the work of becoming yourself.

7　但最重要或最有意义或最美丽或最有趣或最伟大的东西，永远不会来自于模仿。真正困难、真正神奇、让你每一天都真正像从飞机上跳下来的事情是你放弃追求完美，并开始做回自己。

8　This is more difficult, because there is no zeitgeist to read, no template to follow, no mask to wear. Set aside what your friends expect, what your parents demand, what your acquaintances require. Set aside the messages this culture sends to women, through its advertising, its entertainment, its disdain and its disapproval, about how you should behave.

8　这是比较困难的，因为没有时代潮流去理解，没有模板可遵循，没有面具能佩戴。你要抛开朋友们的期望、父母的要求和熟人们的需要。你要抛开文化通过广告、娱乐、以及对"你应该如何表现"的不屑和不满所传达给女性们的信息。

9　Set aside the old traditional notion of female as nurturer and male as leader; set aside, too, the new traditional notions of female as superwoman and male as oppressor. Begin with that most terrifying thing of all, a **clean slate**[10]. Then look, every day, at the choices you are making, and when you ask yourself why you are making them, don't answer to be perfect, find this answer within you: for me, for me. Because these things are who and what I am, and mean to be.

9　你要抛开女人是养育员而男人是领导者的旧传统观念；你还要抛弃女人是女超人而男人是压制者的新传统观念。要从最可怕的事情做起——与往事说再见。然后每天你都要审视你正在做出的选择，当你问自己为什么要做这样的选择时，不要回答是为了完美，而是在内心找到这样的答案：为了我自己，为了我自己。因为我所做的一切都代表着我是谁以及我是什么样的人，我希望成为这样的人。

10　This is the hard work of your life, to make

10　这是你生命之路上的艰难

---

⑩ clean slate *n. 清白历史*

安娜·昆德兰 *Anna Quindlen*

it all up as you go along, to acknowledge once the introvert, the clown, the artist, the reserved, the distraught, the **goofball**[11], the thinker. You will have to bend all your will not to march to the music that all of those great "theys" out there pipe on their flutes. They want you to go to professional school, to wear **khakis**[12], to pierce your navel, to bare your soul. These are the fashionable ways. The music is tinny, if you listen close enough. Look inside. That way lies dancing to the melodies spun out by your own heart. This is a symphony. All the rest are jingles.

11   This will always be your struggle whether you are twenty-one or fifty-one. I know this from experience. When I quit the *New York Times* to be a full-time mother, the voices of the world out there said that I was nuts. When I quit it again to be a full-time novelist, they said I was nuts again. But I am not nuts. I am happy. I am successful on my own terms. Because if your success is not on your own terms, if it looks good to the world but does not feel every day good in your heart, it is not success at all. Remember always the words of Lily Tomlin: If you win the rat race, you're still a rat.

之举，因为当你一路前行时，你要创造这一切，要感谢自己曾经是个内向的人，是个小丑，是个艺术家，是个保守派，是个发狂的疯子，是个傻瓜，是个思想家。你将不得不屈服于你的意志，不要随着那些了不起的"他们"吹出的笛声踏步前进。他们希望你去专业学校，希望你穿卡其裤，希望你戴上肚脐环，希望你倾诉心声。这些都是当下流行的做法。音乐是细腻的，但需要你仔细倾听。你要审视你的内心。你会随着由你自己的内心编织出来的美妙旋律翩翩起舞。这才是一首交响曲，而其余的都是叮当之声。

11   这将是你永远的斗争，无论你是 21 岁的青年人还是 51 岁的中年人。我从自己的经历中懂得了这个道理。当我从《纽约时报》辞职成为一个全职妈妈时，全世界的人都说我疯了。当我再次辞职成为一个全职作家时，他们又说我疯了。但我不是疯子。我是快乐的，因为按照我自己的定义，我是成功的。因为如果你的成功不符合你自己的主张，如果在世人眼里它看起来很好，但它并无法让你每天从内心感到快乐，那它就根本不能算是成功。请记住莉莉·汤姆林的话：如果

---

⑪ goofball ['guːfbɔːl] *n.* 镇静剂；傻瓜

⑫ khakis ['kaːkɪz] *n.* 卡其裤；卡其服装；卡其黄（khaki 的复数）

12　Each of you, all 450 of you, look at your fingers. Hold them like this in front of your face. Each one is crowned by an abstract design that is completely different than those of anyone in this crowd, in this country, or in this world. They are a metaphor for each of you. Each of you is as different as your fingerprints. Why in the world should you be asked to march to any lockstep?

13　The lockstep is easier, but here is why you cannot march to it. Because nothing great or even good comes of it. When writers write to me about following in the footsteps of those of us who string together nouns and verbs for a living, I tell them this: every story has already been told. Once you've read *Anna Karenina*, *Bleak House*, *The Sound and the Fury*, *To Kill a Mockingbird* and *A Wrinkle in Time*, you understand that there is really no reason to ever write another novel. Except that each writer brings to the table, if she will let herself, something that no one else in the history of time has ever had. And that is herself, her personality, her own voice. If she is doing Faulkner imitations, she can stay home.

14　But if she is giving readers something that reflects her character, who she really is, then she is giving them a new and wonderful gift. Giving it to herself, too.

你赢得老鼠比赛，那你还是一只老鼠。

12　你们每个人，所有在座的450人，请看看你们的手指。像我这样在你们面前伸开手指。每根手指都因深奥的设计而自立为王，与在座诸位、与这个国家乃至全世界任何一个人的手指设计都完全不同。它们就是你们的象征。你们每个人正如各自的指纹一样，独一无二。人们有什么理由要求你们迈着相同的步伐前进呢？

13　因循守旧更容易，但是你们不能走那条路，因为任何伟大的东西甚至是好的东西都不会来自于因循守旧。当作家写信给我说要效仿我们这些码字的人来谋生的时候，我这样告诉他们：所有的故事都已经讲了一遍。一旦你读了《安娜·卡列尼娜》、《荒凉山庄》、《喧哗与骚动》、《杀死一只知更鸟》以及《时间的皱纹》，你就明白真的没有理由再写另外一本小说了。除非每个作家推出一本历史上从来没有人读过的书，如果她愿意那么做的话。那就是她自己，她的个性，她自己的声音。如果她模仿福克纳，她可以待在家里。

14　但是如果她拿给读者的东西反映了她的性格，反映了她到底是谁，那么她给予读者的、也是给予她自己的是一个新颖美妙

15   And that is true of music and art and teaching and all other professions. Someone sent me a T-shirt not long ago that read "Well-Behaved Women Don't Make History." They don't make good lawyers, either, or doctors or businesswomen. Imitations are **redundant**[13]. Yourself is what is wanted.

16   You already know this. I just need to remind you. Think back. Think back to first or second grade, when you could still hear the sound of your own voice in your head, when you were too young, too unformed, too fantastic to understand that you were supposed to take on the protective **coloration**[14] of the expectations of those around you. Think of what the writer Catherine Drinker Bowen once wrote, more than half a century ago: "Many a man who has known himself at ten forgets himself utterly between ten and thirty." Many a woman, too.

17   You are not alone in this. We parents have forgotten our way sometimes. I say this as the deeply committed, often flawed mother of three. When you were first born, each of you, our great glory was in thinking you absolutely distinct from every baby who had ever been born before. You were a miracle of singularity, and we knew it in every fiber of our being.

的礼物。

15   这是音乐、艺术、教学和所有其他职业的真谛。前不久有人送我一件 T 恤，上面印着"乖女人不去创造历史"。她们也不会成为好律师、医生或商人。模仿过于泛滥。做你自己才是真正所需。

16   你们已经懂得这个道理。我只是想提醒你们。请回想一下。回想你们上一年级或二年级的时候，那时你们还听不到你自己头脑里的声音，那时你们太小，太不成熟，太异想天开，不明白你们应该披上周围人对你们期望的保护色。想想作家凯瑟琳·德林克·鲍恩在半个多世纪前曾经写下的一句话："很多男人在 10 岁的时候就已经了解自己了，但在 10 岁到 30 岁之间却完全忘了自己。"很多女人也是如此。

17   在这方面你们并不孤单。我们做父母的有时已经忘记了我们是谁。我是以三个孩子的母亲身份说这番话的，作为母亲我尽职尽责，但往往也出现纰漏。当你们每个人刚刚出生的时候，我们最大的荣耀就是认为你们与先前出生的每个婴儿都完全不同。你们是生命独一无二的奇迹，我们从骨子里就知道这一点。

---

⑬ redundant [rɪ'dʌndənt] *adj.* 多余的，过剩的；被解雇的，失业的；冗长的，累赘的

⑭ coloration [ˌkʌlə'reɪʃən] *n.* 着色；染色

18 But we are only human, and being a parent is a very difficult job, more difficult than any other, because it requires the shaping of other people, which is an act of extraordinary **hubris**⑮. Over the years we parents learned to want for you things that you did not want for yourself. We learned to want the lead in the play, the acceptance to our own college, the straight and narrow path that often leads absolutely nowhere. Sometimes we wanted those things because we were convinced it would make life better, or at least easier for you. Sometimes we had a hard time distinguishing between where you ended and where we began.

19 So that another reason that you must give up on being perfect and take hold of being yourself is because sometime, in the future, you may want to be parents, too. If you can bring to your children the self that you truly are, **as opposed to**⑯ some **amalgam**⑰ of manners and mannerisms, expectations and fears that you have acquired as a **carapace**⑱ along the way, you will give them, too, a great gift. You will teach them by example the most important lesson of all not to be terrorized by the narrow and **parsimonious**⑲ expectations of the world, a world that often likes to color within the lines when a spray of paint, a **scrawl**⑳ of crayon, is what is truly wanted.

18 但我们只是普通人，为人父母是一件非常困难的事，比任何其他事都更困难，因为它需要我们塑造别人，这是非常狂妄自大的行为。多年来，我们为人父母的学会了要为你们争取你们自己都不想要的东西。我们学会了要你们在演出中担任主角，让你们接受我们自己上过的大学，让你们走一条笔直但却狭窄的道路，而那条路往往把你们引向了死胡同。有时我们想要那些东西是因为我们相信它会让你们的生活变得更美好，或者至少让你们的生活变得更容易。有时我们很难区分开你们的终点和我们的起点。

19 所以另一个你们必须放弃追求完美抓住自我的原因是，在未来的某个时候，你们可能也想成为父母。如果你们能够向你的孩子们展示真正的自我，而不是一些你们在生活中学到的矫揉造作的礼仪和举止、期望和恐惧混合而成的面具，那么你们也会送给他们一个伟大的礼物。你们将会以身作则，教会他们一则最重要的教训，就是不被世界过于狭隘的期望所吓倒，因为这个世界常常喜欢在线条之间着色，但真

---

⑮ hubris ['hjuːbrɪs] *n.* 傲慢；狂妄自大
⑯ as opposed to 与······截然相反；对照
⑰ amalgam [ə'mælgəm] *n.* [材] 汞合金，[化工] 汞齐；混合物
⑱ carapace ['kærəpes] *n.* 壳；甲壳
⑲ parsimonious [ˌpɑːsə'məʊnɪəs] *adj.* 吝啬的；过于节俭的；质量差的

正被需要的应该是用色彩喷漆、用蜡笔涂鸦。

20 Remember yourself, from the days when you were younger and rougher and wilder, more scrawl than straight line. Remember all of yourself, the flaws and faults as well as the strengths. Carl Jung once said, "If people can be educated to see the lowly side of their own natures, it may be hoped that they will also learn to love their fellow men better. A little less hypocrisy and a little more tolerance toward oneself can only have good results in respect for our neighbors, for we are all too prone to transfer to our fellows the injustice and violence we inflict upon our own natures."

20 记住你们自己吧，从你们更小、更为未加雕琢的时候，从你们乱涂乱写多于划直线的时候。记住你们自己的全部吧，不论缺点和瑕疵还是优势。卡尔·荣格曾经说过："假如人们接受教育之后能看到自己天性卑微的一面，他们就可能有望学着更好地去理解和热爱他们的同胞。对自己少些虚伪，多些宽容，就能产生好的结果，让自己尊重周围的人，因为我们都太容易把加之于我们自身本性上的不公和伤害转向自己的同胞。"

21 Most commencement speeches suggest you take up something or other: the challenge of the future, a vision of the twenty-first century. Instead I'd like you to give up. Give up the backpack. Give up the nonsensical and punishing quest for perfection that dogs too many of us through our lives. It is a quest that causes us to doubt and **denigrate**[21] ourselves, our true selves, our **quirks**[22] and **foibles**[23] and great leaps into the unknown, and that part is bad enough.

21 多数毕业典礼演讲者都会建议大家要开始做这个或做那个：比如迎接未来的挑战，具备21世纪的视野。不过我的建议是让你们放弃。放弃身上的包袱；放弃对完美毫无意义且令人疲惫的追求，我们太多人为了追求完美而耗费了一生。这种对完美的追求致使我们怀疑并贬低我们自己、真实的自我、我们的种种怪癖和弱点，让我们对向未知领域的大飞跃犹豫不决，这种情况糟糕透顶。

[20] scrawl [skrɔːl] *n.* 潦草的笔迹
[21] denigrate ['denɪgreɪt] *vt.* 诋毁；使变黑；玷污
[22] quirk [kwɜːk] *n.* 怪癖；急转；借口
[23] foible ['fɔɪb(ə)l] *n.* 弱点；小缺点；癖好

22　But this is worse: that someday, sometime, you will be somewhere, maybe on a day like this — a berm overlooking a pond in Vermont, the lip of the Grand Canyon at sunset. Maybe something bad will have happened: you will have lost someone you loved, or failed at something you wanted to succeed at.

23　And sitting there, you will fall into the center of yourself. You will look for that core to sustain you. If you have been perfect all your life, and have worn that backpack full of bricks and have managed to meet all the expectations of your family, your friends, your community, your society, chances are excellent that there will be a black hole where your core ought to be.

24　Don't take that chance. Begin today to say no to the Greek chorus that thinks it knows the parameters of a happy life when all it knows is the **homogenization**[24] of human experience. Listen to that voice from inside you, that tells you to go another way. George Eliot wrote, "It is never too late to be what you might have been." It is never too early, either. And it will make all the difference in the world. Take it from someone who learn to leave the backpack full of bricks behind. Every day feels light as a feather. Bless you all.

22　但还有更糟糕的：在将来某一天的某一刻，你们会出现在某个地方，也许就像今天这样子——站在佛蒙特州的一道护堤上俯瞰一塘池水，站在大峡谷的边缘欣赏日落美景。也许某种不幸的事情会发生在你们身上：你们失去所爱的人，或者在你想成功的事情上遭受了失败。

23　坐在那里，你们将成为自我的中心。你们将会寻找支撑你们的核心。如果你们一生都在追求完美，背负着那个装满"砖块"的包袱并设法满足你们的家人、你们的朋友、你们的社区、你们的社会的所有期望，那么很有可能你们的核心会出现黑洞。

24　不要冒那个险。今天就开始对自认为知道幸福生活参数的"希腊合唱团"说不，其实它知道的只是人类经验的同质化。倾听你内心的声音吧，它会告诉你要走另一条路。乔治·艾略特写道："要成为你可能成为的那个人，什么时候都不算晚。"同样的，多早也不算早。这也会使世界变得完全不同。看看那些学会把装满"砖块"的包袱远远抛在身后的人就知道了。要让我们每天都感觉轻松得如羽毛一般。祝福你们大家。

㉔ homogenization [hɒˌmɒdʒənaɪˈzeɪʃən] *n.* 均化；[机] 均化作用